THE MARVELS FOUND IN THE GREAT CITIES AND IN THE SEAS AND ON THE ISLANDS

The Marvels Found in the Great Cities and in the Seas and on the Islands

A Representative of *'Aǧā'ib* Literature in Syriac

Sergey Minov

UNIVERSITY OF CAMBRIDGE
Faculty of Asian and Middle Eastern Studies

OpenBook Publishers

https://www.openbookpublishers.com

Semitic Languages and Cultures 6.

ISSN (print): 2632-6906
ISSN (digital): 2632-6914

ISBN Paperback: 978-1-80064-032-0
ISBN Hardback: 978-1-80064-033-7
ISBN Digital (PDF): 978-1-80064-034-4
DOI: 10.11647/OBP.0237

Cover image: An image from the manuscript of Zakarīyā al-Qazwīnī's *Kitāb 'Aǧā'ib al-maḫlūqāt wa-ġarā'ib al-mauǧūdāt* (1750–1770); Bayerische Staatsbibliothek, Cod. arab. 463, fol. 78r. Courtesy of Bayerische Staatsbibliothek, München.

Cover design: Anna Gatti

لملكة الثالثة عشرة

How many miles to Babylon?
Three score miles and ten.
Can I get there by candle-light?
Yes, and back again ...
If your heels are nimble and your toes are light,
You may get there by candle-light.

I. Opie and P. Opie, *The Oxford Dictionary of Nursery Rhymes* (Oxford: Oxford University Press, 1997).

CONTENTS

Acknowledgments ix

1. Introduction 1
   1.1. Textual tradition 5
   1.2. Language 14
   1.3. Content 17
   1.4. Date and milieu 27

2. Edition and Translation 29
   2.1. Sigla and Conventions 30
   2.2. Recension I 32
   2.3. Recension II 68
   2.4. Synopsis of Recensions 90

3. Commentary 93

4. Indexes 163
   4.1. Index of toponyms 164
   4.2. Index of ethnonyms, demonyms, and personal names 166

5. Bibliography 167

6. Appendix: Manuscript Facsimiles 189

ACKNOWLEDGEMENTS

Since no scholar is an island, I gladly acknowledge my indebtedness to those colleagues of mine without whose support and encouragement this book would never have been written.

While the thought of publishing the *Marvels* has been on my mind since I first came across this fascinating composition in Berlin's Staatsbibliothek in the year 2014, the main bulk of research behind this book was carried out while being a member of the project *Stories of Survival: Recovering the Connected Histories of Eastern Christianity in the Early Modern World*, which is supported by funding from a European Research Council Starting Grant under the European Union's Horizon 2020 research and innovation programme (grant agreement no. 638578). I am deeply grateful to John-Paul Ghobrial, the head of the project, for his generous support, as well as to its other members — Salam Rassi, Lucy Parker, Feras Krimsti, Tobias Graf, and Nora Schmid, whose suggestions have helped me to improve this book significantly.

Moreover, I owe a great debt of gratitude to two *syriacisantes* of Paris — Flavia Ruani, who provided me with some crucial information on the manuscript tradition of the *Marvels*, and Alice Croq, who generously put her impressive knowledge of Muslim and Christian Arabic literature at my disposal. I am also grateful to Sebastian P. Brock, Alessandro Mengozzi, Nikolai Seleznyov, as well as to two reviewers of the book, for their thoughtful comments and corrections. Needless to say, all remaining errors are my own.

In addition to that, I would like to express my thanks to organizers and participants of the two academic venues, where I had a chance to present and discuss my research related to this work: the workshop *Text and Context in Late Antiquity*, put together by Brouria Bitton-Ashkelony (The Hebrew University of Jerusalem) in Zikhron Yaʿakov on 9–10 February 2015, and the conference on *Syriac and Its Users in the Early Modern World c.1500–c.1750*, convened by Lucy Parker (University of Oxford) in Oxford on 15–16 March 2018.

I also wish to express my appreciation to the Bavarian State Library in Munich for permission to use the image from the manuscript Bayerische Staatsbibliothek München, Cod. arab. 463, and to Staatsbibliothek zu Berlin for allowing reproduction of the two manuscripts of the *Marvels* from their collection, i.e., Orient. quart. 802 and Sachau 118.

I am most grateful to Aaron D. Hornkohl for correcting my English, and to the team of Open Book Publishers, especially to Melissa Purkiss and Alessandra Tosi, for their exemplary work.

Last but not least, I would like to thank Prof. Geoffrey Khan for his willingness to accept this book to be published in the recently launched series 'Cambridge Semitic Languages and Cultures', which sets a high bar in the field of academic publishing by following its rigorous standards, while at the same time making scholarly works accessible to everyone thanks to the open access policy.

1. INTRODUCTION

https://doi.org/10.11647/OBP.0237.01

The Arab takeover of the Near East changed the social and cultural landscape of the region, giving birth to a range of new polities dominated by the religion of Islam. The contribution of the Christian 'minority',[1] including that of Syriac-speaking Christians, to the formation of Islamic culture, is a much-discussed and well-documented topic. A relatively less-studied subject, however, is the opposite direction in the never-ceasing process of mutual cultural transfer between Muslims and Christians, that of the influence exercised by the culture of the dominant majority upon Christians.

Scholars have noticed and discussed various areas of the Muslim impact upon practices and beliefs of Christians living throughout the Middle East, including such fields as science, philosophy, legal thought, and even theology. One of the particularly fruitful venues of such interaction was the appropriation by Syriac- and Arabic-speaking Christians of various literary forms and techniques that were developed among Muslim literati. Among examples of this kind, discussed by scholars, one can mention the use by Christian writers of such literary genres and forms as apologetic interreligious disputation-*maǧlis*, *maqāmāt* stories, *ḫamriyyāt* poetry, and *rubāʿiyāt* quatrains.[2] There are

---

[1] On inadequacy of this term for describing the demographic situation during the first several centuries of the Islamic rule, see Tannous (2018a, 340–52). For a general introduction into Christians and Christianity in the world of Islam, see Griffith (2007).

[2] On *maǧlis*, see Griffith (1999); on the development of this genre, see other contributions in Lazarus-Yafeh et al. (1999); on *maqāmāt*: Katsumata (2002); Tannous (2018a, 432); Younansardaroud (2010); on

also examples of whole works that originated in a Muslim milieu, being read and transmitted by Christians, as in the case of some stories from the *One Thousand and One Nights*, such as that of *Sindbad the Sailor*, found in Christian Arabic manuscripts,[3] or the *Story of the Ten Viziers*, translated from the New Persian *Baḵtiār-nāma*, and transmitted both in Arabic and Neo-Aramaic versions.[4]

In this book, I would like to present for the first time a hitherto unpublished Syriac composition, entitled the *Marvels Found in the Great Cities and in the Seas and on the Islands*, which presents its readers with a loosely organized catalogue of marvellous events, phenomena, and objects, natural as well as human-made, found throughout the world. This work is unique in that it bears witness to the adoption by Syriac Christians of another literary mode that was popular among Muslims, the so-called *ʿaǧāʾib*, literally 'marvels', which is paradoxographical literature.[5]

ḫamriyyāt: Taylor (2010); on *rubāʿiyāt*: Mengozzi (2014).

[3] See Braida (2016); Bellino (2019); Mengozzi (Forthcoming).

[4] For the Christian Arabic version, see mss. Paris, BnF Syr. 324 (1889), fols. 3v–66v; Paris, BnF Syr. 331 (1883), fols. 101v–166v; Berlin, Sachau 231; Berlin, Sachau 164, fols. 1r–23r. For the Neo-Aramaic version in the Fellīḥī dialect, see ms. Berlin, Sachau 230. See Mengozzi (Forthcoming).

[5] See Dubler (1986); Bosworth & Afshar (1985); Rodinson (1978); Ron-Gilboa (2017). For a detailed inventory of these works in the Arabic literary tradition, see Demidchik (2004, 119–219). By using the term '*ʿaǧāʾib* literature' I do not imply that there is such a formally defined literary genre, but imagine rather a cluster of the works of diverse

There is a rich and developed tradition of the paradoxographical mode of writing in Arabic and Persian literatures, the earliest preserved specimens of which, such as Buzurg Ibn Šahriyār's *ʿAǧāʾib al-hind* and Abū Dulaf's second *risāla*, go back to the ninth and tenth centuries. This tradition finds its culmination in the most famous composition of Muslim paradoxography, *ʿAǧāʾib al-maḫlūqāt wa-ġarāʾib al-mawǧūdāt*, the encyclopaedia of natural history produced in Arabic by Zakariyā al-Qazwīnī (1203–1283).[6] As for its purpose, this literature had not only erudite or entertaining functions, but a religious dimension as well, as it sought to instil in its audience the feeling of amazement and, thus, advance it in the knowledge of God 'through observing his creations, and contemplating the wonders of his works'.[7] As I am going to demonstrate, the Syriac Christian compiler of the *Marvels* appropriated this mode of writing creatively, both following its conventions and adjusting it to the needs of his audience.

---

genres, often closely related to geographical literature, that have in common a pronounced tendency to present natural and human-made phenomena and objects that are meant to evoke the feeling of astonishment. For an argument against the existence of a literary genre of *ʿaǧāʾib*, see von Hees (2005); cf. also Bellino & Mengozzi (2016, 433).

[6] For a general introduction into his life and work, see von Hees (2002); Demidchik (2004, 45–118).

[7] According to the passage from *Asrār al-maḫlūqāt* of al-Ġazālī, quoted by von Hees (2005, 106).

1.1. Textual tradition

The Syriac text of the *Marvels* is attested in the following four manuscripts, described here in chronological order:

V = Vatican, Biblioteca Apostolica, Borgia sir. 39; paper, 31/31.5 × 21.5/22 cm, 298 fols., 1 col., ca. 1680.[8]

The manuscript is written in a partially vocalized East Syrian script. Although its final section, which may have included a colophon, is lost, the scribal notes found on fols. 162v, 219r, and 281v provide information that this manuscript was produced by a scribe named Yaldā (ܝܠܕܐ) for a church dedicated to Mary in the village of Karsabā (ܟܪܣܒܐ). In a detailed investigation of Borgia sir. 39, Joseph-Marie Sauget comes to the conclusion that this scribe should be identified as the priest Yaldā bar Daniel, a member of an established East Syrian scribal dynasty in Alqosh, and that the manuscript was produced around the year 1680, at the beginning of Yaldā's prolific scribal career, which spanned the period of approximately 1679 to 1725.[9] It should also be mentioned that we know of at least five other manuscripts that

---

[8] For a comprehensive codicological description, see Sauget (1981). A digital reproduction of the manuscript is available online at https://digi.vatlib.it/view/MSS_Borg.sir.39.

[9] See Sauget (1981, 49–62). Of the manuscritps produced by Yaldā, at least twenty four have survived. On Yaldā and the Naṣrō family of Alqosh, to which he belonged, see also Wilmshurst (2000, 247–50); Murre-van den Berg (2015, 93–94).

were commissioned from different scribes of Alqosh for the church of Mary in Karsabā (also spelled as Karsāpā) during the seventeenth century.[10]

Borgia sir. 39 is an anthology of writings, mostly comprising hagiographical works, with the addition of some parabiblical and other texts. The text of the *Marvels* is located on fols. 111r–115v: it follows an edifying story about a boy killed by his teacher (fols. 109v–111r), and is followed by the *Fables of Aesop* (fols. 115v–122v). The title of the work as well as its concluding sentence are rubricated. Throughout the text, rubricated subtitles and introductory words, such as 'a marvel' or 'marvels', are used as well.

L = London, British Library, Or. 4528; paper, 17 × 10 cm, 248 fols., 1 col., 1737.[11]

The manuscript is written in a partially vocalized East Syrian script. According to the information provided in the extended colophon (fols. 244r–245r), it was produced by the priest ʿAbdīšōʿ bar Qūrǧībeg (ܥܒܕܝܫܘܥ ܒܪ ܩܘܪܓ̰ܝܒܓ) in the village of Qūdšānīs (ܩܘܕܫܢܝܣ) in the region of Bārwār (ܒܪܘܪ), in the year of the Greeks 2048 (i.e., 1737). The scribe also relates that he carried out his task during the reign of 'Mār Shemʿon, Catholicos and Patriarch of the East'. Taking into consideration the date and

---

[10] For the references, see Wilmshurst (2000, 240), who tentatively identifies this village with 'the village of Khōrsābād in the Mosul plain, several miles east of Telkepe'.

[11] For a brief description, see Margoliouth (1899, 47).

place where the manuscript was produced, we can safely identify this hierarch as Šemʿōn XIV Šlemōn (1700–1740). This indicates that ʿAbdīšōʿ was a member of the East Syrian community.

As for its content, Or. 4528 is an anthology of diverse works that includes parabiblical texts, such as Pseudo-Basil's *History of Joseph*, as well as hagiographical, exegetical, chronological, and some other compositions. The text of the *Marvels* is located on fols. 73v–78v: it follows a brief question and answer addressed to an unnamed doctor (fol. 73v) and is followed by the *Story of Arsanis* (fols. 78v–81r). The title of the work is rubricated. Throughout the text, rubricated subtitles and introductory words, such as 'there is', 'another' or the first words of a unit, are used as well.

B1 = Berlin, Staatsbibliothek zu Berlin, Orient. quart. 802 (Berlin Syr. 59); paper, 21.5 × 15.5 cm, 80 fols., 1 col., 18th c.[12]

The manuscript, written in a partially vocalized East Syrian script, was produced by the scribe and priest Īšō bar Ḥediršā (ܐܝܫܘܥ ܒܪ ܚܕܝܪܫܐ), who left several scribal marks (fols. 41r, 75r, 80v). According to Eduard Sachau, who dates it to the beginning of the eighteenth century, it was produced in the vicinity of Urmia.[13] The confessional affiliation of the scribe should, most likely, be regarded as East Syrian, given the kind of script used,

---

[12] For a description, see Sachau (1899, 1:200–204). For a facsimile of the manuscript, see Appendix.

[13] Sachau (1899, 1:204).

and the absence of any explicit identity markers that would point in another direction.

Orient. quart. 802 is an anthology of diverse writings, for the most part parabiblical and hagiographical. The text of the *Marvels* is located on fols. 68v–72v: it follows a brief notice on St Melania (fol. 68r) and is followed by a geographical composition attributed to Andronicus (fols. 72v–75r). The title of the work as well as its concluding sentence are rubricated. Throughout the text, rubricated subtitles and introductory words, such as 'there is' or the first words of a unit, are used as well.

B2 = Berlin, Staatsbibliothek zu Berlin, Sachau 118 (Berlin Syr. 86); paper, 16.5 × 10.5 cm, 31 fols., 1 col., 17th–18th cc.[14]

This composite manuscript binds together portions from various manuscripts, written in a vocalized East Syrian script, although by different hands. Unfortunately, none of the included parts features a colophon or a scribal mark with a date or other information. While Sachau tentatively dates the script of the manuscript to the eighteenth century,[15] Richard Gottheil, who published one of the works that it contains, dates its script to the seventeenth century.[16]

---

[14] For a description, see Sachau (1899, 1:317–19). For a facsimile of the manuscript, see Appendix. I am grateful to Alessandro Mengozzi for sharing with me images of the relevant folios.

[15] Sachau (1899, 1:319).

[16] Gottheil (1888, 208).

A collection of various works, it includes compositions dealing with natural history and human nature. The text of the *Marvels* is preserved only partially, represented by two folios, 7 and 8: they follow a folio containing a section of an unidentified zoological work (fol. 6) and are followed by a hexaemeric composition,[17] also partially preserved (fols. 9a–13b). Throughout the text, rubricated subtitles and introductory words, such as 'a marvel' or 'marvels', are used.

The two textual witnesses V and L should be grouped together since they are almost identical in regard to the sequence of units as well as their content, except for minor textual variants. Most significant among the differences are the absence of unit I.40 in L, and the relocation in L of unit I.23 after I.19, and of unit I.16 after I.64. It should be pointed out that although the manuscript containing L is somewhat younger than that of V, the former is not derived directly from the latter, as one can conclude from some cases where L offers better readings than V.[18] To this group of manuscripts also belongs B2, comprising two disparate folios. As far as their content allows us to judge, this version contains the same units in precisely the same order as V, that is: fols. 7r–v — the second half of I.27, I.28, I.29; fols. 8r–v — the end of I.41,

[17] It seems to be identical to the *Wonders of the Six Days of Creation*, preserved completely in ms. Cambridge, Cambridge University Library, Add. 2017, fols. 113r–126r; see Wright (1901, 2: 556–57).

[18] Cf. I.31 — 'six digits' in L vs 'three digits' in V; I.32 — toponym *Balōs* in L vs *Klāmīs* in V.

I.42, I.43, I.44, I.45, I.46, the beginning of I.47. The text in these folios is identical to that of V.

The textual witness B1 differs from V and L to a considerable degree. On the one hand, it lacks not a small number of units, such as I.8–12, I.23, I.25–27, I.33, I.41, I.43, I.47–53, I.56. On the other hand, it contains several units that are absent from V and L, such as II.29, II.36–38, II.41, II.43–48, II.52–53, II.57. Moreover, in several cases of shared units, B1 provides better readings than V and L.[19] It is possible, then, that B1 preserves at least some units in a form closer to that of the original version of the *Marvels*.

Based on these observations, it seems reasonable to divide all textual witnesses of the *Marvels* into two main groups: Recension I, represented by V, L and B2, and Recension II, represented by B1. At the moment, it is difficult to establish with certainty which of the two recensions preserves a version of the text that stands closer to the original version of the work, and which is a result of its later reworking. It should be pointed out, however, that even the oldest textual witness of Recension I, i.e., manuscript V, cannot be regarded as an autograph of the work's compiler since it contains mistakes and copying errors.[20]

[19] Cf. toponym *Waqwaq* in II.32 vs *Baqāwās* in V and *Bāqāwās* in L of I.42. Cf. also such units, derived from the *Alexander Romance*, as II.40 and II.42.

[20] Besides several cases, where V has readings inferior to those of L, the unit I.65 that concludes it seems to be out of place, with a more suitable concluding unit being the preceding one, i.e. I.64, as in B1. Cf. also the

Moreover, one cannot exclude the possibility that some of the textual units that are absent from Recension I, but appear in Recension II,[21] were not a part of the original composition. In fact, given the fluid textual tradition of our work, whose atomistic literary structure makes it easily amenable to alteration and rearrangement, it might be futile to try to reconstruct the original text of the *Marvels*.

In addition to the Syriac version, there are also a Neo-Aramaic and, closely related to it, Arabic version of the *Marvels*. Found in the same single manuscript, London, British Library, Or. 9321 (fols. 231v–244r), both versions have been published recently by Francesca Bellino and Alessandro Mengozzi.[22] The two versions of the *Marvels* are included in an anthology of texts in North-Eastern dialects of Neo-Aramaic that was compiled on behalf of the German scholar Eduard Sachau by the Chaldean priest Gabriel Quryaqoza during the last decade of the nineteenth century. While the content of the Neo-Aramaic and Arabic versions of the *Marvels* in this textual witness is practically identical, it comprises only about a third of the original Syriac composition. As for their textual affinity, their text corresponds

couple of truncated and almost identical units I.62 and I.65 vis-à-vis the corresponding unit II.40.

[21] I.e., units II.29, II.36–38, II.41, II.43–48, II.52–53, II.57.

[22] Bellino & Mengozzi (2016).

closely, both in the sequence of units and in their content,[23] to the part of Recension I that encompasses units I.1 to I.25.

According to Bellino and Mengozzi, who were not aware of the existence of a complete Syriac version of the *Marvels*, the *Vorlage* behind the Neo-Aramaic version was 'a Christian Arabic text, written or transmitted in East Syrian milieu'.[24] Although they do refer to the Syriac fragments of the *Marvels* from ms. Sachau 118 in their discussion,[25] Bellino and Mengozzi were not able to identify them as coming from the same composition. The main reason for this is that these fragments come from the part of the work that, for some reason, was not translated into Arabic and Neo-Aramaic.

As has been suggested by Bellino and Mengozzi, it was most likely Gabriel Quryaqoza himself who translated the text of the *Marvels* from Arabic into Neo-Aramaic.[26] While this suggestion seems plausible, there are still several difficult questions that are posed by the published Arabic and Neo-Aramaic versions of our work.

Thus, the task of establishing the exact nature of the relationship between the two versions poses a certain challenge. On the one hand, one comes across evidence that suggests the primacy of the Arabic version, namely, instances where its text stands closer to the Syriac original than to that of the Neo-

[23] It lacks only unit I.23.

[24] Bellino & Mengozzi (2016, 449).

[25] Bellino & Mengozzi (2016, 434).

[26] Bellino & Mengozzi (2016, 449).

Aramaic version. One such case, pointed out by Bellino and Mengozzi, is the translation of the Syriac toponym *Taymnā* 'the South' in unit I.22/II.17 with the similarly sounding toponym *al-Taymā*ʾ[27] in the Arabic and with the general *daštā* 'the plain' in the Neo-Aramaic version.[28] An even more telling example comes from unit I.9/II.9, where the Syriac noun *qūmrē* 'chains, bonds' is rendered as 'moons' — *aqmār* in the Arabic and *sērē* in the Neo-Aramaic version. As one can recognize at once, it is the Arabic version that mistranslates the Syriac original, most likely as a result of confusion over the nominal derivatives of the root *qmr* (attested both in Syriac and Arabic, albeit with different meanings), whereas the Neo-Aramaic version follows the choice made by the Arabic translation. On the other hand, however, there are readings that go in the opposite direction, such as the case of the Syriac noun *esṭūnē* 'columns' in the same unit I.9/II.9 being faithfully reproduced in the Neo-Aramaic version, while rendered as *ahrām* 'pyramids' in the Arabic one.[29] One possible explanation for this inconsistency is that the author of the Neo-Aramaic version carried out his translation on the basis of the Arabic version, while making occasional use of the Syriac original.

In their discussion, Bellino and Mengozzi seem to hold the opinion that the Arabic version is a full or abridged copy of the aforementioned Christian Arabic *Vorlage*. In light of the much

---

[27] I.e., the oasis of Tayma in north-west Arabia.

[28] Bellino & Mengozzi (2016, 449).

[29] See also Bellino & Mengozzi (2016, 440).

longer Syriac version of the work, however, the abridged and derivative character of the Arabic version becomes evident. What remains unclear is who and for what purposes produced this truncated translation of the *Marvels*. One possibility is that it was made impromptu by Gabriel Quryaqoza, or one of his associates, for the sake of inclusion in the anthology that he was preparing for Sachau. Another possibility is that this version was already in existence before this project. Since there is no textual evidence so far that would confirm the latter, the former scenario appears to be more likely.

1.2. Language

In the absence of any unequivocal textual evidence that would confirm the hypothesis of Bellino and Mengozzi about a Christian Arabic *Vorlage* of the *Marvels,* I find it preferable to regard this work as an original Syriac composition. So far, there seem to be no unambiguous linguistic or other markers that would allow us to establish with certainty that it was translated from Arabic. The heavy reliance on Muslim sources by its compiler, as well as the appearance in the text of Arabic and Persian loan-words, cannot be taken as decisive arguments in favour of it being translated *as a whole* from either of these languages.[30]

---

[30] This, of course, does not preclude the possibility that some individual units of the *Marvels* were translated from Arabic. This is relevant, especially, for those units that find close parallels in the works of Muslim authors, but might also apply in the case of some explicitly Christian units, such as the story of the ape-martyr (I.48).

The language of the *Marvels* in all four of the textual witnesses is standard Classical Syriac. However, it exhibits a number of peculiarities: some of them reflect the influence of the Islamicate cultural milieu, in which the work was produced and circulated, while others bear witness to its socio-linguistic matrix, as it exhibits the impact of the Neo-Aramaic dialect that was, apparently, spoken by the compiler or, alternatively, by the scribes who copied his work.

In what concerns the former aspect, it manifests itself in the appearance of a significant number of Arabic and Persian loan-words or calques. Given the nature of the work, many of them are found among toponyms or references to natural phenomena: the cities of *Baghdad* (I.43), *Basra* (I.49–50, II.52), and *Tus* (I.43), *Qōnyā* for Iconium (I.12), *Hejaz* (I.22/II.17), *Serendib* for Sri Lanka (I.33, I.51), the *Sea of Qūlzam* for the Red Sea (I.58/II.49, II.53), the fabulous tree of *Waqwaq* (I.42/II.32), the island *Barṭīl* (I.64/II.58), the explicitly marked as 'Persian' gloss *gālīm gōš* to refer to the 'ear-people' (I.28/II.19). In addition to these, there are also cases like the weight measurement unit *qafīz* (I.44/II.33), the nouns *hağ* and *hağāyē* for 'pilgrimage' and 'pilgrims' (I.47), and the ethnonym *parangāyā* for a Frankish man (I.46/II.35).

In this regard, one should also mention the use by the scribe of V of the Garshuni sign for marking the letter *ğamal*, in order to render the consonant *ğ*, absent from Classical Syriac, in cases of such borrowed nouns and toponyms as *hağ* 'pilgrimage' and *hağaye* 'pilgrims' (I.47), *Ādurbayğ*, i.e., Azerbaijan (I.23), *Bēt Dlīğ* (I.24–25), *Qātāğ* (I.25). Yet, as the case of *Hejaz* spelled as ܚܓܐܙ (I.22) demonstrates, he was not consistent in following this path.

The same inconsistency characterizes the approach of the scribe of L, who sometimes uses *ǧamal*, but more often does not.[31]

The influence of everyday speech in the text of the *Marvels* can be recognized, first of all, in the cases of phonetic spellings of Classical Syriac words, such as ܡܚܝܐ as ܡܗܝܐ (I.17), or ܢܚܬܐ as ܢܗܬܐ (II.12). More interesting, however, are instances of the intrusion of Neo-Aramaic vocabulary in the text or the use of intratextual vernacular glosses to explain some Classical Syriac words. As for the former, one could point out the Neo-Aramaic *spāqē* 'jars' used alongside the Classical Syriac *gūrnē* (I.5/II.5), and the Neo-Aramaic *gamešē* 'buffalo bulls' used instead of the Classical Syriac *gāmūšē* (I.51). As for the glosses, one comes across the Classical Syriac noun *šūšmānē* 'ants' glossed with the Neo-Aramaic *šekwānē* (I.10). In a similar manner, the Syriac noun *gālē* 'turtles' is glossed with the Neo-Aramaic *qrāyē* (I.54/II.54).

At this point, it is difficult to establish with certainty whether this Neo-Aramaic stratum belongs to the original text of the work or whether it was introduced later, during the process of its transmission by East Syrian scribes. However, because the Neo-Aramaic noun *spāqē*, 'jars' in I.5/II.5 is not marked as a gloss, but appears as an organic element of the text in both recensions, the former scenario seems entirely plausible.

---

[31] Contrary to the scribe of V, he uses this letter to spell *Heǧāz* (I.22), *ǧālīm ǧōš* (I.28), *haǧ* (I.48).

1.3. Content

In what concerns the general structure of the *Marvels*, it is rather simple, being made up of a sequence of units of varying length, in which various wondrous objects or events are described. These units are grouped roughly into three main parts, that is, the marvels of the cities, marvels of the seas, and marvels of the islands. This tripartite division is signalled in the title of Recension I, as well as marked by additional paratextual means, such as subheadings written in red ink.[32] In Recension I, there are two subheadings: 'About marvels of springs and waters' before I.13, and 'About marvels that are in the Eastern islands and beyond' before I.28. Recension II, likewise, features two subheadings: 'About rivers' before II.8, and 'Again, marvels in the Eastern islands' before II.19. It should be noted that the content of some of the units within the subsections marked by these subheadings does not always fit their proclaimed subject. Another paratextual feature of the work is the marker 'marvel/marvels', also written in red ink, that introduces most of the textual units.

As one reads through the text of the *Marvels*, it becomes apparent that its compiler derived this diverse material from a wide range of sources, written as well as oral. It is, however, only on rare occasions that he indicates the origin of individual units.

---

[32] It should be pointed out that the scribes of all four of the manuscripts of the *Marvels* resorted to the paratextual strategy of rubricated titles, subtitles, and introductory words ('a marvel', 'marvels', 'another', and others) in order to make it easier for readers to navigate the text.

Thus, only in one case, I.48, a written source, 'the book of Mār Basil', that he used is explicitly mentioned (on this, see below). In what concerns oral sources, the compiler discloses them more often: by providing names of his informants, which include Joseph, the brother of ʿAbdīšōʿ of Elam (I.12), a certain Anās (I.40/II.31), Qūryāqōs of Mosul (I.41, I.47), and Rabban Emmanuel (II.47), or by referring to them in general terms ('merchants' in I.42, 'they' in I.46 and I.49). Yet, there might be even more oral accounts, incorporated into our work, whose origin is not made explicit by the compiler. One such case is, probably, the cluster of four textual units dealing with the region of Bitlis in Kurdistan (I.24–27). Given the narrow territorial focus of these units, as well as the fact that none of them seems to find close parallels in the major Arabic and Persian paradoxographical or geographical compositions, it seems justified to regard them as the elements of local folklore that reached the compiler of the *Marvels* not via literary sources, but through the process of oral transmission.[33]

1.3.1. *Christian background*

In what concerns the composition's milieu and the confessional identity of its author, there is no doubt that it was produced by a Christian. Setting aside the fact that it is preserved in Syriac, the language used during the Middle Ages exclusively by Christians, the work features several distinctively Christian themes and images.

---

[33] Note that unit I.25 features a local proverb.

To begin with, one should point out Christian names of several among the compiler's informants, such as Joseph, the brother of Mār ʿAbdīšōʿ of Elam (I.12), the priest Qūryāqōs of Mosul (I.41, I.47), and Rabban Emmanuel (II.47).

In addition to that, one comes across several instances of the compiler's dependence on Christian written sources. There is only one instance when he mentions explicitly a Christian work used by him, that is, when he introduces the story about the ape-martyr in I.48 as coming from 'the book of Mār Basil' (i.e., Basil of Caesarea). And indeed, this account has a very close parallel in the Arabic version of the *Questions of Basil and Gregory.*[34] However, most of the Christian sources, on which our compiler apparently relied, remain unnamed. Nevertheless, one can single out at least two Syriac compositions that were likely used by him, whether directly or indirectly.

One of them is the Syriac version of Pseudo-Callisthenes's *Alexander Romance,*[35] in which a number of units connected with the figure of Alexander the Great find close parallels, such as the scorpion-legged people (I.31/II.22), the people with dogs' teeth

[34] For the text and discussion, see Commentary below.

[35] Edited in Budge (1889). Of course, in its origin the *Romance* is a late antique composition, usually considered to be authored by a non-Christian writer; for a general information, see Nawotka (2017). Its Syriac version could be categorized as a Christian work only conditionally, in the sense of it being produced and transmitted in the Syriac Christian milieu. On reception of the *Romance* and popularity of the figure of Alexander among Syriac Christians, see Gero (1993); Brock (2011); Kotar (2013); Doufikar-Aerts (2016); Stoneman (2017); Nawotka (2018).

(I.34/II.24), the headless people (I.35/II.25), the raven-like people (I.37/II.27), the ass-legged people (I.38/II.28), the wolf and leopard (I.53), Alexander and the two talking birds (I.61/II.39), Alexander and the two talking trees (I.63/II.42), the people with lions' heads (II.29), the horned serpents (II.37), the animal bigger than an elephant (II.38), Alexander and the growing trees (II.40/I.62, 65), the partridge-looking bird (II.41), the half-human animal (II.43), the animals attacking Alexander's troops (II.44), the threatening bats (II.45), the bird on a tree-top (II.46). It is noteworthy that all these parallels come from chapter 7 of the third book of the *Romance,* comprising the letter of Alexander to Aristotle, in which the king describes his journey to India.[36]

Another written source that might have been used by the compiler seems to be the Syriac *Book of Natural Beings,*[37] in which several units dealing with rivers or seas find close counterparts, such as the river Bāeṭlas (I.13/II.18), the Sea of Reeds (I.14/II.9), the place ʾEwrīqōs (I.15/II.10), the river that flows one day during the week (I.16/II.11), the river that flows on the Sabbath (I.19/II.14), and the river of sand (I.20/II.15).

[36] This section of the *Romance* played an important role in the development of paradoxographical tradition in medieval Europe, where it often circulated as an independent work. See Zuwiyya (2011, 17, 322–23); Kim (2017).

[37] Edited in Ahrens (1892), it is a medieval naturphilosophical compilation, comprising 125 chapters, about one-third of which come from the Syriac version of the *Physiologus*.

It should be emphasized, however, that in the case of neither the units that find parallels in the *Alexander Romance* nor those that are similar to the *Book of Natural Beings* is there unambiguous evidence of direct textual dependence of the compiler of the *Marvels* on either of the two written sources. A most likely explanation for this textual dissimilarity is that material from the two works reached the compiler by way of oral transmission, hence the concise character of many such units in comparison with the original passages.

Furthermore, the text of the *Marvels* features several references to Christian religious beliefs or practices. One should point out such cases as the mention of *ḥnānā*, the mixture of blessed oil, water, and dust from the tombs of saints (I.18/II.13), and the mention of Antichrist (I.64/II.58). However, the most striking expression of the Christian background of the work's compiler is found in two grotesque stories, one following the other in units I.47 and I.48.

The former story (i.e., I.47) is, perhaps, the most unusual apologetic attempt to affirm the primacy of Syriac as the primeval language. The notion of Syriac primacy is old and goes back to Late Antiquity, found in such Syriac works as the *Cave of Treasures*.[38] The compiler of the *Marvels* or, to be more precise, the source he used for this unit, offers a novel argument in support of this idea, by presenting the account of a child who grew up alone in the desert while suckling on the breast of his dead mother and who, when brought back to human society by his father, started to speak Syriac. Typologically, this argument

---

[38] See Rubin (1998); Moss (2010); Minov (2013, 165–75).

follows the pattern established already in Greco-Roman antiquity, in the famous story recounted by Herodotus (*Hist.* 2.2) about an experiment conducted by the pharaoh Psammetichus, who had ordered that a couple of new-born children be brought up without a person speaking with them, in order to see what would be the first words they speak and, thus, establish what nation is oldest in the world. The story in I.47 employs a similar logic while embedding it within the grotesque narrative framework, where a half-decayed corpse is able to breastfeed.

An equally bizarre account in unit I.48 explores another important Christian theme: the notion of baptism as a primary marker of belonging to the community. It does so by telling a story of the martyrdom of the offspring of a woman and an ape. Longing to become a full member of the Christian community, but denied the sacrament of baptism by the bishop on account of his ambiguous status, the half-human protagonist of the story finds an alternative path to obtain his goal, by inflicting on himself voluntary martyrdom and, thus, being baptized by his own blood. Much like the previous story, this narrative continues the late antique tradition of the Christian understanding of martyrdom as the second baptism, but does so by resorting to grotesque imagery.

These two stories serve as an excellent example of how the rhetoric of monstrosity and grotesque narrative conventions typical of Islamic *ʿaǧāʾib* literature were appropriated by Syriac Christians and employed to convey distinctively Christian messages of the Syriac language as an essential identity marker and of the crucial role of baptism as a *sine qua non* for belonging within the Christian community. Regardless of the original context of these stories, the compiler's decision to include them in his compilative work bears witness to the importance of the issues they problematize in the milieu in which the *Marvels* were composed and circulated.

1.3.2. *Muslim background*

Alongside the Christian elements, the text of the *Marvels* exhibits numerous traces of indebtedness to the Muslim geographical and literary tradition. Most significant among them is the choice of the literary form itself, as indicated explicitly in the work's title. The Syriac plural noun *tedmrātā* in the title of our work corresponds to Arabic *ʿaǧāʾib* 'marvels, wonders' that appears in the title of many works. The title of the *Marvels*, thus, evokes titles of such Arabic compositions as 'Marvels of India' (*ʿAǧāʾib al-Hind*) by Buzurg Ibn Šahriyār and 'Marvels of the Sea' (*ʿAǧāʾib al-baḥr*) by several other authors, which are listed in the *Fihrist* by Ibn al-Nadīm (10th c.).[39]

It should be pointed out that, so far, there is no compelling evidence proving that the *Marvels* as a whole was derived from any of the Arabic or Persian paradoxographical compositions that are known to us. One cannot, however, rule out entirely the possibility that such a composition existed and was available to the Christian compiler of our work. In that regard, Ibn al-Nadīm

[39] Cf. several works entitled 'Marvels of the Sea': *Fihrist* 3.1 (by Hišām al-Kalbī), 3.3 (by Abū al-ʿAnbas al-Ṣaymarī and by Ibn al-Šāh al-Ṭāhirī); ed. Sayyid (2009, I.2:305, 468, 472).

provides us with an interesting testimony. He opens a brief section dealing with *ʿağāʾib* works in chapter 8 of his catalogue with the following report:

> There is the book known as *The Book of Ṣaḫr al-Maġribī*, which was written by ...[40] It contains thirty stories: ten about the wonders of the land, and ten about the wonders of the dawn, and ten about the wonders of the sea.[41]

There are two noteworthy details in this concise description of an apparently lost work. First of all, like the *Marvels*, it is a relatively brief and simply organized composition. Second, it had a tripartite structure, similar to what we see announced in the title of the *Marvels*. Moreover, its 'the wonders of the land' section corresponds to 'the marvels of the great cities' in the *Marvels*, while 'the wonders of the sea' part corresponds to 'the marvels in the Eastern islands'. Of course, these similarities are not specific enough to presume that the *Marvels* was modelled after the lost book of Ṣaḫr al-Maġribī. The testimony of Ibn al-Nadīm is still significant, however, as a witness that, alongside extended and sophisticated *ʿağāʾib* compositions, such as the works of Buzurg

---

[40] The manuscript has a blank space at this point, indicating, probably, that Ibn al-Nadīm intended to add the name of the book's author later.

[41] *Fihrist* 8.1: وهي كتاب يعرف بكتاب صخر المغربي، وألفه ... ويحتوي على ثلاثين حديثا: عشرة في عجائب البر وعشرة في عجائب السحرة وعشرة في عجائب البحر; ed. Sayyid (2009, II.1:332); trans. Dodge (1970, 2:724). The reading *saḥara* 'dawn' is somewhat problematic in this context. Cf. ed. Flügel (1871–1872, 308), who gives instead the noun *šağara* 'tree'.

Ibn Šahriyār or Zakariyā al-Qazwīnī, there existed more modest representatives of this genre, which offered not much more than a simple catalogue of the wonders of nature and culture.

The presence of a significant number of Arabic and Persian loan-words or calques in the vocabulary of the *Marvels* has already been discussed above. In addition to these cases, one comes across many parallels between geographical and mythological traditions incorporated into our work and the works of Muslim authors. Most of them come from geographical or paradoxographical works, such as *Kitāb al-masālik wa-l-mamālik* by Ibn Ḫordāḏbeh,[42] *Aḫbār al-ṣīn wa-l-hind* by Abū Zayd al-Sīrāfī,[43] *ʿAǧāʾib al-hind* by Buzurg Ibn Šahriyār,[44] *ʿAǧāʾib al-maḫlūqāt* by Zakariyā al-Qazwīnī,[45] and some others. Sometimes these parallels can be narrowed down to particular works or authors, such

---

[42] Cf. the descriptions of Alexandria and its lighthouse (I.2–3/II.2–3), the mirror in Alexandria (I.4/II.4), the lighthouse of brass (I.5/II.5), the wall between the Caspian and Mediterranean seas (I.7/II.7), the city with seven gates (I.8), the brass columns in Egypt (I.9), the brass horseman in Andalus (I.10), the pyramids of Egypt (I.11), the raining place Maṭlāyā (I.21/II.16), the rain in Hejaz (I.22/II.17), the tree climbers of Serendib (I.33), the buffalos of Serendib (I.51), the bull-fish (I.60), and the island of Antichrist (I.64/II.58).

[43] Cf. the stories about the big fish (I.58–59/II.49–50), and the fish called ‘sea-locust’ (II.53).

[44] Cf. the stories of the giant fish and sailors (I.58/II.49), the bridge made from the fish rib (II.52), and the whale stranded ashore (II.57).

[45] Cf. the descriptions of the river in Azerbaijan (I.23), and the various kinds of human monsters (I.28/II.19, I.30/II.21, I.34–36/II.24–26).

as the story about a child raised by a dog (I.49), which finds a very similar account in *Kitāb al-ḥayawān* by al-Ǧāḥiẓ. Some of them, however, such as the image of the legendary insular tree of Waqwaq (I.42/II.32), are attested in such a diverse range of Arabic and Persian sources, that any attempt to establish the exact source used by our compiler would be impossible.

Especially remarkable are rare occasions when the compiler of the *Marvels* introduces Islamic religious vocabulary or traditions. In what concerns the former, he uses the Arabic loanword *ḥaǧ* and its derivative *ḥaǧāyē* to refer to 'pilgrimage' and 'pilgrims', respectively, in I.47. As for the latter, in I.64/II.58, he represents Antichrist by locating him on the island of Barṭīl, full of sounds of musical instruments. In doing so, he follows Muslim conventions about the corresponding eschatological figure of Daǧǧāl, who is often represented in Arabic sources as chained to a mountain on a distant island in the sea.

It remains an open question as to how exactly the Syriac Christian compiler of the *Marvels* became acquainted with this rich assortment of Muslim geographical and anthropological lore. Although the possibility of his dependence on some specific *ʿaǧāʾib* composition cannot be ruled out completely, it does not seem particularly likely, as I was unable to discover an Arabic or Persian work that would contain all these traditions. A more plausible scenario, thus, is that he culled these traditions while perusing a number of existing Muslim geographical and paradoxographical works, such as those by Ibn Ḫordāḏbeh or al-Qazwīnī, and reworked them according to his taste, as he rendered this material into Syriac.[46] At the same time, a possibility of the oral transmission of at least some of these traditions, which one can easily imagine becoming a part of the folklore of the Islamicate world, should also be taken into consideration.

1.4. Date and milieu

The anonymous and compilative character of the *Marvels* makes the task of determining the date of its composition particularly challenging. The *terminus ante quem* of ca. 1680, provided by the date of the oldest textual witness in which it is attested (i.e., Borgia sir. 39), could be pushed to a somewhat earlier date, given the fact that this manuscript does not present an autograph. The *terminus post quem* is, however, much more difficult to establish. Such linguistic markers as the appearance of a gloss in New Persian (I.28/II.19) and the mention of a Frankish man (I.46/II.35) certainly point to a post-Crusader period. Moreover, the story about the victims of the 'great plague' in Basra (I.49) might indicate the time after the onslaught of the Black Death in the middle of the fourteenth century. At the moment, the period between the fifteenth and the first half of the seventeenth century appears to be the most plausible time of the work's composition.

In what concerns the milieu, from which the composition originates, it may be said with a fair degree of confidence that it was produced by a member of the East Syrian Christian

[46] For examples of the use of Muslim Arabic works on natural science by such Christian authors of 'Syriac Renaissance' as Barhebraeus and Jacob bar Shakko, see Takahashi (2004, 293–97; 2002; 2006).

community, most likely, in Northern Mesopotamia. As for a more exact location of the place where the compiler of the *Marvels* might have carried out his work, it cannot be established with absolute certainty. It should, however, have been one of the urban centres, where a literate member of the East Syrian community might be exposed both to Arabic (and/or Persian) Muslim culture as well as to oral traditions from such regions as Central Anatolia (cf. I.12), Kurdistan (cf. I.24–27), and the Persian Gulf (cf. I.40). In a manner of speculation, a city like Mosul, the commercial hub of north-eastern Iraq, seems to be a likely option. In that direction points also the fact that one of the compiler's informants, the priest Quryāqos (I.41, I.47), is said to be a native of this city. However, other cities with significant East Syrian communities, such as Alqōš or Urmia, cannot be ruled out completely.

2. EDITION AND TRANSLATION

https://doi.org/10.11647/OBP.0237.02

2.1. Sigla and Conventions

[...] indicates emendations or extended abbreviations in the Syriac text; in the English translation, indicates renderings based on emendations or variant readings;

<...> indicates readings that are added in the margins or between the lines of the main text;

|...| indicates folio numbers of Syriac manuscripts;

(...) indicates a supplied word or words;

Manuscripts

B1 Berlin, Staatsbibliothek zu Berlin, Orient. quart. 802 (Berlin Syr. 59);

B2 Berlin, Staatsbibliothek zu Berlin, Sachau 118 (Berlin Syr. 86);

L London, British Library, Or. 4528;

V Vatican, Biblioteca Apostolica, Borgia sir. 39;

For the sake of readability, I have chosen to reproduce the original text of the *Marvels* with the standard and non-confessional Estrangelo typeface, most commonly used in academic editions of Syriac texts. Another editorial decision was to omit vocalization, which in all four manuscripts is partial and does not seem to deviate in any significant manner from the standard rules of Classical Syriac grammar. The vocalization was retained, however, where it could be of importance for establishing correct pronunciation or meaning of words, as in the case of toponyms, proper names, and rare or corrupt forms. Those who are interested in the vocalization can easily access it directly in the facsimiles of the manuscripts, reproduced in Appendix (B1, B2) or available online (V).

The text of the *Marvels* is presented as divided into separate units. This division, meant to facilitate analysis of the work's content and comparison between the two recensions, is based on the rubricated words, such as 'a marvel', 'marvels', 'another', etc., which introduce many of the units in the manuscripts or, when they are absent, on the content of the units.

For transcribing Syriac, I use a slightly modified version of the simplified system of transcription that was outlined by Sebastian P. Brock and adopted by the Library of Congress.[1] Unless specified otherwise, all translations of Syriac and Arabic texts in the commentary part are mine.

[1] The description is available online at https://www.loc.gov/catdir/cpso/romanization/syriac.pdf.

2.2. Recension I: Text (V)

ܬܘܒ ܒܝܕ ܐܠܗܐ ܟܬܒܝܢܢ ܬܕܡܪ̈ܬܐ ܕܐܝܬ ܒܡܕܝܢ̈ܬܐ ܪܘܪ̈ܒܬܐ ܘܒܝ̈ܡܡܐ ܘܒܓܙܪ̈ܬܐ.

1 ܐܠܟܣܢܕܪܘܣ ܒܢܐ ܡܕܝܢܬܐ ܡܢ ܠܘܩܐ. ܒܐܬܪܐ ܕܐܓܝܦܛܘܣ ܒܓܙܪܬܐ ܚܕܐ. ܕܪܘܣܛܘܬܗ ܐܪܒܥܐ ܦܪ̈ܣܐ. ܘܗܘܐ ܒܗ ܓܪ̈ܐ ܣܓܝ̈ܐܐ. ܘܐܝܬܝܗ ܡܕܝܢܬܐ ܪܒܬܐ. ܘܫܒܝܚܬܐ ܘܠܝܬ ܒܗ ܬܪ̈ܥܐ.

2 ܐܬܒܢܝܬ ܐܠܟܣܢܕܪܝܐ ܘܪܗܘܡܐ ܒܬܠܬܡܐܐ ܫܢ̈ܝܢ. ܘܠܐ ܡܣܝܢ ܗܘܘ ܕܢܫܠܡܘܢ ܠܡܒܢܝܗܝܢ ܒܫܘܡܠܝܐ. ܟܕ ܒܢܝܢܗܘܢ ܡܬܚܡܝܢ ܗܘ̈ܝ ܒܣܘܕܪ̈ܐ ܐܘܟܡܐ. ܕܠܐ ܢܦܪ̈ܩܘܢ ܡܢ ܡܫܠܡܘܬ ܣܪܘܬܐ. ܘܡܢܣ̈ܝܐ ܘܠܝܚܐ ܘܣܩܠܐ ܘܒܢܝܢܐ ܕܡܕܝܢܬܐ.

3 ܘܐܝܬ ܗܘܐ ܒܐܠܟܣܢܕܪܝܐ ܡܕܝܢܬܐ ܡܢܪܬܐ ܚܕܐ ܕܐܬܒܢܝܬ ܥܠ ܓ̈ܠܠܐ |fol. 111v| ܚܕ ܕܙܓܘܓܝܬܐ. ܘܐܝܬ ܗܘܐ ܒܗ ܡܚܙܝܬܐ ܐܠܦܝܢ ܡܘܕܥܢܐ ܫܒܐ ܡܢ ܡܕܝܢ̈ܬܐ ܐܚܪ̈ܢܝܐ ܕܠܐ ܡܫܢܝܐ.

4 ܘܐܝܬ ܗܘܐ ܒܐܠܟܣܢܕܪܝܐ ܡܣܝܬܐ ܚܕܐ ܕܬܠܝܐ ܒܪܫܗ ܡܢܪܬܐ. ܘܥܠ ܡܢ ܕܝܠܗ ܗܘܐ ܬܘܬܒܗ. ܚܕܐ ܗܘܐ ܠܗ ܠܦܘܣܛܝܣܛܘܠܝܘܢ ܡܕܝܢܬܐ. ܘܥܠ ܡܫܝܚܬܐ ܕܒܣܡܐ ܡܠܘܗ ܒܝܡܐ.

Title ܒܝܕ ܐܠܗܐ] om. L

1a ܡܢ ܠܘܩܐ. ܒܐܬܪܐ ܕܐܓܝܦܛܘܣ] om. L

1b ܕܪܘܣܛܘܬܗ] ܕܪܘܣܛܘܬܗ ܐܪܒܥ L 1c ܒܗ] ܠܗ L

2c ܒܣܘܕܪ̈ܐ] ܒܣܕܪ̈ܐ L | ܢܦܪ̈ܩܘܢ] ܢܬܠܒܫܘܢ L

3b ܗܘܐ] om. L 4a ܗܘܐ] om. L 4b ܡܢܪܬܐ] ܕܡܢܪܬܐ L

2.2. Recension I: Translation

Again, with God's help, I write down marvels that are found in the great cities and in the seas and on the islands.

1 Alexander built a city of brass on some island in the country of Andalus, the width of which is four months. And he placed many treasures in it. And it is a great and sealed city, and there are no gates in it.

2 Alexandria and Rome were built over a period of three hundred years. And they (i.e., the inhabitants) were not able to walk in their midst during the daytime, (but only) when their eyes were covered with black veils so that they would not be dazzled by the exceeding whiteness and splendour and rays and adornments and buildings of the city.

3 And there was in the city of Alexandria a lighthouse that was built upon dew[2] of glass. And there were six hundred thousand Jews in it, besides other countless nations.

4 And there was in Alexandria a mirror that was hung on the top of the lighthouse. And anyone who would sit under it would see the city of Constantinople and every ship that was going out of it into the sea.

[2] Arabic version: 'hill'; Neo-Aramaic version: 'mountain, hill'.

5 ܘܐܝܬ ܒܚܕܐ ܕܘܟܬܐ ܡܢܪܬܐ ܕܢܚܫܐ ܘܥܠ ܪܫܗ̇ ܦܪܚܐ ܚܕ
ܕܢܚܫܐ. ܘܒܝܘܡܬܐ ܕܒܐܕܪ ܕܝܠܗܘܢ ܢܒܥܝܢ ܟܢ̈ܫܐ ܡܢ ܗܿܝ
ܡܢܪܬܐ. ܘܫܬܝܢ ܡܢܗ̇ ܟܠܗܘܢ ܒܢܝ̈ܢܫܐ ܕܡܬܟܐܒܝܢ ܠܬܡܢ
ܘܡܬܐܣܝܢ ܠܟܘܪ̈ܗܢܝܗܘܢ. ܘܡܠܝܢ ܟܠܗܘܢ ܡܦ̈ܩܐ ܕܗܘܝܢ ܒܒܬܝ̈ܗܘܢ.
ܘܠܫܢ̈ܝܐ ܕܐܝܬ ܬܡܢ. ܒܬܪ ܒܐܕܪ ܦܣܩܐ ܡܢܪܬܐ ܕܟܢ̈ܫܐ.
ܘܠܐ ܬܘܒ ܡܢܪܬܐ ܐܝܟ ܒܥܕܢܗ̇.

6 ܘܐܝܬ ܠܡܕܝܢܬܐ ܕܐܝܬ ܠܗ̇ ܫܒܥܐ ܫܘܪ̈ܐ ܚܕ ܠܓܘ ܚܕ. ܘܒܝܬ
ܫܘܪܐ ܠܫܘܪܐ ܫܒܥܐ ܡܝ̈ܠܐ. ܘܟܠ ܬܠܬܐ ܡܝ̈ܠܐ ܚܕ ܦܪܣܚܐ.
ܘܒܝܬ ܫܘܪܐ ܠܫܘܪܐ ܦܪ̈ܕܝܣܐ ܘܢܨܒ̈ܬܐ ܘܡܥܝ̈ܢܐ ܘܫܩ̈ܝܐ
ܘܐܪ̈ܣܘܬܐ.

7 ܐܝܬ ܫܘܪܐ ܕܒܢܐܘܗܝ ܡ̈ܠܟܐ ܡܢ ܡܫܚܐ ܕܓܒܪ ܘܒܢܝܢܐ ܠܫܡܐ
ܕܦܘܪܫܐ. ܡܬܚܫܐ ܕܬܡܢܝܐ ܢܦ̈ܫܢ.

8 ܬܕܡܘܪܬܐ. ܕܡܕܝܢܬܐ ܚܕܐ ܘܐܝܬܝܗ̇ ܡܕܝܢܬܐ ܪܒܬܐ. ܕܐܝܬ
ܗܘܘ ܠܗ̇ ܫܒܥܝܢ ܬܪ̈ܥܐ. ܘܐܝܬܘܗܝ ܗܘܐ ܒܓܘܗ̇ ܕܡܕܝܢܬܐ
ܡܢ ܢܚܫܐ ܘܡܢ ܦܪܙܠܐ. ܘܢܦܩܝܢ ܡܢ ܬܚܬ ܒܪܘܗ̇ ܕܡܠܟܐ
ܐܪܒܥܐ ܢܗܪ̈ܘܬܐ ܪܘܪ̈ܒܐ.

5b-c ܟܢ̈ܫܐ ܡܢ ܗܿܝ ܡܢܪܬܐ] ܡܢ ܗܿܝ ܡܢܪܬܐ ܟܢ̈ܫܐ L   5e ܒܬܪ] ܘܒܬܪ L

6a ܘܐܝܬ] ܐܝܬ L | ܠܡܕܝܢܬܐ] ܡܕܝܢܬܐ L | ܠܓܘ] ܠܓܘ ܡܢ L

7a ܕܓܒܪ] ܕܒܪ L

8a ܕܡܕܝܢܬܐ] ܐܝܬ ܡܕܝܢܬܐ L | ܘܐܝܬܝܗ̇ ܡܕܝܢܬܐ] om. L | ܕܐܝܬ] ܘܐܝܬ L

8c ܕܡܠܟܐ] ܕܡܕܝܢܬܐ ܗܕܐ L

5 And in a certain place, there is a lighthouse[3] of brass, and on its top a horseman of brass. And on the day of their festival, the water flows forth from this lighthouse. And all the people who are assembled there drink from it and water their cattle and fill all the jars they have with them and the vessels that are there. After the festival, the stream of water ceases and no longer flows as it used to.

6 And there is a city that has seven walls, one within the other. And between one wall and the other, there are seven miles. And every three miles is one parasang. And between one wall and the other, there are orchards, and rivers, and vineyards, and canals, and mills.

7 There is a wall that the kings built from the Sea of the Khazars (i.e., the Caspian Sea) to the Sea of Syria (i.e., the Mediterranean Sea). (Its) length — eight days.

8 *A marvel:* [There is] a certain city, which is a great city, that has seventy gates. And the city was built of brass and iron. And four great rivers flow forth from beneath the king's throne.

[3] Or 'minaret'.

9 ܬܕܡܘܪܬܐ. ܐܝܬ ܗܘܐ ܒܐܪܥܐ ܕܡܨܪܝܢ ܐܘܣܛܘܢܐ. ܘܒܪܫܗ ܕܟܠ ܐܘܣܛܘܢܐ ܩܘܡܬ̈ܐ ܕܢܫܪܐ. ܘܢܛܦܝܢ ܗܘܘ ܡ̈ܝܐ ܡܢ ܕܘܟ̈ܝܬܐ ܕܩܘܡܬ̈ܐ ܒܪܘܡܐ ܠܦܠܓܗ ܕܐܘܣܛܘܢܐ. ܘܠܐ ܒܒܪܢܫ ܗܘܘ ܡܢ ܦܠܓܗ ܕܐܘܣܛܘܢܐ ܘܠܬܚܬ. ܘܠܐ ܡܬܦܣ̈ܩܝܢ ܗܘ̈ܝ، ܠܦ̈ܘܩܐ ܠܐ ܠܠܝܐ ܘܠܐ ܐܝܡܡܐ.

10 ܬܕܡܘܪܬܐ. ܐܝܬ ܗܘܐ ܒܐܪܥܐ ܕܐܢܛܠܘ̈ܣ ܗܢܘ ܕܝܢ ܕܡܘܪܛܢܘܣ. ܦܪܫܐ ܚܕ ܕܢܚܫܐ ܕܪܟܝܒ ܥܠ ܣܘܣܝܐ ܕܢܚܫܐ ܘܐܝܕܗ ܦܫܝܛܐ ܐܝܟ ܗ̇ܘ ܕܡܚܘܐ ܐܘܪܚܐ. ܘܐܡܪܝܢ ܕܠܝܬ ܡܝܐ ܘܠܗܠ ܕܡܕܒܪܬܐ ܕܡܕܒܪܐ. ܘܟܠ ܡܢ ܕܥܒܪ ܥܠ ܦܪܫܐ ܗ̇ܘ. ܒܠܥܝܢ ܠܗ ܫ̈ܐܕܐ. ܗܢܘ |fol. 112r| ܕܝܢ ܝܚܝ̈ܕܝܐ ܕܐܝܬ ܬܡܢ.

11 ܬܕܡܘܪܬܐ. ܘܐܝܬ ܒܐܪܥܐ ܕܡܨܪܝܢ ܒܢܝܢܐ ܚܕ ܐܘܪܟܗ ܐܪܒܥܡܐܐ ܐܡ̈ܝܢ. ܘܦܬܝܗ ܐܪܒܥܡܐܐ ܐܡ̈ܝܢ. ܘܒܬܘܟ ܠܟܠ ܡܢܗ ܕܣܠܡ ܒܣܠܡ ܗܘܐ ܒܢܝܢܐ. ܥܠ ܡܠܟܐ ܕܐܝܬ ܒܗ <ܣܠܟܐ> ܢܚܘܪܘܗܝ. ܘܒܚܘܪܐ ܦܫܝܛܐܝܬ ܡܢ ܒܢܝܢܐ. ܘܟܠܗܘܢ ܡ̈ܠܟܐ ܕܟܠܡܐ ܠܐ ܡܨܝܢ ܠܡܚܘܪܘܬܗ.

9d ܗܘܘ] ܗܘܘ ܡ̈ܝܐ L

9e ܠܠܝܐ] ܒܠܠܝܐ L | ܐܝܡܡܐ] ܒܐܝܡܡܐ. ܘܕܘܟ̈ܝܬܐ ܕܡ̈ܝܐ ܗܘܝܢ ܢܘܪ̈ܐ L

10a ܕܝܢ] L om. | ܕܡܘܪܛܢܘܣ] ܡܘܪܛܢܘܣ L

10e ܗܢܘ ܕܝܢ ܝܚܝ̈ܕܝܐ] L om.

11a ܘܐܝܬ] ܐܝܬ L   11b ܐܪܒܥܡܐܐ ܐܡ̈ܝܢ] ܗܟܢ L

11d ܣܠܟܐ] V Added in superscript

9 *A marvel:* In the land of Egypt, there were columns, and on the top of each column brass chains. And the water dropped from the places of the chains until halfway down the column, but it did not pass below the midpoint of the column. And drops did not stop day and night.[4]

10 *A marvel:* In the land of Andalus, that is Qōrnetōs, there was a brass horseman riding a brass horse. And his hand is stretched out, as of someone who beckons and says, ‘From now on, there is no inhabited place’. And the ants, that is *šekwānē,*[5] that are there devour everyone who passes beyond that horseman.

11 *A marvel:* In the land of Egypt, there is a building whose length is four hundred cubits; and its width is four hundred cubits. And there is written on it, ‘We built this building. Every king who has the power in himself, let him pull it down!’ And to destroy is easier than to build, but all the kings of the world are not able to pull it down.

[4] L add. ‘And the places of that water are green’.

[5] I.e. Neo-Aramaic ܫܟܘܢ̈ܐ ‘ants’.

12 ܬܕܡܘܪܬܐ. ܐܫܬܟܚ ܠܝ ܝܘܣܦ ܐܚܘܗܝ ܕܡܪܝ ܒܒܪܝܫܘܥ
ܕܚܠܡ. ܕܚܙܐ ܠܒܪܐ ܒܡܘܬܒܐ ܡܕܝܢܬܐ. ܘܠܒܪܐ ܗܘ
ܪܘܗܡܝܐ ܐܢܬܘܗܝ ܗܘܐ. ܘܐܝܬ ܗܘܐ ܠܗ ܫܒܥܐ ܦ̈ܠܚܐ
ܦܪ̈ܕܝܣܐ ܕܒܢ̈ܝ ܒܣܦܗ ܡܢ [ܢܬܘܬܐ] ܕܐܒܗ̈ܘܗܝ. ܘܟܠ
ܦܪ̈ܕܝܣܐ ܫܘܪܗ ܡܢܗ. ܘܠܗ ܚܙ̈ܘܗܝ. ܘܠܐ ܡܬܚܠܦ ܦܪ̈ܕܝܣܐ
ܒܣܒܪܗ.

ܥܠ ܬܕܡܘܪܬܐ ܕܡܒܘ̈ܥܐ ܘܢܗܘܪܬܐ.

13 ܐܝܬ ܚܕ ܢܗܪܐ ܕܡܬܩܪܐ ܟܐ̈ܦܠܘܣ ܬܠܬ ܫܢ̈ܝܢ ܡܢ ܫܢܝܪ
ܐܢܛܘܟܝܐ ܡܢܪܡ ܡ̈ܝܗ ܠܫܡܝܐ. ܘܬܠܬ ܫ̈ܢܝܢ ܡܬܟܠܝܐ
ܡܪ̈ܕܘܬܗ. ܘܢܫܝܐ ܕܒܬܪܗ ܕܡܪ̈ܕܘܬܗ.

14 ܬܕܡܘܪܬܐ. ܢܗܪܐ ܕܢܘܦ ܒܪ ܢܦܠ ܒܗ ܒܪܢܫܐ ܐܘ ܒܥܝܪܐ
ܒܢܗܪܐ ܕܐܝܬܘܗܝ، ܚܝܐ ܘܐܝܬ ܒܗ ܢܦܫܐ. ܠܐܦ ܠܟܠ ܡܢ ܕ̈ܢܦܠ.
ܘܒܪ ܡܝܐ ܠܐܒܐ ܒܓܘܗ.

15 ܬܕܡܘܪܬܐ. ܘܐܝܬ ܒܢܗܪܐ ܕܘܟܬܐ ܚܕܐ ܕܡܬܩܪܐ ܐܦܘܪܝܩܘܣ.
ܙܕܐ ܘܡܬܦܫܩ ܒܢܘܢܐ ܬܠܬ ܝܘܡܝܢ. ܘܡܬܟܠܝܐ ܡܪ̈ܕܘܬܗ
ܬܠܬ ܫܢ̈ܝܢ. <ܡܫܡܫܢܐ ܕܪ̈ܟܐ. ܘܡܢ ܒܬܪ> ܒܕܡܘܬܐ ܕܡܬܚܙܝܐ
ܐܪܟܐ ܕܡܫܝܚܐ.

LV ܡܬܘܪܬܐ [ܢܬܘܬܐ 12d   L ܗܘܐ [ܗܘܘ 12c

L ܕܡܪ̈ܕܝܬܐ [ܕܡܪ̈ܕܝܬܗ 13c

V Added [ܡܫܡܫܢܐ ܕܪ̈ܟܐ. ܘܡܢ ܒܬܪ | L ܕܪ̈ܟܐ ܒܡܫܡܫܘ [ܕܪ̈ܟܐ 15c
in the left margin by the same hand.

12 *Marvels:* Joseph, the brother of Mār ʿAbdīšōʿ of Elam, told us that he saw a man in the city of Qōnyā. And that man was a Greek,[6] and he had seven thousand gardens, bought with his money from the [inheritance][7] of his parents. And each garden has its own wall that surrounds it, and no garden overlaps another.

About marvels of springs and rivers.

13 There is a river that is called Bāeṭlas. Its waters flow to the sea for three hours from the beginning of the day. And its flow stops for three hours, and the place of its flow dries up.

14 *A marvel:* The Sea of Reeds:[8] when a man or an animal falls into it, as long as he is alive and there is breath in him, he floats upon the water. But when he dies, he sinks in the water.

15 *Marvels:* And in the sea, there is a certain place that is called ʾEwrīqōs. It flows and stops three times during the day, and its flow pauses for three hours. [Its depth] is five hundred cubits. And afterward, it withdraws until the dry land appears.

---

[6] Lit. 'Roman'.

[7] While the manuscript has 'abundance', the emendation follows the reading الورث 'inheritance' of the Arabic version.

[8] In this context, the Dead Sea.

16 ܬܕܡܘܪܬܐ. ܘܐܝܬ ܒܣܘܪܝܐ ܚܕ ܢܗܪܐ ܕܡܪܕܐ ܒܫܒܬܐ ܚܕ
ܝܘܡܐ. ܘܡܫܠܡ ܟܠܗ̇، ܘܒܫܒܬܐ ܢܝ̈ܚܬܐ ܐܫ̈ܬܬܐ
ܡܬܦܣܩ. ܒܕܡܐ ܕܡܬܚܙܝܐ ܐܪܥܐ ܝܒܝܫܬܐ.

17 ܬܕܡܘܪܬܐ. ܐܝܬ ܒܐܪܥܐ ܙ̇ܒܘܠܘܢ ܐܝܬ ܒܐܪܐ ܕܡܦܩܐ ܡ̈ܝܐ
ܘܡܠܝܚܐ ܘܚܠܝܐ. ܘܡܬܦܣܩܝܢ ܡ̈ܝܐ ܒܫܘܝܐ. ܙܒܢ ܡ̈ܝܐ
ܡ̈ܠܝܚܐ. ܘܗܘܝܢ ܡܠܝܚܐ ܚܠܝܐ ܘܚܘܪܐ. ܘܠܐ ܗܘܐ ܒܗ ܠܡܫܬܝܐ
ܕܢܦܠܐ ܘܐܦܠܐ ܪܫܝܐ. ܘܢܦܠܐ ܦܐܫ ܒܕܘܟܬܗ [ܒܫܘܝܐ]. ܟܕ
ܠܝܬ ܒܗ ܠܡܫܬܝܐ ܕܡܠܝܚܐ.

18 ܬܕܡܘܪܬܐ. ܒܐܬܪܐ ܕܦܠܣܛܝܢ̈. ܐܝܬ ܡܥܝܢܐ ܒܟܐܦܐ
ܕܡܪܕܐ ܕܡܐ. ܘܪܚܫ ܘܠܥܠܡܗ ܘܪܦܘܬܗ ܣܠܩ. ܘܪܕܐ
|fol. 112v| ܘܡܛܐ ܘܗܘܐ ܟܦܪܐ ܣܘܣܡܐ. ܟܕ ܠܝܬ ܒܗ
ܠܡܫܬܝܐ ܘܠܐ ܪܫܝܐ ܕܕܡܐ. ܘܥܠܝܡ ܡܢܗ ܚܝ̈ܠܐ.

19 ܬܕܡܘܪܬܐ. ܒܐܬܪܐ ܕܗܦ̈ܩܝܐ ܐܝܬ ܢܗܪܐ ܕܪܕܐ ܒܝܘܡܐ
ܕܫܒܬܐ. ܘܫܪܟܐ ܕܝܘ̈ܡܬܐ ܡܬܦܣܩ.

20 ܐܝܬ ܢܗܪܐ ܚܕ ܕܡܪܕܐ ܟܠܗ ܚܠܐ ܡܒܥܐ. ܕܠܐ ܡ̈ܝܐ. ܘܠܐ
ܡܨܐ ܒܪܢܫܐ ܘܠܐ ܒܥܒܪܐ ܘܠܐ ܦܫܝܛܐ ܠܡܥܒܪ ܒܗ.
ܘܒܝܘܡܐ ܕܫܒܬܐ ܡܬܟܠܝܐ ܡܪܕܝܬܗ. ܘܢܝܚ ܕܘܒܬܐ
ܕܡܪܕܝܬܗ ܠܐܦ̈ܝ ܡܥܪܒܐ.

16 In L this unit follows unit I.64.

17a ܐܝܬ ܙ̇ܒܘܠܘܢ] ܙ̇ܒܘܠܘܢ L | ܕܡܦܩܐ] ܘܡܦܩܐ L 17b ܘܡܬܦܣܩܝܢ] ܕܡܬܦܣܩܝܢ L | ܒܫܘܝܐ] ܒܫܒܝܐ L 17d ܒܫܘܝܐ] ܒܫܘܝܘܬܐ V ܒܫܒܝܐ L

18a ܕܦܠܣܛܝܢ̈] ܕܦܠܣܛܝܢ̈ܐ L 18b ܣܠܩ] ܐܝܟ ܕܡܐ L

19a ܕܗܦ̈ܩܝܐ] ܕܗܦܩܪܐ L 19b ܡܬܦܣܩ] ܡܬܦܣܩ. ܐܝܬ ܢܗܪܐ ܚܕ ܒܐܕܘܪܒܝܓܢ. ܕܪܕܝܢ ܡܢܗ ܡ̈ܝܐ ܘܡܒܥܝܢ. ܘܗܘܝܢ ܟܐ̈ܦܐ. L

20b ܘܠܐ ܦܫܝܛܐ ܠܡܥܒܪ ܒܗ] ܕܢܥܒܪ ܒܗ ܘܠܐ ܦܫܝܛܘܬܐ L

16 *Marvels:* And there is a river in Syria that flows one day during the week, and its waters increase. And during the other six days, they stop until the dry land appears.

17 *Marvels:* There is a well in the land of Knīgar that brings forth water and salt and naphtha (i.e., crude oil). And [when] the water stops in a pool, the salty waters flow forth and turn into sweet and white salt, and it has neither taste nor smell of naphtha. And the naphtha remains in its place in the pool, while there is no (more) taste of salt in it.

18 *A marvel:* In the country of Pūštīdar, there is a spring in a stone that runs blood. And its smell and taste and stench are [like those of blood]. And it flows and dries up and turns into red dust that has no taste or smell of blood. And they take from it *ḥnānā*.

19 *Marvels:* There is a river in the country of Spārē that flows on the day of the Sabbath and stops on the remaining days.[9]

20 There is a river that flows entirely with dry sand without (any) water. And neither man, nor animal, nor ship can cross it. And on the day of the Sabbath, its flow stops. And (people) see the place of its flow in the direction of the West.

---

[9] L add. 'In Azerbaijan, there is a river from which waters flow, and dry up, and turn into stones'. (= I.23)

21 ܬܕܡܪ̈ܬܐ. ܐܝܬ ܒܐܬܪܐ ܕܪ̈ܗܘܡܝܐ ܥܠ ܫܡܐ ܕܐܒܓܪ ܐܬܪܐ
ܕܡܬܩܪܐ ܓ̇ܠܠܒܐ. ܠܐ ܡܬܦܣܩ ܡܢܗ ܡܛܪܐ ܠܐ ܣܬܘܐ
ܘܠܐ ܩܝܛܐ. ܘܐܦܠܐ ܡܨܝܢ ܠܡܚܒܫܘ ܓ̈ܠܠܬܐ ܐܠܐ ܠܓܘ ܒ̈ܬܐ.

22 ܬܕܡܪ̈ܬܐ. ܒܐܬܪܐ ܕܬܝܡܢܐ ܘܕܡܕܢܚܐ ܗܘܐ ܟܠܗ ܡܛܪܐ.
ܘܒܣܬܘܐ ܗܘܐ ܩܝܛܐ.

23 ܬܕܡܪ̈ܬܐ. ܐܝܬ ܢܚܠܐ ܚܕ ܒܐܕܪ̈ܒܝܓܢ. ܕܪܕܝܢ ܡܢܗ ܟ̈ܐܦܐ.
ܘܡܦܩܝܢ ܗܘܝܢ ܡܢܗ ܒܟ̈ܐܦܐ.

24 ܬܕܡܪ̈ܬܐ. ܒܒܝܬ ܕܠܒ̈ܝܐ ܡܕܝܢܬܐ ܒܡܪܒܥܬܐ ܕܡܪܢܬܐ
ܕܡܬܩܪܝܐ ܓܒܓܘ. ܐܝܬ ܡܥܡܕܐ ܚܕ ܙܥܘܪܐ ܥܠ ܣܦܬܗ
ܕܝܡܐ. ܘܡܢܕܪܐ ܟ̈ܐܦܐ ܣܘ̈ܡܩܐ ܘܫܚܘ̈ܪܐ ܐܝܟ ܚܠܐ ܬܘܩܦܐ.
ܘܐܝܬ ܒܓܠܓܠܗ ܫܪܒܘܬܐ ܘܓܘܢܗ ܐܝܟ. ܘܪܕܝܢ ܘܢܦܩܝܢ
ܒܢܗܪܐ. ܘܡܦܩܝܢ ܟ̈ܐܦܐ ܫ̈ܦܝܢ ܣܘ̈ܡܩܐ ܒܟ̈ܐܦܐ ܘܒܪ̈ܩܐ.

25 ܬܕܡܪ̈ܬܐ. ܐܝܬ ܒܐܬܪܐ ܕܡܬܩܪܐ ܩ̈ܠܦܪ ܒܝܬ ܣܝ̈ܢܝ ܠܒܝܬ
ܕܠܒ̈ܝܐ. ܛܘܪܐ ܚܕ ܡܥܡܘܣܬܐ ܕܪܫܗ ܚܕ ܦܪܣܚܐ. ܘܐܝܬ ܠܗ
ܡܣܩ̈ܠܐ ܡܢ ܬܪܝܨܘ ܠܟܒ̈ܐ. ܘܡܬܬܢܝܐ ܕܬܪܝܨܘ ܐܝܟ
ܡܡܠܐ. ܘܢܦܩ ܡܢܗ ܢܗܪܐ. ܘܡܥܝܢܐ ܠܚ̈ ܡܢ ܠܟܒܗ
ܕܛܘܪܐ. ܡܥܢܐ ܡܢ ܢܣܡ. ܘܢܦܩ ܘܡܥܝܢܐ ܠܟܒܐ ܕܒܝܬ
ܕܠܒ̈ܝܐ ܠܐܬܪܐ ܕܡܬܩܪܐ ܓ̈ܠܠܒܝ. ܘܠܟܒܐ ܐܚܪܢܐ ܟܠܗ
ܡܬܦܪܣܢ ܡܢ ܬܡܢܐ. ܘܡܢ ܡܬܦܣܩ ܢܗܪܐ ܘܡܟܐ ܡܟܡܟܡ.

21a ܕܐܒܓܪ] ܕܒܓܪ L   21c ܠܓܘ] ܠܓܘ ܡܢ L

22a ܟܠܗ] ܟܠܗ ܩܝܛܐ L

23 In L this unit follows unit I.19.

24a ܕܠܒ̈ܝܐ] ܕܠܒܝܙ L   24d ܐܝܟ] ܐܝܟ ܩܪܡܘܣܘ L

25b ܕܠܒ̈ܝܐ] ܕܠܒܝܙ L   25d ܠܟܒܗ] ܠܟܒ̈ܐ L

25f ܕܠܒ̈ܝܐ] ܕܠܒܝܙ L | ܠܐܬܪܐ] ܘܠܐܬܪܐ L | ܟܠܗ] ܟܠܗ ܩܝܛܐ L

25g ܘܡܢ] ܘܡܢ ܬܫܪܝܢ L

21 *Marvels:* In the country of Romans, there is a place on the Sea of the Khazars (i.e., the Caspian Sea), which is called Maṯlayā. It does not stop raining there, in winter as well as in summer. And they cannot even store crops, unless inside the houses.

22 *Marvels:* In the country of the South and of the Hejaz, it rains during the whole [summer], and it is summer in the winter.

23 *Marvels:* In Azerbaijan, there is a river from which waters flow, and dry up, and turn into stones.

24 *Marvels:* In the city of Bēt Dlīğ (i.e., Bitlis), in the vicinity of a town called ʿAmas, there is a small fount on the seashore, and it flows with water that is red and sour like strong vinegar. And it has a sharp taste, and its colour is like (that of) [minium]. And it flows and runs into a river, and those red waters become stones and pebbles.

25 *Marvels:* In the place called Pānōr, between Ḥīzān and Bēt Dlīğ, there is a mountain whose top measures one parasang. And it has ascents on both sides, and beneath both of them there is a sort of fount, and from it, a river comes out and waters one of the sides of the mountain. Beginning with Nisan, it comes out and waters the side of Bēt Dlīğ, the place called Ṭāṭīq, while (on) the other side they are afflicted by thirst the whole [summer]. And [from Teshrin], the river stops, and its fount dries up.

ܘܐܦ ܠܓܒܐ ܐܚܪܢܐ ܕܦܘܪܐ ܒܬܚܘܡܐ ܕܢܚܝܢ ܒܐܬܪܐ
ܕܡܬܩܪܐ ܩܐܬ̈ܠܓ. ܘܪܕܐ ܒܠܗ ܣܬܘܐ. ܘܠܐ ܢܬܪܝܡ ܡܢܗ
ܡܕܡ. ܘܡܬܬܠܝܡ ܒܗ ܒܢ̈ܝ ܐܬܪܐ ܡܬܠܐ. |fol. 113r| ܘܐܡܪܝܢ
ܕܬܘܪܢܐ ܒܬ̈ܠܝܗ. ܘܣܘܣܢܐ ܒܩܐܬ̈ܠܓ.

26 ܬܕܡܘܪܬܐ. ܬ̈ܠܝܦ ܡܢܝܬܐ ܒܐܬܪܐ ܕܒܝܬ ܕܝܠܡ. ܐܝܬ ܝܡܐ
ܚܕ ܒܡܪܒܥܘܬܐ ܕܡܢܝܬܐ. ܘܐܝܬ ܒܓܘ ܝܡܐ ܡܒܘܥܐ ܕܡ̈ܝܐ
ܬ̈ܠܝܐ ܘܡܢܒܥ ܠܡܒܥܐ. ܘܢܦܠ ܣܦܪܗ ܕܚܕ ܓܒܪܐ ܪܒܐ ܒܓܘ
ܗ̇ܘ ܡܒܘܥܐ. ܘܐܦ ܒܐܬܪܐ ܐܚܪܢܐ ܒܡܒܘܥܐ ܕܬ̈ܠܝܐ.
ܡܬܚܙܝܢܐ ܕܒܣܪܐ ܢܘܡܝܢ.

27 ܬܕܡܘܪܬܐ. ܐܝܬ ܛܘܒ ܒܐܬܪܐ ܕܒܝܬ ܕܝܠܡ ܒܛ̈ܘܪܐ ܢܗܪܐ
ܒܚܝܠܐ ܘܪܘܝܐ. ܘܐܝܬ ܒܗ ܒܢܗܪܐ ܕܒܝܬܐ ܚܕܐ ܪܘܫܝܬܐ
ܐܝܟ ܐܓܡܐ. ܘܡܬܡܚܝܟܬ ܕܒܝܬܐ ܗ̇ܝ ܓܙܪܬܐ ܚܕܐ
ܝܒܘܪܬܐ. ܘܦܠܝܫܐ ܒܠ ܥ̈ܘܩ ܡ̈ܝܐ. ܘܒܣܘܡܐ ܕܓܙܪܬܐ ܫܠܝܐ
ܗ̇ܝ ܓܙܪܬܐ ܠܟܠ ܡܢ ܡ̈ܝܐ. ܘܐܬܝܐ ܘܒܠܝܐ ܒܕܘܒܬܐ
ܒܚܝܠܬܐ. ܘܒܒܪܝܢ ܒܢ̈ܝܢܫܐ ܒܠܗ̇ ܐܝܟ ܓܙܪܐ ܒܝܡܐ
ܠܬܥܒ ܥܡ̈ܝܢ. ܘܡܢ ܣܦܪܐ ܓܙܪܬܐ ܠܕܘܒܬܗ̇. ܘܐܦ ܡܣܬܡܟܠ
ܐܢܫ ܒܠܗ̇ ܦܐܙ ܒܕܘܒܬܗ ܒܝܡܐ ܠܓܙܪܬܐ ܐܚܪܬܐ.
ܕܫܠܝܐ ܛܘܒ ܠܗ̇ ܕܘܒܬܐ. ܘܒܒܪ ܘܐܙܠ ܘܡܬܦܪܐ ܗ̇ܘ ܢܗܪܐ
ܕܣܦܝܢܬܐ.

25b ܩܐܬ̈ܠܓ] ܩܬܠܓ L

26a ܬ̈ܠܝܦ] ܒܬܠܝܦ L | ܕܝܠܡ] ܕܝܠܙ L

26e ܡܬܚܙܝܢܐ ܕܒܣܪܐ] ܘܡܬܚܙܝܢܐ ܕܒܣܪܝܢܐ ܒܣܪܝܢ L

27a ܕܒܝܬ ܕܝܠܡ] ܕܝܠܙ L

27j ܕܣܦܝܢܬܐ] ܢܗܪܐ ܕܣܦܝܢܬܐ L

And it comes out on the other side of the mountain, in the territory of Ḥizān, in the place called Qātāğ. And it flows (there) the whole winter, but they do not benefit at all from it. And the locals have a proverb about it, and they say, 'Gain in Ṭāṭīq, and loss in Qātāğ'.

26 *Marvels:* [In] the town of Ṭāṭōn in the country of Bēt Dlīğ, there is a sea in the vicinity of the town. And in the midst of the sea, there is a fount of sweet-water, and it is close to the dry land. And the staff of one of the shepherds fell into that fount, and it came out in the water spring in a different country, located ten days afar.

27 *Marvels:* Again, in the country of Bēt Dlīğ, in Ṭārōn, there is a deep and narrow river. And in this river, there is a wide place, like a pond, and in the middle of that place a small island, and it floats upon the surface of the water. And on Fridays, that island raises above the water and comes and stops at a deep place. And people cross over it as if upon a bridge for nine hours. And then the island returns to its place. And if a man comes upon it, he stays in his place until the next Friday, when it rises up again to that place, and he crosses and leaves. And that river is called '[the River] of Sin'.

ܥܠ ܬܕܡ̈ܪܬܐ ܕܐܝܬ ܒܓܙܪ̈ܬܐ ܡܕ̈ܝܢܬܐ ܘܦܓܪ.

28 ܐܝܬ ܒܓܙܪܬܐ ܚܕܐ ܒܢ̈ܝܢܫܐ ܕܐܝܬ ܠܗܘܢ ܐܕ̈ܢܐ ܐܪ̈ܝܟܐ ܘܦܬ̈ܝܬܐ ܕܡܟܣܝܢ ܠܗܘܢ ܡܢ ܪ̈ܫܝܗܘܢ ܘܥܕܡܐ ܠܪ̈ܓܠܝܗܘܢ. ܕܗܘܬ ܒܠܐ. ܘܡܬܬܘܪܝܢ ܦܬܐܝܬ ܟ̈ܠܝܡ ܒܦܓܪ.

29 ܬܕܡܘܪܬܐ. ܐܝܬ ܒܓܙܪܬܐ ܡܕ̈ܝܢܬܐ ܓܙܪܬܐ ܚܕܐ ܕܡܬܩܪܝܐ ܦܢܘܪ. ܘܐܝܬ ܒܗ ܒܢ̈ܝܢܫܐ ܟܠܒ̈ܢܐ. ܕܪ̈ܫܝܗܘܢ ܐܝܟ ܟܠ̈ܒܐ. ܘܟܕ ܢܒܚܘܢ ܠܘܬܗܘܢ ܒܡܠ̈ܬܐ ܢܒܚܘܢ ܘܢܦܩܘܢ ܒܫܘܪܐ ܕܐܝܬ ܬܡܢ. ܘܢܬܒܪܟܘܢ ܥܠ ܚܠܐ ܕܢܗܘܐ ܕܗܘܬ ܢܠܐ. ܘܠܐ ܥܒܪ ܒܗܘܢ ܒܓܪܐ ܘܠܐ ܙܘܡܝܐ ܘܠܐ ܫܝܦܐ. ܘܐܦ ܐܢܫ ܡܢ ܒܢ̈ܝܢܫܐ ܢܬܩܪܒ ܠܘܬܗܘܢ ܒܝܕ ܕܚܘܠܬܐ. ܟܕ ܥܠܬܗ ܡܐܬ.

30 ܬܕܡܘܪܬܐ. ܘܐܝܬ ܒܡܕܒܪܐ ܕܥܪ̈ܒܝܐ. ܐܢܫܐ ܕܐܝܬ ܠܗܘܢ ܐ̈ܠܝܬܐ. ܐܝܟ ܐ̈ܠܝܬܐ ܕܥܪ̈ܒܐ. ܘܟܕ ܚܙܝܢ ܒܢ̈ܝܢܫܐ ܥܪܩܝܢ ܡܢܗܘܢ. ܘܥܪ̈ܒܝܐ ܕܐܬܪܐ ܗܘ ܐܟܠܝܢ ܠܗܘܢ.

31 ܬܕܡܘܪܬܐ. ܢܦܩ ܥܠ ܐܠܟܣܢܕܪܘܣ ܒܢ̈ܝܢܫܐ ܕܪ̈ܓܠܝܗܘܢ ܐܝܟ |fol. 113v| ܪ̈ܓܠܐ ܕܥܩܪ̈ܒܐ. ܘܐܝܬ ܗ̈ܘܝ ܠܗܘܢ ܬܠܬ ܨ̈ܒܥܢ ܒܟܠ ܚܕܐ ܪ̈ܓܠܐ.

ܥܠ ܬܕܡ̈ܪܬܐ ܕܐܝܬ ܒܓܙܪ̈ܬܐ ܡܕ̈ܝܢܬܐ ܘܦܓܪ.] L om.

28b ܪ̈ܫܝܗܘܢ] ܪܫܗܘܢ L | ܠܪ̈ܓܠܝܗܘܢ] ܠܪܓܠܝܗܘܢ. ܘܐܬܬܣܝܡ ܠܗܘܢ L

28c ܟ̈ܠܝܡ ܒܦܓܪ] ܟ̈ܠܝܡ ܒܦܓܪ L

29d ܕܢܗܘܐ] ܕܢܗܘܐ ܠܗܘܢ L

30a ܬܕܡܘܪܬܐ] L om. 30b ܒܢ̈ܝܢܫܐ] ܠܒܪ̈ܢܫܐ L

31a ܢܦܩ] ܢܦܩܘ L 31b ܬܠܬ] ܫܬ L

On marvels that are in the Eastern islands and beyond.

28 On a certain island, there are people who have long and wide ears that cover them from their heads to their [feet] instead of a cloak. And in Persian, they are called *gālīm gōš*.

29 *Marvels:* In the Eastern islands, there is an island called Karnāš, and on it, there are dog-people, whose males are like dogs. And when enemies approach them, they enter and swim in the river, which is there. And they roll in the sand, so that it would serve [them] instead of armour; and neither arrow, nor spear, nor sword can reach them. And if a regular man would cleave to their women by way of intercourse, he dies immediately.

30 *Marvels:* And in the desert of the Arabs, there are people who have fat tails, like those of sheep. And when they see [a man], they flee from him. And the Arabs of that country eat them.

31 *Marvels:* The people whose legs are like the legs of scorpions went out against Alexander, and they had three[10] digits on each leg.

[10] 'Six' in L and B1 in II.22.

32 ܬܕܡܘܪܬܐ. ܒܪܘܬܐ ܚܕܐ ܐܝܬ ܕܡܡܘܪ̈ܝܫ ܐܟܠܝܢ ܒܢܝܢܫܐ ܟܕ ܗ̇ܘ ܚܝ. ܠܐ ܕܟܣܝܢ ܠܗ. ܐܠܐ ܦܣܩܝܢ ܠܓܘܪܗ. ܘܐܟܠܝܢ ܠܗ ܟܕ ܗ̇ܘ ܚܝ ܟܕ ܠܐ ܡܐܬ ܗ̣ܘ ܘܐܦܠܐ ܡܟܐܒܐ. ܘܒܪܘܬܐ ܡܬܩܪܝܐ ܟܠܿܚܝܦ. ܐܟܠܝܢ ܒܗ̇ ܒܢܝܢܫܐ.

33 ܬܕܡܘܪܬܐ. ܐܝܬ ܒܦܢܕܝܢ ܒܢܝܢܫܐ ܕܫܠܡܝܢ ܠܓ̈ܡܠܐ ܐܪ̈ܢܒܐ. ܟܕ ܠܐ ܡܫܟܚܝܢ ܪ̈ܓܠܝܗܘܢ ܥܠ ܓ̈ܡܠܐ.

34 ܬܕܡܘܪܬܐ. ܚܙܐ ܐܠܟܣܢܕܪܘܣ ܒܢܝܢܫܐ ܕܐܝܬ ܠܗܘܢ ܥܝ̈ܢܐ ܐܝܟ ܕܟܠ̈ܒܐ.

35 ܘܚܙܐ ܬܡܢ ܒܢܝܢܫܐ ܕܪ̈ܝܫܝܗܘܢ ܘܦܪ̈ܨܘܦܝܗܘܢ ܘܥܝ̈ܢܝܗܘܢ ܒܚܕ̈ܝܗܘܢ.

36 ܘܐܝܬ ܒܢܝܢܫܐ ܕܥܩ̈ܒܝܗܘܢ ܘܪ̈ܓܠܝܗܘܢ ܐܝܟ ܟܪ̈ܥܐ ܐܪ̈ܢܒܐ. ܟܕ ܠܝܬ ܒܪܟܐ ܒܥܩ̈ܒܝܗܘܢ. ܘܡܬܬܘܪܝܢ ܒܪ̈ܟܝ ܪ̈ܓܠܐ. ܘܪܗܛܝܢ ܪ̈ܓܠܝܗܘܢ ܥܠ ܓ̈ܡܠܐ ܕܡܒܬܪ̈ܐ ܕܐܝܬ ܠܗܬܘܢ. ܘܫܠܡܝܢ ܒܗܘܢ ܐܝܟ ܐܢܫ ܕܫܠܡ ܒܣܘܣܝܐ. ܘܐܟܠܝܢ ܡܢ ܦܐܪ̈ܐ ܕܐ̈ܝܠܢܐ. ܘܡܟܐ ܕܚܙܐ ܠܒܢܝܢܫܐ ܥܪܩܝܢ ܘܠܒܝܢ ܠܗ ܘܪܕܦܝܢ ܠܗ ܥܠ ܓ̈ܡܠܬܗ. ܘܡܟܪܟܝܢ ܪ̈ܓܠܝܗܘܢ ܥܠ ܥܩ̈ܒܬܗ ܘܚܢܩܝܢ ܠܗ.

32b ܠܗ. ܐܠܐ] ܠܗ ܟܡܐ ܕܗ̇ܘ ܚܝ. ܐܠܐ ܡܟܐ ܕܡܐܬ L | ܠܓܘܪܗ] ܓܘܪܗ L

32c ܚܝ] ܚܝ. ܗ[ܘ] L | ܡܟܐܒܐ] ܡܟܐܒ L | ܘܒܪܘܬܐ] ܘܒܪܘܬܐ ܗ̇ܝ L

32d ܟܠܿܚܝܦ] ܓ̇ܠܗܦ L | ܐܟܠܝܢ] ܕܐܟܠܝܢ L

36c ܓ̈ܡܠܐ] ܓ̈ܡܠܐ ܪ̈ܘܪܒܐ L   36e ܠܗ] L om.

36f ܪ̈ܓܠܝܗܘܢ ܥܠ ܥܩ̈ܒܬܗ] ܪ̈ܓܠܝܗܘܢ ܥܠ ܨܘܪܗ L

32 *Marvels:* There is an island whose inhabitants eat people while they are still alive. They do not slay him, but cut his throat and eat him while he is alive, without roasting or boiling. And the island is called Klāmīs;[11] they eat people there.

33 *Marvels:* In Serendib (i.e., Sri Lanka), there are people who climb the tall trees without putting their feet on the trees.

34 *Marvels:* Alexander saw people who have teeth like those of dogs.

35 And moreover, he saw people with their head and their mouth and their eyes on their chest.

36 And there are people whose thighs and legs are like long straps, because there are no bones in their thighs. And they are called 'strap-feet'. And they cast their legs upon the pear trees that they have there, and climb with their help like a man who climbs with a rope, and eat the fruit of the trees. And when they see a human, they jump and seize him and mount on his shoulders. And they twist their legs around his shoulders and strangle him.

---

[11] *Balōs* in L and B1 in II.23.

37 ܬܕܡܘܪܬܐ. ܘܐܝܬ ܒܢ̈ܝܢܫܐ. ܕܕܡܘ̈ܬܗܘܢ ܐܝܟ ܕܕܡܘܬܐ ܕܒܥܝ̈ܪܐ. ܘܪܫܝܡ ܒܒ̈ܢܝܢܫܐ ܒܓܘܦܐ ܬܪܢܓܠܬܐ. ܘܫܦܝܪܐ. ܘܩܠܝܠ ܡܫܟܚܐ ܡܢ ܚܠܩܬܗ ܕܐܠܟܣܢܕܪܘܣ.

38 ܘܐܝܬ ܐܢܫܐ ܕܪ̈ܓܠܝܗܘܢ ܐܝܟ ܪ̈ܓܠܐ ܕܣܘܣܝܐ. ܘܫܪܟܐ ܕܗ̈ܕܡܐ ܕܠܗܘܢ ܐܝܟ ܒ̈ܢܝܢܫܐ.

39 ܬܕܡܘܪܬܐ. ܘܐܝܬ ܐܢ̈ܫܝܢ ܒܡܕܢܚܐ ܟܕ ܠܐ ܐܝܬ ܠܗܘܢ ܩܕܠܐ ܥܠ ܥܠܝܐܝܬ. ܘܠܐ ܪ̈ܫܝܐ ܘܠܐ ܐܦ̈ܝܐ. ܘܦܘ. ܕܝܠܗ ܥܝ̈ܢܐ ܒܚܕܝ̈ܗܘܢ. ܟܐܠܝܢ ܕܚܙܝܢ ܡܢ ܫܟܝܚܘܬܐ ܕܥܡܡ̈ܐ ܕܒܕܝܪܐ ܠܗܟܢ ܥܒܕܝܢ.

40 ܬܕܡܘܪܬܐ. ܐܫܬܡܥ ܠܝ ܐܢܫ ܕܫܡܥܗ ܦܛܪܘܣ ܕܣܒܐ ܒܚܘܪܬܐ ܕܓܒܝ. ܒܪܢܫܐ ܚܕ ܕܡܢ ܚܝܘܗܝ ܘܠܗܠܟܬ ܚܕ ܦܬܪܐ ܘܚܙܐ ܒܪܝܫܐ ܘܬܪܝܢ ܪ̈ܫܐ. ܘܡܢ ܚܝܘܗܝ ܠܗܠܟܬ ܐܪܒܥ ܐ̈ܝܕܝܐ. ܘܠܝܬ ܗܘܐ ܡܢ ܫ̈ܕܝܐ ܥܠ ܢܦܫܬܐ ܕܐܒܘܗܘܢ. ܘܡܢ ܡܝܬ ܚܕ ܡܢܗܘܢ ܦܫ ܠܡܥܒܕܗ ܬܠܝܐ ܒܥܒܪܗ ܢܩܡܝܢ. ܘܡܝܬ ܗܘ ܐܦ ܠܒܬܪ ܐܚܪܢܐ. |fol. 114r|

ܘܫܦܝܪܐ] ܘܫܦܝܪܐ ܪܫܝܡ ܬܪܢܓܠܬܐ L 37b

ܘܩܠܝܠ ܡܫܟܚܐ] ܘܡܫܟܚܐ ܩܠܝܠ L 37c

ܐܝܟ] om. L 38b

ܠܐ ܐܝܬ] ܠܝܬ L 39a

The whole unit is absent from L. 40

37 *Marvels:* And there are people whose appearance is like the appearance of ravens, and they throw stones and sticks straight at men. And they killed many from the army of Alexander.

38 And there are people whose legs are like the legs of an ass, whereas the rest of their limbs are like those of humans.

39 *Marvels:* And there are people in the East who have no hair whatsoever, and neither eyebrows nor eyelids. And when the sun shines upon their faces, they enter the water because of the sun's heat for as long as nine hours.

40 *Marvels:* The man called Anās told us that he saw on the island of Kīš a man who from his chest downwards had one body and one belly, and (upwards) from his chest — two heads and four arms. And they were quarrelling with one another about the inheritance of their father. And when one of them died, his body remained hanging upon his companion for three days, and that other side (also) died.

41 ܐܫܬܡܥ ܠܝ ܡܫܝܚܐ ܡܘܪ̈ܝܩܘܦ ܒܡܘܠܟܐ. ܬܠܬܐ. ܕܒܝܬ ܒܪ ܙܕܩ
ܗܘܝܢ ܒܝܡܐ ܠܘܡܒܠ ܕܡܒ̈ܬܠ. ܚܙܝܢ ܒܐܦܐ ܪܒܬܐ ܡܬܝܒܬ
ܡܢܐ. ܘܒܠܝܢܗ ܠܓܢܐ ܗܕܐ ܥܒܕ ܕܡܠܐ ܒܪ̈ܬܠ. ܘܒܗ ܚܙܝܢܗܝ
ܗܒܪܝ ܕܡܢ ܠܘܒܒܐ ܐܫܬܘܕܝ. ܘܡܪܒܝܢܗ ܠܐܠܦܐ ܠܘܬܗ
ܕܢܣܒܬ ܠܘܬܗ. ܘܒܗ ܚܙܐ ܠܐܠܦܐ. ܢܦܩ ܒܦܐ ܘܒܚܝܘ. ܘܐܪܒܥܐ
ܢܦܫܗ ܒܝܡܐ ܘܗܘܢܐ ܘܐܙܠ.

42 ܬܕܡܘܪ̈ܬܐ. ܐܡܪܝܢ ܬܠܬܐ ܕܐܝܬ ܒܓܙܪ̈ܬܐ ܐ̈ܢܫܐ ܕܠܒܝܢ
ܒܢܝܫܐ ܘܦ̈ܬܝܬܐ ܘܡܬܢܦܫܐ ܣܘܬܐ. ܘܡܬܬܪܐ ܐܢܫܐ
ܕܩ̈ܦܘܦ. ܘܒܗ ܡܬܒܪܝܢ ܦܪܝܢ ܘܐܙܠܝܢ. ܘܐܡܪܝܢ ܕܢܦܫܐ
ܣܘܬܐ ܡܢ ܡܟܐ ܘܐܒܠܐ ܠܗܘܢ.

43 ܬܕܡܘܪ̈ܬܐ. ܠܓܢܐ ܚܕ ܐܙܕܘܓ ܒܒܓ̈ܕܕ. ܘܡܠܝܢܗ ܠܐܢܬܬܗ
ܘܐܙܠ ܠܦܠܘܦ. ܘܒܠܝܠܬ ܐܢܬܬܗ. ܘܥܡ ܒܘܠܐ ܒܪܝܫܗ ܒܝܘܡ
ܘܐܪܒܥܐ ܢ̈ܦܫܝ. ܘܒܗ ܠܕܬ. ܐܝܬ ܗܘܐ ܠܗ ܠܒܘܠܐ ܥܢ̈ܐ.

44 ܬܕܡܘܪ̈ܬܐ. ܐܢܬܬܐ ܕܡܢ ܚܕܐ ܡܠܕܬ ܥܬܝܡ ܒܢܝܐ. ܒܬܠܬܝܢ
ܘܫܒܥ ܙܒ̈ܢܝܢ. ܘܒܟܠ ܥܕܬܐ ܙܒܢܬܐ ܘܬܪ̈ܬܝܢ ܣܓܝܐ ܗܘܬ.
ܐܡܪܝܢ ܗܘܘ ܡܠܕܬ ܒܗܕܐ ܕܒܢ̈ܝܐ ܒܗ̇ܝ ܕܒܗܕܐ ܐܢܬܬܗܝ ܥܬܝܡ
ܡܩܝܡܐ.

41a ܬܠܬܐ] om. L   41b ܕܡܒ̈ܬܠ] ܕܡܒ̈ܬܠ L | ܪܒܬܐ] ܪܒܒܬܐ L
41c ܗܕܐ] ܗܕܐ ܘܥܒܕ ܚܙܘܐ L | ܥܒܕ] ܘܥܒܕ L
41d ܠܐܠܦܐ] ܐܠܦܐ L   41e ܚܙܐ] ܚܙܗ L | ܘܐܪܒܥܐ] ܘܐܪܒܥ L
42b ܘܡܬܢܦܫܐ] ܘܡܬܢܦܫܐ ܒܗܘܢ L   42c ܕܩ̈ܦܘܦ] ܕܩ̈ܦܘܦ L
43a ܬܕܡܘܪ̈ܬܐ] ܬܕܡܘܪܬܐ B2 | ܒܒܓ̈ܕܕ] ܒܒܓܕܕ L
44c ܗܘܘ] ܗܘܘ ܠܗ L | ܐܢܬܬܗܝ] ܗܘܐ L

41 We have been told by the priest Qūryāqōs of Mosul, a merchant, 'When we were sailing on the sea towards Myaṭāl, we saw a big rock in the midst of the sea, and upon it an old man, [good-looking], fair-bearded (and) naked. And when we saw him, we thought that he escaped a shipwreck. And we brought the ship near him so that he might get down to us. And when he saw the ship, he struck the rock and laughed. And he threw himself into the sea and swam and got away'.

42 *Marvels:* The merchants say that on the islands, there are trees that bear humans and birds, and life is breathed [into them]. And it is called the tree of Baqāwās.[12] And when they fully develop, they fly away and leave. And they say that a beast comes out of the sea and eats them.

43 *Marvels:* A certain man got married in Baghdad, and he took his wife and went to Ṭōs (i.e., Tus). And his wife became pregnant, and the fetus remained in her womb twenty-four months. And when she gave birth, the infant had teeth.

44 *Marvels:* A certain woman, then, gave birth to sixty children in thirty-five times. And every year, she would miscarry once and again. They would say, 'She gave birth to a *kōr* of children', because one *kōr* contains sixty *qpīzē*.[13]

---

[12] *Waqwaq* in B1 in II.32.

[13] Both *kōr* and *qpīzā* are measures of capacity.

45 ܬܕܡܘܪ̈ܬܐ. ܐܢܬܬܐ ܚܕܐ ܝܠܕܬ ܒܡܪܝܢ ܒܢ̈ܝܐ ܒܫܒܥܐ ܒܝܪ̈ܚܐ ܘܚܝܘ ܟܠܗܘܢ.

46 ܬܕܡܘܪ̈ܬܐ. ܘܐܡܪܝܢ ܕܓܒܪܐ ܚܕ ܦܪܢܓܝܐ ܝܠܕܬ ܠܗ ܐܢܬܬܗ ܫܒܥܐ ܒܢ̈ܝܢ ܒܚܕܐ ܟܪܣܐ ܘܚܝܘ ܟܠܗܘܢ.

47 ܬܕܡܘܪ̈ܬܐ. ܐܫܬܟܚ ܠܝ ܡܫܟܐ ܦܘܪ̈ܦܘܪܣ ܒܡܘܠܝܐ. ܕܓܒܪܐ ܚܕ ܐܙܠ ܠܢܦܩ ܗܘ ܘܐܢܬܬܗ. ܘܟܕ ܡܛܐ ܠܦܠܓܗ̇ ܕܐܘܪܚܐ. ܡܝܬܬ ܐܢܬܬܗ ܒܫܒܝܠܗ̇. ܫܩܠܗ̇ ܓܒܪܐ ܘܩܒܪܗ̇ ܒܕܘܟܬܐ ܫܬܝܩܬܐ ܒܡܕܒܪܐ. ܘܐܡܪ ܕܟܕ ܗܦܟܢܐ ܢܦܩ ܐܢܐ ܠܗ̇ ܒܥܒܪ. ܘܟܕ ܗܦܟܘ ܫܢ̈ܝܐ ܡܢ ܣܓܝ. ܐܙܠ ܒܐܘܪܚܐ ܐܚܪܬܐ. ܘܟܬܪ ܫܒܥܐ ܫܢ̈ܝܢ ܬܘܒ ܐܙܠ ܠܣܓܝ ܘܐܙܠ ܒܐܘܪܚܐ ܠܗ̇ ܕܕܘܟܬܐ. ܘܐܫܟܚܗ̇ ܠܐܢܬܬܗ ܒܗ̇ ܡܫܬܐ. ܘܦܠܓܗ̇ ܬܫܬܐ ܒܗ̇ ܒܠܐ. ܘܦܠܓܗ̇ ܒܠܝܐ ܒܗ̇ ܠܐ ܡܥܒܕܐ ܒܣܘܪܗ ܘܠܐ ܐܬܚܒܠ. ܘܦܠܓܐ ܒܠܝܗ̇ ܒܗ̇ ܢܡ ܣܠܒܐ ܡܢ ܬܪ̈ܝܗ̇. ܘܟܕ ܚܙܝܗ̇ ܦܠܓܐ |fol. 114v| ܒܪܗ. ܘܗܘ ܐܒܘܗܝ, ܙܟܐ ܫܕܪܗ ܠܘܬ ܒܪܗ. ܘܪܗܛ ܒܬܪܗ ܘܠܒܒܗ. ܘܟܕ ܐܟܠܘܗܝ, ܠܒܕܬܐ ܐܫܬܘܕܥ ܠܠܫܢܐ ܣܘܪܝܐ. ܐܡܪܝܢ ܕܫܪܝܪܐܝܬ ܕܠܫܢܐ ܩܕܡܝܐ ܕܒܗ ܡܠܠ ܐܠܗܐ ܥܡ ܐܕܡ. ܐܪܡܝܐ ܗ̇ܘ. ܗܢܘ ܕܝܢ ܣܘܪܝܐ.

46a ܚܕ] L om.

47a ܒܡܘܠܝܐ] L om.

47c ܒܫܒܝܠܗ̇] ܒܫܒܝܠܐ ܕܒܥܠܐ L | ܫܩܠܗ̇] ܘܫܩܠܗ ܗܘ ܘܐܡܪܗ L | ܓܒܪܐ] ܓܒܪܐ ܗܘ L | ܘܩܒܪܗ̇] ܘܩܒܪ ܐܢܘܢ L

47d ܗܦܟܢܐ] ܗܦܟ ܐܢܐ L | ܢܦܩ ܐܢܐ] ܢܦܩܢܐ L | ܠܗ̇] ܠܗ ܠܒܥܠܐ L

47h ܒܣܘܪܗ] ܒܣܘܪܗ̇ L   47k ܠܠܫܢܐ] ܠܫܢܐ L

47l ܕܠܫܢܐ] ܗܘܘ ܠܫܢܐ L   47m ܕܝܢ] L om.

45 *Marvels:* A certain woman gave birth to twenty children in five pregnancies, and all of them lived.

46 *Marvels:* They say about a certain Frankish man (that) his wife bore him seven children in one womb, and all of them lived.

47 *Marvels:* We have been told by the priest Qūryāqōs of Mosul that a certain man went on a pilgrimage together with his wife. And when they reached the middle of the way, his wife died in childbirth. [And that] man took [him (i.e., the new-born baby) and his mother and put them] in some hidden place in the desert. And he said, 'When I return, I will take [the baby] with me'. And when the pilgrims returned from the pilgrimage, they went by another road. And after seven years, he again went on the pilgrimage, and he went on the way to that place. And he found the dead woman, her lower half-decayed and her upper half with its flesh unchanged and uncorrupted, and upon her the child sucking milk from her breasts. And when the child saw him, he fled away. And the father became inflamed with love for his son, and he ran after him and caught him. And when they brought him into the church, he recognized the Syriac language. They say that the first language in which God spoke to Adam was indeed Aramaic, that is Syriac.

48 ܬܕܡܪ̈ܬܐ. ܐܬܡܠܠ ܡܢ ܚܕܐ ܕܡܢܝ، ܩ̈ܠܝܡܦ ܐܝܬ ܗܘܐ ܕܝܢ
ܒܩܠܝܒܝܩܐ ܡܕܝܢܬܐ. ܐܢܬܬܐ ܚܕܐ ܕܕܡܟܬ ܥܡ ܗܘܦܐ ܚܕܐ.
ܘܒܛܢܬ ܘܝܠܕܬ ܒܪܐ ܕܒܪܐ ܟܠܗ ܠܓܘܫܡܗ ܕܡܘܬ ܗܘܦܐ.
ܘܦܪ̈ܨܘܦܗ ܐܝܟ ܦܪ̈ܨܘܦܐ ܕܒ̈ܢܝܢܫܐ. ܘܡܐܟܠ ܗܘܐ ܠܒܪܬܐ.
ܘܫܟܒ ܗܘܐ ܒܬ̈ܘܠܬܐ ܐܠ̈ܡܫܐ. ܘܒܬܪ ܒܙܒܢ ܥ̈ܒܝܢ ܒܚܕܐ
ܡܕܝܢܬܐ ܘܠܐ ܐܫܟܚܘܗ، ܘܗܘܬ ܒܟܬܐ ܡܥܪܬܐ ܥܠ ܗܕܐ.
ܡܢܗܘܢ ܐܡܪܝܢ ܗܘܘ ܕܠܐ ܡܬܡܠܟܐ ܡܢ ܡܕܝܢܬܐ. ܘܡܢܗܘܢ
ܐܡܪܝܢ ܗܘܘ ܕܠܐ ܥܘܐ ܠܡܕܝܢܬܐ. ܘܐܡܪ ܕܝ̈ܘܣܝܦܘܣ ܐܦܣܩܘܦܐ
ܕܐܬ̈ܝܘܦܣ. ܕܐܢܐ ܠܐ ܡܚܠ ܐܢܐ ܠܡܕܝܢܬܐ. ܢܦܩܝܢ ܕܚܙ̈ܘܬܐ
ܠܡܚ̈ܙܝܬܐ. ܘܥܠܡܐ ܠܡܠܬܗ ܒܠܫܢܗܘܢ. ܘܒܪ ܐܬܐ ܠܩܝ̈ܪܝܦ
ܡܠܟܐ ܠܡܕܝܢܬ ܩܘܠܝܒܝܩܐ. ܒܚܕܐ ܡܢܗܘܢ ܕܫܢܝ̈ܘܗܝ ܠܫܢ̈ܝܐ
ܘܠܝ̈ܠܕܐ ܘܠܐܠܦ̈ܝܐ. ܐܬܐ ܗ̇ܘ ܡܫܠܛ ܓܘܪ̈ܬܐ. ܘܩܡ ܩܕܡ
ܡܠܟܐ ܘܐܡܪ ܕܐܢܐ ܒܪܢܫܐ ܐܢܐ. ܘܠܡܫܝܚܐ ܡܫܒܚܢܐ.
ܘܐܦ ܡܠܟܐ. ܘܦܩܕ ܕܢܚܙܘܢܝܗܝ، ܘܢܫܩܠܘܢ ܠܗ ܥܒ̈ܕܐ ܘܡܣ̈ܪܝܐ
ܡܫܒ̈ܚܬܐ. ܘܗܟܢܐ ܗܘܐ ܘܐܡܪ. ܡܠܟܐ ܒܟܘܪܐ ܕܡܫܒܚܬܐ.
ܘܦܩܕ ܘܐܬܝܘܗ ܙܘܓܐ ܘܡܕܝܢܬܐ ܘܐܪܬܘܗ ܡܢ ܫܐܕ̈ܐ.

48b ܒܩܠܝܒܝܩܐ] ܒܩܠ̈ܝܒܝܩܐ L | ܗܘܦܐ ܚܕܐ] ܗܘܦܐ ܚܕ L

48d ܘܦܪ̈ܨܘܦܗ ܐܝܟ] ܦܪ̈ܨܘܦ L | ܦܪ̈ܨܘܦܐ ܕܒ̈ܢܝܢܫܐ] ܒܢ̈ܝܢܫܐ L

48f ܒܟܬܐ] ܒܟܬܐ L

48g ܐܡܪܝܢ ܗܘܘ ܕܠܐ ܡܬܡܠܟܐ ܡܢ ܡܕܝܢܬܐ. ܘܡܢܗܘܢ] om. L

48i ܕܐܬ̈ܝܘܦܣ] ܕܐܬܝܘܦܣ L

48k ܡܠܟܐ] om. L | ܩܘܠܝܒܝܩܐ] ܩܘܠܝܩܝܐ L

48l ܘܠܝ̈ܠܕܐ ܘܠܐܠܦ̈ܝܐ] ܘܠܐܠܦ̈ܝܐ ܘܠܝ̈ܠܕܐ L | ܓܘܪ̈ܬܐ] ܓܘܪ̈ܬܗ L

48m ܡܫܒܚܢܐ] ܡܫܒܚ ܐܢܐ L

48n ܘܢܫܩܠܘܢ ܠܗ] ܘܢܫܩܠܘܢܗܝ L

48p ܘܐܬܝܘܗ] ܕܐܬܝܘܗ L

48 *Marvels:* It was told in the book of Mār Basil that in the city of Callinicum a certain woman had slept with an ape. And she got pregnant and gave birth to a male child, whose whole body was like that of an ape, and (his) face (was) like a human face. And he used to go to the church and listen to the divine scriptures. And after twenty years, he sought baptism, but they did not baptize him. And there was a great debate on this account: some said that he should not be denied baptism, while some said he is not worthy of baptism. And Dionysios, the bishop of Athens, said, 'I will not baptize the likenesses of unclean beasts!' And everyone agreed with his word. And when the king Tiberius came to the city of Callinicum, he requested from them to sacrifice to demons and idols and graven images. And that misshapen one came and stood before the king, and said, 'I am Christian, and I worship Christ'. And the king became angry and ordered that they should beat him and inflict upon him tortures and lacerations and blows. And the king cried out and in a fiery rage said and ordered, and they brought pitch and brimstone and boiled them together.

ܘܫܠܡܘܗܝ ܠܒܪ ܡܘܣܐ. ܘܫܕܐܘܗܝ ܒܓܘܗ. ܘܡܪܚܡ ܗܘܐ
ܘܐܡܪ. ܕܐܢܐ ܟܪܣܛܝܢܐ ܐܢܐ ܘܠܡܫܝܚܐ ܣܓܕܢܐ. ܘܡܟܐ
ܘܐܡܪ ܡܪܝ ܝܫܘܥ ܡܫܝܚܐ. ܢܗܘܐ ܠܝ ܡܕܣܐ ܗܢܐ ܓܘܪܢܐ
ܕܡܥܡܘܕܝܬܐ. ܘܒܕܘܟܬ ܥܡܕܐ ܘܐܡܪܘ ܟܠܗܘܢ ܐܒܗ̈ܬܐ
ܕܗ̇ܘ ܡܗܝܡܢܐ ܗܘܐ ܒܝܘܡܐ ܕܩܝܡܬܐ. ܘܥܡ ܣܗ̈ܕܐ
ܘܡܘ̈ܕܝܢܐ ܘܙܕܝܩ̈ܐ ܝܪܬ ܡܠܟܘܬܐ ܕܫܡܝܐ.

49 ܬܕܡܘܪ̈ܬܐ. ܐܫܬܥܝܘ ܠܝ ܕܒܡܕܝܢܬܐ ܚܝܪܐ. ܓܕܫܘ ܡܬܘܬܢܐ
ܪܒܢܐ. ܘܚܙܐ ܓܒܪܐ ܚܕ ܠܟܠܬܐ ܚܕܐ ܕܒܥܠܐ ܒܒܝܟܐ
ܠܚܢܬܐ ܚܕ. ܕܠܐ ܦܫܘ ܒܗ ܐܢܫ ܡܢ ܡܬܘܬܢܐ. ܘܐܙܠ ܟܠ
ܒܬܪܗ. ܘܚܙܐ ܠܛܠܝܐ |fol. 115r| ܘܒܗܘܪܐ ܟܕ ܡܫܦܦ ܟܠ
ܐܝ̈ܕܘܗܝ. ܘܐܬܐ ܘܩܡ ܩܕܡ ܟܠܬܐ ܘܩܡ ܡܢܗ ܚܠܒܐ. ܘܫܩܠ
ܠܛܠܝܐ ܗ̇ܘ ܘܪܒܝܗ. ܘܩܪܝܢ ܗܘܘ ܠܗ ܒܪ ܟܠܬܐ.

48a ܘܫܠܡܘܗܝ] ܘܫܠܡܘܢܘܗܝ L | ܘܡܪܚܡ] ܘܗ̇ܘ ܡܪܚܡ L

48b ܣܓܕܢܐ] ܣܓܕ ܐܢܐ L

48c ܓܘܪܢܐ] ܘܙܢܐ L

48d ܘܒܕܘܟܬ] ܘܕܘܟܬ L

49a ܐܫܬܥܝܘ] ܐܫܬܥܝܘܢ L | ܠܝ] ܐܢ̈ܫܝܢ L | ܕܒܡܕܝܢܬܐ] ܕܒܡܕܝܢܬܐ L |
ܚܝܪܐ] ܕܚܝܪܐ L | ܓܕܫܘ] ܓܕܫ L

49c ܦܫܘ] ܦܫ L 49d ܐܝ̈ܕܘܗܝ] ܐܝ̈ܕܘܗܝ ܘܪ̈ܓܠܘܗܝ L

49e ܘܩܡ] ܘܩܡ ܗܘܐ L

And they took the ape's son and threw him into it. And he proclaimed and said, 'I am Christian, and I worship Christ!' And he cried out and said, 'Our Lord Jesus Christ, Let this cauldron be for me a baptismal font and instead of baptism!' And all the Fathers said that he will be counted as a believer on the day of resurrection and will inherit the kingdom of heaven together with martyrs, confessors, and righteous ones.

49 *Marvels:* They told us that in the city of Basra, there was a great plague. And a certain man saw a bitch entering through a hole into a house in which no people were left after the plague. And he followed her and saw a small child, crawling on his hands [and his legs]. And he came and stood up before the bitch and sucked her milk. And he took that child and raised him, and they used to call him 'Son of a Bitch'.

50 ܬܕܡܘܪܬܐ. ܘܒܗ ܒܗܿܘ ܙܒܢܐ ܡܝܬ ܒܒܝܪܐ ܚܡܫܝܢ ܐ̈ܠܦܝܢ ܒܢ̈ܝܢܫܐ. ܒܚܕ ܢܘܡܣܐ ܘܥܡܠ ܓܒܪܐ ܡܢ ܒܢ̈ܝ ܡܕܝܢܬܐ ܓܘ̈ܠܒܐ ܕܬܡ̈ܪܐ. ܟܠ ܐܡܬܝ ܕܥܒܪܝܢ ܗܘܘ ܒܪ̈ܘܚܬܐ ܕܬܚ̈ܘܬܐ. ܪܡܐ ܥܠ ܚܕܐ ܓܘܠܒܐ ܒܪܡܘܪܐ ܕܣܝܦܐ. ܘܒܪܡܫܐ ܡܚܐ ܐܢܘܢ ܘܫܠܡ ܡܢܝܢܗ ܡܢ̈ܝܢܗܘܢ ܠܚܡܫܝܢ ܐ̈ܠܦܝܢ ܒܢ̈ܝܢܫܐ.

51 ܐܚܪܢܐ. ܐܝܬ ܒܣܪ̈ܢܕܝܒ ܓܙ̈ܝܪܬܐ ܙܘܪ̈ܒܐ ܕܠܝܬ ܠܗܘܢ ܕܘܢ̈ܒܐ.

52 ܐܚܪܢܐ. ܐܝܬ ܛܘܪܐ ܚܕ ܚܘܘ̈ܬܐ ܕܟܠܗܝܢ.

53 ܚܙܐ ܐܠܟܣܢܕܪܘܣ ܕ̈ܐܒܐ ܘܢܡܪ̈ܐ. ܕܘܢ̈ܒܝܗܘܢ ܐܝܟ ܕܘܢ̈ܒܐ ܕܒܥܝ̈ܪܐ.

54 ܐܚܪܢܐ. ܐܝܬ ܒܝܡܐ ܓ̈ܠܐ. ܫܡܗ ܕܝܢ ܩܛ̈ܝܐ. ܚܠܝܫ ܡܢܝܢܗܘܢ ܚܡܫܝܢ ܐܢ̈ܫܝܢ ܚܘܕܪܗ. ܘܒܪܘܡܐ ܕܟܠ ܡܢܝܢܗܘܢ ܐܠܦ ܒܬ̈ܝܢ.

55 ܘܐܝܬ ܒܗ ܢܘܢܐ ܕܡܘܬ ܓܡܠܐ.

50a ܡܝܬ] ܡܝܬܘ L   50b ܓܒܪܐ] ܓܒܪܐ ܚܕ L

50c ܟܠ] ܗܘܐ   50e ܡܢܝܢܗ] L om. | ܒ̈ܢܝܢܫܐ] L om.

51 ܐܚܪܢܐ] ܬܕܡܘ[ܪܬܐ] L | ܓܙ̈ܝܪܬܐ] ܓܙܝܪ̈ܬܐ L

52 ܐܚܪܢܐ] ܬܕܡ[ܘܪܬܐ] L | ܚܕ] ܚܕ ܕܐܝܬ ܒܗ L

54 The whole unit is absent from L.

55 The whole unit is absent from L.

50 *Marvels:* And at that time, twenty thousand people died in Basra on one day. And a certain man from among the citizens took date stones, (and) whenever biers of the dead would pass, he would throw a stone into an earthen jar. And he would count them in the evening. And their number came to twenty thousand people.

51 *Another:* In Serendib, there are large buffalo bulls that have no tails.

52 *Another:* There is a mountain, [whereon there are] devouring snakes.

53 Alexander saw a wolf and a leopard, whose tails were like the tails of scorpions.

54 *Another:* In the sea, there are turtles, that is *qrāyē,*[14] each of them twenty cubits in circumference. And they have one thousand offspring each in its belly.

55 And there is in it a fish there that looks like a camel.

[14] I.e., Neo-Aramaic ܩܪ̈ܝܐ ‘turtles’.

56 ܐܚܪܢܐ. ܘܐܝܬ ܒܝܡܐ ܕܡܕܢܚܐ ܬܪ̈ܬܝܢ ܓܙܪܬܐ. ܚܕܐ ܡܢܗܘܢ ܠܐ ܡܬܐܬ ܒܗ̇ ܐܢܫ ܟܠ ܟܠܗ. ܘܟܕ ܟܠܐ ܠܡܥܒܪܗ ܘܟܠܠ ܚܝܠܗ. ܘܦܫܐ ܠܫܘܬܗ. ܘܡܗܘܠܝܢ ܠܗ ܐܢ̈ܫܘܗܝ ܘܡܥܒܪܝܢ ܠܗ ܠܗ̇ ܓܙܪܬܐ ܐܚܪܬܐ. ܘܟܕ ܡܛܐ ܠܗ̇ ܓܙܪܬܐ ܐܚܪܬܐ. ܒܪܫܥܬܗ ܡܐܬ.

57 ܬܕܡܘܪܬܐ. ܘܐܝܬ ܒܡܨܪܝܢ ܓܙܪܬܐ ܚܕܐ ܕܟܠ ܝܘܡܐ ܕܗܘܝܢ ܥܠ ܡܛܪܐ ܡܪ̈ܥܝܢ ܐܢ̈ܫܘܗܝ ܠܫܡܝܐ. ܘܒܥܝܢ ܡܢ ܐܠܗܐ. ܘܐܬܐ ܥܠܝܗܘܢ ܡܛܪܐ ܒܪܫܥܬܗ.

58 ܬܕܡܘܪܬܐ. ܐܝܬ ܒܝܡܐ ܕܩܘܦܠܝܪ ܢܘܢܐ ܐܘܪܟܗ ܡܐܬܝܢ ܐܡ̈ܝܢ. ܕܚܠܝܡ ܡܢܗ ܒܡܒ̈ܪܝ ܐܠܦܐ. ܘܟܕ ܣܠܩ ܠܗ ܢܦܩܝܢ ܟܠ ܢܘܢܐ. ܘܡܥܒܕ ܥܠܗ ܕܢܘܢܐ ܘܒܠܥ.

59 ܐܝܬ ܒܗ ܢܘܢܐ ܐܘܪܟܗ ܡܐܬܝܢ ܐܡ̈ܝܢ. ܘܒܟܪܣܗ ܕܢܘܢܐ ܢܘܢܬܐ ܐܚܪܬܐ. ܘܒܟܪܣܗ̇ ܕܐܚܪܬܐ ܐܪܒܥܐ ܢ̈ܘܢܐ ܚܕ ܒܟܪܣܐ ܕܚܒܪܗ. ܐܝܟ ܩܠܦܐ ܕܒ̈ܨܠܐ ܚܕ ܠܓܘ ܚܕ.

56a ܐܚܪܢܐ] ܬܕܡ[ܘܪܬܐ] L | ܘܐܝܬ] ܐܝܬ L

56b ܡܢܗܘܢ] ܡܢܗܝܢ L

56e ܐܚܪܬܐ] om. L

57b ܥܠ ܡܛܪܐ] ܠܡܛܪܐ L

58a ܢܘܢܐ] ܢܘܢܐ ܚܕ L | ܐܘܪܟܗ] ܕܐܘܪܟܗ L

58b ܕܚܠܝܡ] ܘܕܚܠܝܡ L   58c ܥܠܗ ܕܢܘܢܐ] om. L

59a ܐܝܬ] ܘܐܝܬ L | ܢܘܢܐ] ܢܘܢܐ ܐܚܪܢܐ L

59a–b ܘܒܟܪܣܗ ܕܢܘܢܐ ܢܘܢܬܐ ܐܚܪܬܐ. ܘܒܟܪܣܗ̇ ܕܐܚܪܬܐ] ܘܐܝܬܝܗܘܢ L

59c ܠܓܘ] ܠܓܘ ܡܢ L

56 *Another:* In the Western sea there are two islands. On one of them no one dies at all. And when his body wears out, and his strength fails, and he hates his life, his people take him and bring him to the other island. And when he reaches that other island, he dies at once.

57 *Marvels:* In India there is an island where, on any day when they need rain, they raise their hands to heaven and beseech God, and the rain comes to them at once.

58 *Marvels:* In the Sea of Qūlzam there is a fish whose length is two hundred cubits. The sailors are afraid of it, and when they see it, they strike a piece of wood, and it hears the sound of wood and flees.

59 There is in it a fish whose length is two hundred cubits. And in the belly of this fish there is another smaller fish, and in the belly of the other (fish) four fishes, one inside of another, like the peels of onion, one inside of another.

60 ܘܐܝܬ ܒܗ ܢܗܪܐ ܦ̈ܪܬܗ ܐܝܟ ܕܬܘܪܐ ܠܒܪܐ ܘܡܝܢܩܐ. ܘܡܢ
ܠܒܪܗ ܒܒܪܝܢ [ܡܪ̈ܥܝܬܐ].

61 ܬܕܡܘܪܬܐ. ܚܙܐ ܐܠܟܣܢܕܪܘܣ ܬܪ̈ܬܝܢ ܦ̈ܪܚܬܐ ܕܡܬܩܪܝܢ
|fol. 115v| ܐܝܟ ܕܡܠܘܬܐ ܕܒܢ̈ܝܢܫܐ. ܘܡܡܠܠܝܢ ܗ̈ܘܝ ܐܝܟ
ܒܢ̈ܝܢܫܐ. ܘܐܘܕܥܘ ܠܗ ܥܠ ܡܠܘܬܗ ܕܡܠܟܐ ܐܠܟܣܢܕܪܘܣ. ܘܥܠ
ܠܡܟܪܙ ܕܗܘܐ. ܘܥܠܘܗܝ ܥܠ ܢܝܚܘܬܗ. ܕܠܐ ܗܦܟ ܚܝ̈ܘܗܝ ܡܢ
ܥܠܡܐ.

62 ܘܚܙܐ ܬܘܒ ܐܠܟܣܢܕܪܘܣ ܬܪܝܢ ܐ̈ܝܠܢܐ ܕܡܢ ܦܐܪܐ ܘܡܒܕܡܐ
ܠܒܢ̈ܝ ܐܢܫܐ ܝܗܒܝܢ ܗܘܘ.

63 ܘܚܙܐ ܬܘܒ ܐܠܟܣܢܕܪܘܣ ܬܪܝܢ ܐ̈ܝܠܢܐ ܙܘܓܐ. ܘܡܡܠܠܝܢ
ܐܝܟ ܒܢ̈ܝܢܫܐ ܘܡܠܠ ܒܗܘܢ ܚܕ ܡܢܗܘܢ ܠܡܠܟܐ ܢܘܢܐ.
ܘܐܚܘܝܘ ܠܡܠܟܐ ܙܡܝܪܬܐ. ܘܐܘܕܥܘܗܝ ܥܠ ܡܘܬܗ. ܘܗܦܟ
ܡܢ ܬܡܢ ܘܡܝܬ.

64 ܟܪܬܐ ܚܕܐ ܕܡܬܩܪܝܐ ܦܪܛܝܠ. ܡܫܬܡܥ ܒܗ ܩܠܐ ܕܙܡܪܐ
ܘܩܠ̈ܐ ܘܟܢܪ̈ܐ ܒܠܗ ܠܠܝܐ. ܘܐܡܪܝܢ ܐܢܫܝܢ ܡܢ ܒܢ̈ܝ
ܐܬܪܐ. ܗܘ ܕܡܢ ܬܡܢ ܢܦܩ ܒܪ ܐܢܫܐ. ܕܗܘܐ ܦܠܛܝܢܘܣ.

60a ܠܒܪܐ] ܘܠܒܪܐ L 60b ܡܪ̈ܥܝܬܐ] ܡܘܪ̈ܥܝܬܐ V ܡܘܪܥܝܬܐ L

61b ܘܡܡܠܠܝܢ] ܘܡܡܠܠܝܢ L | ܗ̈ܘܝ] om. L

61c ܘܐܘܕܥܘ] ܘܐܘܕܥ L 61d ܚܝ̈ܘܗܝ] ܒܚܝ̈ܘܗܝ L

63b ܒܗܘܢ] ܒܗܘܢ L | ܢܘܢܐ] ܢܘܢܐ ܡܡܠܠ L

63d ܘܡܝܬ] ܘܡܝܬ ܒܗ ܒܡܕܝܢܬܗ L

64a ܡܫܬܡܥ] ܘܡܫܬܡܥ L

64b ܘܟܢܪ̈ܐ] ܘܟܢܪܐ L | ܒܢ̈ܝ] om. L

64c ܦܠܛܝܢܘܣ.] ܬܕܡܘܪܬܐ. ܘܐܝܬ ܒܡܕܝܢܬܐ ܚܕ ܢܗܪܐ. ܕܡܪܝܐ ܒܥܠܬܐ
ܚܕ ܢܘܡܐ ܘܡܢܝܢ ܡܝ̈ܗ. ܘܥܠܬܐ ܢܝ̈ܚܬܐ ܐܝ̈ܟܢܐ ܡܬܦܩܩܝܢ ܒܗܘܢ
ܕܡܬܚܙܝܢ ܐܢܫܐ ܡܫܬܢܝܬܐ. L add.

60 And there is in it a fish that looks like a bull that gives birth and suckles. And they make [shields][15] from its skin.

61 *Marvels:* Alexander saw two birds whose appearance was like the appearance of humans, and they were talking like humans. And they related the death of the king Alexander and everything that is going to happen. And they reproached him for his covetousness, that he is not satisfied in his life with the world.

62 And again, Alexander saw two trees that grew shorter from the morning until evening.

63 And again, Alexander saw two great trees, and they spoke like humans. And one of them talked to him in the Greek language, and another in the Latin language. And they made known to him about his death. And he returned from there and died.

64 An island called Barṭīl: the sound of singing and tambourines and [timbrels] is heard there during the whole night. And the people from among the locals say that from there will come the son of perdition, who is Antichrist.[16]

[15] V 'bolts'; L 'clothes'. The emendation follows the reading of B1 in II.51.

[16] L add. '*Marvels:* And there is a river in Syria that flows one day during the week, and its waters increase. And during the other six days they stop until the dry land appears' (= I.16).

65 ܘܚܙܐ ܬܘܒ ܐܠܟܣܢܕܪܘܣ ܐܝ̈ܠܢܐ ܕܡܢ ܨܦܪܐ ܘܥܕܡܐ ܠܦܠܓܗ
ܕܝܘܡܐ ܪ̈ܒܝܢ ܗܘ̈ܝ. ܘܡܢ ܦܠܓܗ ܕܝܘܡܐ ܘܥܕܡܐ ܠܥܕܢ ܪܡܫܐ
ܘܒܨܪ̈ܢ ܗܘ̈ܝ.

ܫܠܡ ܬܕܡܪ̈ܬܐ ܘܠܐܠܗܐ ܫܘܒܚܐ ܐܡܝܢ.

Desinit ܫܘܒܚܐ] ܫܘܒܚܐ ܐܡܝܢ

65 And again, Alexander saw trees that grew taller from the morning until midday and grew shorter from midday until evening time.

Completed are the marvels, and glory to God. Amen.

2.3. Recension II: Text (B1)

ܬܘܒ ܒܬܒܠܐ ܬܕܡܪ̈ܬܐ ܕܐܝܬ ܒܡܕܝܢ̈ܬܐ ܪ̈ܘܪܒܬܐ.

1 ܒܢܐ ܐܠܟܣܢܕܪܘܣ ܡܕܝܢܬܐ ܡܢ ܠܣܛܐ ܒܐܬܪܐ ܕܐ̱ܝܓܘܦܛܘܣ
ܒܓܙܪܬܐ ܚܕܐ. ܕܪܘܚܬܗ̇ ܐܪܒܥܐ ܦܪ̈ܣܐ. ܘܫܘܩ ܒܗ̇
ܢܗܪܐ ܡܫܩ̈ܝܢܐ. ܘܐܘܪܟܗ̇ ܡܕܝܢܬܐ ܪܒܬܐ ܘ[ܫܒܥܬܐ]
ܘܠܝܬ ܠܗ̇ ܬܪ̈ܥܐ.

2 ܐܬܒܢܝܬ ܐܠܟܣܢܕܪܝܐ ܘܪ̈ܗܘܡܐ ܒܬܠܬ ܡܐܐ ܫܢ̈ܝܢ
ܘܦܫܘ ܒܡܠܘ̈ܫܝܢ ܫܒܥܝܢ ܫܢ̈ܝܢ ܠܐ ܡܨܝ̈ܢ ܗܘܘ ܕܢܫܠܡܘܢ
ܒܠܒ̈ܗܘܢ ܒܐܣܟܡܐ. ܟܕ ܒܢ̈ܝܢܗܘܢ ܡܬ̈ܩܢܝܢ ܗܘ̈ܝ ܒܡܫܪܐ
ܐܘ̈ܟܡܐ. ܕܠܐ ܢܬܠܚܝܢ ܡܢ ܗܦܟܐܘܬ ܫܘܪ̈ܬܐ ܘܦܚ̈ܡܐ
ܘܙܠ̈ܩܐ ܘܫܩܠܐ ܘܒܢ̈ܝܢܐ ܕܡܕܝܢܬܐ.

3 ܘܐܝܬ ܗܘܬ ܒܐܠܟܣܢܕܪܝܐ ܡܕܝܢܬܐ ܚܕܐ ܕܐܬܒܢܝܬ ܟܠ
ܠܠܐ ܚܕ ܕܠܒܢ̈ܬܐ. ܘܐܝܬ ܗܘܘ ܒܗ̇ ܫܬܡܐܐ ܐܠܦܝܢ
ܡܘܪ̈ܕܝܐ. ܣܛܪ ܡܢ ܒܢ̈ܝܢܐ ܐܚܪ̈ܢܐ ܕܠܐ ܡܢܝܢ.

4 ܘܐܝܬ ܗܘܬ ܒܐܠܟܣܢܕܪܝܐ ܡܫܘܚܬܐ ܚܕܐ ܕܬܠܬܐ ܒܪ̈ܫܗ̇
ܕܡܕܝܢܬܐ. ܘܟܠܗܝܢ ܕܝܬܒ ܗܘܐ ܬܘܬܒܗ̇ ܚܙܐ ܗܘܐ ܠܗ̇
ܠܘܦܠܘܦܠܘܣ ܡܕܝܢܬܐ. ܘܟܠ ܡܫܘܚܬܐ ܕܩܘܡܐ ܡܢܗ̇
ܒܡܐܐ <ܚܙܝܢ ܗܘܘ ܠܗ̇>.

1c ܘܫܒܥܬܐ] ܘܫܒܥܝܢܬܐ B1

4d ܚܙܝܢ ܗܘܘ ܠܗ̇] Added in the right margin by the same hand. B1

2.3. Recension II: Translation

Again, I write down the marvels that are found in the great cities.

1 Alexander built a city from brass in the country of Andalus on some island, the width of which is four months. And he placed many treasures there. And it is a great and sealed city, and it has no gates.

2 Alexandria and Rome were built over the course of three hundred years. And for seventy years, their inhabitants were not able to walk in their midst during the daytime, (but only) when their eyes were covered with black veils, so that they would not be harmed by the exceeding whiteness and splendour and rays and adornments and buildings of the city.

3 And there was in Alexandria a lighthouse that was built upon a dew of glass. And there were six hundred thousand Jews in it, besides other countless nations.

4 And there was in Alexandria a mirror that was hanging on the top of the lighthouse. And every one who would sit under it saw the city of Constantinople. And they would see every ship that went out of it by sea.

5 ܘܐܝܬ ܒܚܕܐ ܕܘܟܬܐ ܡܢܪܬܐ ܐܚܪܬܐ ܕܢܚܫܐ. ܘܟܠ ܪܫܗ ܦܪܫܐ ܚܕ ܕܢܚܫܐ. ܘܒܝܘܡܐ ܕܥܐܕܐ ܕܝܠܗܘܢ ܢܒܥܝܢ ܡ̈ܝܐ ܡܢ ܗ̇ܘ ܡܢܪܬܐ ܘܫܬܝܢ ܡܢܗܘܢ ܟܠܗܘܢ ܒܢܝ̈ܢܫܐ ܕܡܬܘܥܕܝܢ ܠܬܡܢ. ܘܡܫܩܝܢ ܠܒܥܝܪܗܘܢ ܘܡܠܝܢ ܟܠܗܘܢ ܣܩ̈ܠܐ ܕܗܘܝܢ ܒܒܬܝܗܘܢ ܘܠܓܘܪ̈ܒܐ ܕܐܝܬ ܬܡܢ. ܘܒܬܪ ܥܐܕܐ ܦܣܩܐ ܡܪܕܝܬܐ ܕܡ̈ܝܐ. ܘܠܐ ܬܘܒ ܡܪܕܝܐ ܐܝܟ ܒܥܕܢܗ̇.

6 ܐܝܬ ܡܕܝܢܬܐ ܕܐܝܬ ܠܗ̇ ܫܒܥܐ ܫܘܪ̈ܐ ܚܕ ܠܓܘ ܡܢ ܚܕ. ܘܒܝܬ ܫܘܪܐ ܠܫܘܪܐ ܫܒܥܐ ܡ̈ܝܠܐ. ܘܟܠ ܬܠܬܐ ܡ̈ܝܠܐ ܚܕ ܦܪܣܚܐ. ܘܒܝܬ ܫܘܪܐ ܠܫܘܪܐ ܦܪ̈ܕܝܣܐ ܘܢܨܒ̈ܬܐ |fol. 69r| ܘܟܪ̈ܡܐ ܘܫܩ̈ܝܐ ܘܪ̈ܚܘܬܐ.

7 ܐܝܬ ܫܘܪܐ ܕܒܢܐܘܗܝ ܡ̈ܠܟܐ. ܡܢ ܡܚܐ ܕܓܒ̈ܪܐ ܘܒܕܡܐ ܠܒܢܐ ܕܣܘܪܝܐ ܐܪܘܥܐ ܕܬܡܢܝܐ ܢܩ̈ܡܝܢ.

ܥܠ ܢܗܪ̈ܘܬܐ.

8 ܢܗܪܐ ܕܡܬܩܪܐ ܓ̇ܐܠܝܘܣ ܬܠܬ ܫܢܝܢ ܡܢ ܫܘܪܝ ܐܫܬܡܛܐ ܡܪܕܝܢ ܡ̈ܝܘܗܝ ܠܝܡܐ. ܘܬܠܬ ܫܢܝܢ ܡܬܟܠܝܐ ܡܪܕܝܬܗ. ܘܝܒܫܐ ܕܘܟܬܐ ܕܡܪܕܝܬܐ.

5 And there is in a certain place another lighthouse[17] of brass, and on its top a horseman of brass. And on the day of their festival, water would flow from this lighthouse and all the people who were assembled there, would drink from it and water their cattle and fill all the jars they had with them and the vessels that are there. And after the festival, the stream of water ceases and does not flow anymore as it used to.

6 There is a city that has seven walls, one inside another, and between one wall and another seven miles. And every three miles is one parasang. And between the walls: orchards, and rivers, and vineyards, and channels, and mills.

7 There is a wall, which the kings built from the Sea of the Khazars (i.e., the Caspian Sea) to the Sea of Syria (i.e., the Mediterranean Sea). (Its) length: eight days.

On rivers.

8 The river called Baʾṭlas: from the beginning of days, its waters flow to the sea for three hours. And its flow stops for three hours, and the place of the flow dries up.

---

[17] Or ‘minaret’.

9 ܝܡܐ ܕܣܘܦ ܟܕ ܢܦܠ ܒܗ̇ ܒܥܝܪܐ ܐܘ ܒܪܢܫܐ. ܒܝܡܐ
ܕܐܝܬܘܗܝ ܚܝܐ ܘܐܝܬ ܒܗ ܢܦܫܐ ܠܐ ܛܒܥ ܠܥܠ ܡܢ ܡ̈ܝܐ.
ܘܟܕ ܡܐܬ ܛܒܥ ܒܡ̈ܝܐ.

10 ܐܝܬ ܒܝܡܐ ܕܡܬܩܪܐ ܕܡܬܩܪܝܐ ܐܘܪܝܩܢܘܣ ܕܪ̈ܐ
ܘܡܬܦܣܩܐ ܒܝܘܡܐ ܬܠܬ ܙܒ̈ܢܝܢ ܘܡܬܚܠܦܐ ܡܪ̈ܕܝܬܗ
ܚܕܐ ܥܠܝܐ ܡܬܥܠܝܢܐ ܕܡ̈ܝܐ. ܘܡܢ ܒܬܪ ܗܕܐ
ܕܡܬܚܙܝܐ ܐܪܥܐ ܝܒܫܐ.

11 ܐܝܬ ܢܗܪܐ ܚܕ ܕܡܪܕܐ ܒܫܒܬܐ ܚܕ ܝܘܡܐ. ܘܫܠܝܢ
ܡ̈ܝܘܗܝ. ܘܫܒܬܐ ܝܘ̈ܡܐ ܐܚܪ̈ܢܐ ܡܬܦܣܩܝܢ ܒܕܡܐ
ܕܡܬܚܙܝܐ ܐܪܥܐ ܝܒܝܫܬܐ.

12 ܒܐܬܪ ܕܓܒ̈ܠܝܐ ܐܝܬ ܒܪܐ ܚܕܐ ܕܡܟܣܝܐ ܥ̈ܢܢܐ ܘܚܠܝܐ
ܘܢܘܦܐ. ܘܡܢ ܕܡܬܦܫܩܝܢ ܥ̈ܢܢܐ ܒܡܛܪܐ. ܕ̈ܕܝܢ ܥ̈ܢܢܐ
ܚ̈ܠܝܢܐ ܘܗܘܝܢ ܡܠܚܐ ܚܠܝܐ ܘܚܡܪܐ ܘܠܐ ܗܘܐ ܒܗ̇
ܛܒܥܐ ܕܢܘܦܐ ܘܐܦܠܐ ܐܪܥܐ. ܘܢܘܦܐ ܦܐܫ ܒܕܘܟܬܗ
[ܒܣܘܣܝܐ] ܟܕ ܠܝܬ ܒܗ ܛܒܥܐ ܕܚܠܝܐ.

13 ܒܐܬܪܐ ܕܩܘܫܛ ܐܝܬ ܡܥܝܢܐ ܒܐܦܐ ܕܡܪܕܝܐ ܪܕܝܐ ܕܡܝܐ
ܪ̈ܕܝܢ ܘܠܒܒܗ ܘܪܦܝܘܬܗ ܐܝܟ ܕܡܝܐ. ܘܪܕܐ ܘܒܥܐ
ܘܗ̇ܘܐ ܒܦܪܐ. ܣܘܡܟܐ ܟܕ ܠܝܬ ܒܗ ܠܐ ܛܒܥܐ ܘܠܐ
ܪܝܫܐ [ܕܕܡܐ] ܘܥܒܠ ܡܢܗ ܚܝ̈ܐ.

12e ܒܣܘܣܝܐ] ܒܣܘܣܘܬܐ B1

13d ܕܕܡܐ] ܕܪܡܐ B1

9 The Sea of Reeds:[18] when a man or animal falls into it, as long as he is alive and there is breath in him, he floats upon the water, but when he dies, he sinks into the water.

10 In the sea there is a place called ʾEwrīqōs. It flows and stops three times during a day. And its flow rises for five hundred cubits in one hour. And afterward, it withdraws until the dry land appears.

11 There is a river that flows one day during the week, and its waters increase. And during the other six days, they stop until the dry land appears.

12 In the land of Kānīlāz, there is a well that brings forth water and salt and naphtha (i.e., crude oil). And when the waters stop in a pool, the salty waters flow away, and there remains sweet and white salt that has neither taste nor smell of naphtha. And the naphtha remains in its place in the pool, while there is no (more) taste of salt in it.

13 In the country of Pūštī, there is a spring in a rock that flows with blood, and its smell and taste and stench are like those of blood. And it flows and dries up and turns into red dust that has no taste or smell of blood. And they take from it *ḥnānā*.

[18] In this context, the Dead Sea.

14 ܒܐܬܪܐ ܕܦܪ̈ܣܝܐ ܐܝܬ ܢܗܪܐ ܕܪܕܐ ܒܝܘܡܐ ܕܫܒܬܐ.
ܘܫܪܟܐ ܕܝܘ̈ܡܬܐ ܡܬܦܣܩ. ܘܡܬܩܪܐ ܢܗܪܐ ܫܒܬܝܐ.

15 ܒܐܬܪܐ ܕܦܪܩ ܐܝܬ ܢܗܪܐ |fol. 69v| ܢܗܪܐ ܚܕ ܕܡܪܕܐ
ܚܠܐ ܡܢܥܐ ܕܠܐ ܡ̈ܝܐ. ܘܠܐ ܡܨܐ ܒܪܢܫܐ ܘܠܐ ܒܥܝܪܐ
ܘܠܐ ܡܫܟܚܐ ܠܡܥܒܪ ܒܗ. ܘܝܘܡܐ ܕܫܒܬܐ ܡܬܟܠܝܐ
ܡܪ̈ܕܝܬܗ. ܘܫܪܟ ܕܝܘܡܬܐ ܕܡܪ̈ܕܝܬܗ ܠܐܦ ܡܥܒܪܐ.

16 ܒܐܬܪܐ ܕܪ̈ܗܘܡܝܐ ܥܠ ܝܡܐ ܕܒܪ̈ܪ ܐܬܪܐ ܕܡܬܩܪܐ
ܓܠ̈ܠܐ. ܠܐ ܡܬܦܣܩ ܡܢܗ ܡܛܪܐ. ܠܐ ܣܬܘܐ ܘܠܐ
ܩܝܛܐ. ܘܐܦܠܐ ܡܨܝܢ ܠܡܥܒܪܗ ܓ̈ܠܠܬܐ. ܐܠܐ ܠܚܘ ܡܢ
ܒ̈ܬܐ.

17 ܒܐܬܪܐ ܕܬܝܡܢܐ ܘܕܟܘܫ̈ܝܐ ܗܘܐ ܟܠܗ ܩܝܛܐ ܡܛܪܐ.
ܘܒܣܬܘܐ ܗܘܐ ܩܝܛܐ. ܩܝܛܐ ܕܬܡܢ ܣܬܘܐ. ܘܣܬܘܐ
ܩܝܛܐ.

18 ܒܒܝܬ ܕܠܒܙ ܡܕܝܢܬܐ ܒܡܪܒܥܘܬܐ ܕܩܪܝܬܐ ܕܡܬܩܪܝܐ
ܓܡܣܘ ܐܝܬ ܡܥܡܕܐ ܚܕ ܙܥܘܪܐ ܥܠ ܫܦܘܪܗ ܕܝܡܐ
ܘܡܪ̈ܕܐ ܡ̈ܝܐ ܣܘܡ̈ܩܐ ܘܣܡܘ̈ܩܐ ܐܝܟ ܚܠܐ ܬܘܡܦܐ
ܘܐܝܬ ܒܛܒܥܗ ܚܪܝܦܘܬܐ. ܘܓܘܢܗ ܐܝܟ ܣܘܪܩܐ
ܘܪܕܝܢ ܘܪܡܝܢ ܒܢܗܪܐ. ܘܐܘܪܚܐ ܕܡ̈ܝܐ ܣܘܦܐ ܣܘܡ̈ܩܐ
ܒܟ̈ܦܐ ܘܒܪ̈ܩܐ.

14 In the country of Spārē, there is a river that flows on the day of the Sabbath and stops on the remaining days. And it is called the 'Sabbatical river'.

15 In the country of Persia there is a river that flows with dry sand, without any water. And neither man nor animal nor ship is able to cross it. And on the day of the Sabbath, its flow stops. And (people) see the place of its flow in the direction of the West.

16 In the country of Romans, (there is) a place on the Sea of the Khazars which is called Maṭlāyā. It does not stop raining there, in winter as well as in summer. And they cannot even store crops, unless inside the houses.

17 In the country of the South and of the Hejaz, it rains during the whole summer, and in winter it is summer. Summer there is winter and winter is summer.

18 In the country of Bēt Dlīš, in the vicinity of the town called ʿAms, there is a certain small spring on the seashore, and it flows with water that is red and sour like strong vinegar. And it has a sharp taste, and its color is like that of minium. And it flows and runs into a river, and the course of those red waters is (made of) stones and pebbles.

ܬܘܒ ܬܕܡܘܪܬܐ ܒܓܙܪܬܐ ܕܡܕܝܢܚܬܐ

19 ܐܝܬ ܒܓܙܪܬܐ ܚܕܐ ܒ̈ܢܝܢܫܐ ܕܐܝܬ ܠܗܘܢ ܩ̈ܪܢܐ ܐܪ̈ܝܟܐ ܘܩ̈ܛܝܢܐ ܕܡܟܬܫܝܢ ܠܗܘܢ ܡܢ ܪ̈ܚܩܗܘܢ ܘܡܕܒܪܐ ܠܪ̈ܓܠܝܗܘܢ. ܕܘܟܬ ܓܠܐ ܘܡܬܬܩܢܝܢ ܩ̈ܪܢܐ. ܦܪܣܐܝܬ ܩܪܝܢ ܠܗܘܢ ܓܠܝܡ ܟ݂ܘܪ.

20 ܐܝܬ ܓܙܪܬܐ ܚܕܐ ܕܡܬܩܪܝܐ ܙ̈ܢܓ. ܘܐܝܬ ܒܗ̇ ܒ̈ܢܝܢܫܐ ܠܒ̈ܢܝܢܫܐ. ܕܪ̈ܫܝܗܘܢ ܐܝܟ ܟܠܒ̈ܐ. ܘܟܕ ܢܟܠܘܢ ܠܘܬܗܘܢ ܡܠܟ̈ܐ ܢܟܠܘܢ ܘܢܫܩܘܢ ܒܫܡܪܐ ܕܐܝܬ ܬܡܢ. ܘܢܦܪܢܓܠܘܢ ܟܠ ܚܠܐ ܕܢܗܘܐ ܠܗܘܢ ܕܘܟܬ ܙܢܓܐ. ܘܠܐ ܚܙܐ ܒܗܘܢ ܠܐ ܠܐܓܪܐ ܘܠܐ ܙܘܒܢܐ ܘܠܐ ܫܘܩܐ. ܘܐܦ ܐܢܫ ܡܢ ܒ̈ܢܝܢܫܐ ܢܛܘܦ ܠܒ̈ܢܝܗܘܢ ܒܙܢܐ ܕܙܘܘܓܐ |fol. 70r| ܒܪ̈ܫܟܬܗ ܡܟܐܬ.

21 ܘܐܝܬ ܒܡܕܒܪܐ ܕܥܪ̈ܒܝܐ ܐܪ̈ܢܐ ܕܐܝܬ ܠܗܘܢ ܐܠܝ̈ܬܐ ܐܝܟ ܐܠܝ̈ܬܐ ܕܥܪ̈ܒܐ. ܘܟܕ ܚܙܝܢ ܠܒܪ̈ܢܫܐ ܥܪܩܝܢ ܡܢܗ. ܘܡܪ̈ܥܝܬܐ ܕܐܬܪܐ ܗܘ ܐܟܠܝܢ ܠܗܘܢ.

22 ܢܩܡ ܥܠ ܐܠܟܣܢܕܪܘܣ ܐܝܬ ܒ̈ܢܝܢܫܐ ܕܪ̈ܓܠܝܗܘܢ ܐܝܟ ܪ̈ܓܠܐ ܕܡܥܪ̈ܒܐ. ܘܐܝܬ ܗܘ̈ܝ ܠܗܘܢ ܥܝܢ ܩܕܡ ܒܟܠ ܚܕܐ ܪܓܠܐ.

23 ܐܝܬ ܓܙܪܬܐ ܚܕܐ ܕܡܬܩܪܝܐ ܐܟܠܝܢ ܒ̈ܢܝܢܫܐ. ܟܕ ܗܘ ܚܝ ܠܐ ܕܚܣܝܢ ܠܗ. ܐܠܐ ܦܣܩܝܢ ܠܦܓܪܗ. ܘܐܟܠܝܢ ܠܗ ܟܕ ܗܘ ܚܝ. ܟܕ ܠܐ ܡܩܛܠܝܢ. ܘܐܦܠܐ ܡܒܫܠܐ. ܘܒܓܙܪܬܐ ܐܝܬ ܒܠܘܦ.

Again, marvels in the Eastern islands.

19 On one island, there are people who have long and wide ears that cover them from their head to their feet instead of a cloak. And they are called 'ears'. In Persian, they call them *glīm gōš*.

20 There is one island called Karnāš, and on it, there are dog-people, whose males are like dogs. And when enemies approach them, they enter and swim in the river which is there. And they roll in the sand, which serves them instead of armour, so that neither arrow nor spear nor sword can reach them. And if a regular man would cleave to their women by way of intercourse, he is going to die immediately.

21 And in the desert of the Arabs, there are people who have fat tails like those of the sheep. And when they see humans, they flee from them. And the Arabs of that country eat them.

22 It appeared to Alexander (that) there are people whose legs are like those of scorpions, and they had six digits on each leg.

23 There is an island whose inhabitants eat people while they are still alive. They do not slaughter him, but cut off his flesh and eat him while he is alive, without roasting or boiling. And the island is Balōs.

24 ܚܙܐ ܐܠܟܣܢܕܪܘܣ ܒܢ̈ܝܢܫܐ ܕܪ̈ܫܝܗܘܢ ܐܝܟ ܪ̈ܫܐ ܕܟܠܒ̈ܐ.

25 ܘܚܙܐ ܬܘܒ ܒܢ̈ܝܢܫܐ ܕܠܝܬ ܠܗܘܢ ܪܫܐ ܘܦܘ̈ܡܝܗܘܢ ܘܥܝ̈ܢܝܗܘܢ ܒܚܕ̈ܝܗܘܢ.

26 ܘܐܝܬ ܒܢ̈ܝܢܫܐ ܕܥܩ̈ܒܝܗܘܢ ܘܪ̈ܓܠܝܗܘܢ ܐܝܟ ܒܩܪ̈ܐ ܐܪ̈ܒܥܐ. ܟܕ ܠܝܬ ܓܪܡܐ ܒܥܩ̈ܒܝܗܘܢ. ܘܡܗܠܟܝܢ ܒܬܪ̈ܝܢ ܪ̈ܓܠܐ. ܘܪܡܝܢ ܪ̈ܓܠܝܗܘܢ ܥܠ ܐ̈ܝܠܢܐ ܪܘܪ̈ܒܐ ܕܡܕܝܢ̈ܬܐ ܕܐܝܬ ܠܘܬܗܘܢ ܘܫܠܝܛܝܢ ܒܗܘܢ ܐܝܟ ܐܢܫ ܕܫܠܛ ܒܥܓܠܐ ܘܐܟܠܝܢ ܡܢ ܦܐܪ̈ܐ ܕܐ̈ܝܠܢܐ. ܘܡܐ ܕܚܙܝܢ ܠܒܪܢܫܐ ܥܒܪܝܢ ܘܠܒܟܝܢ ܠܗ ܘܪܟܒܝܢ ܥܠ ܟܬ̈ܦܬܗ ܘܡܟܪܟܝܢ ܪ̈ܓܠܝܗܘܢ ܥܠ ܟܬ̈ܦܬܗ ܘܚܢܩܝܢ ܠܗ.

27 ܘܐܝܬ ܒܢ̈ܝܢܫܐ ܕܨܘܬܗܘܢ ܐܝܟ ܕܨܘ̈ܬܐ ܕܚܡܪ̈ܐ. ܘܥܕܝܢ ܒܒܢ̈ܝܢܫܐ ܒܐܦ̈ܐ ܛܪܘܣܐܝܬ ܘܫܘܚܪ̈ܐ. ܘܩܛܠܝܢ ܣܓܝ̈ܐܐ ܡܢ ܚܝ̈ܠܘܬܗ ܕܐܠܟܣܢܕܪܘܣ.

28 ܘܐܝܬ ܕܪ̈ܓܠܝܗܘܢ ܐܝܟ ܪ̈ܓܠܐ ܕܚܡܪܐ ܘܫܪܟܐ ܕܦ̈ܓܪܐ ܐܝܟ ܒܢ̈ܝܢܫܐ.

29 ܘܐܝܬ ܐܢܫܝܢ ܕܪ̈ܫܝܗܘܢ ܐܝܟ ܪ̈ܫܐ ܕܐܪܝܐ. ܘܐܝܬ ܠܗܘܢ ܕܘܢܒܐ ܐܝܟ ܕܟܠܒܐ.

24 Alexander saw people whose teeth are like the teeth of dogs.

25 And moreover, he saw people who have no head, and their mouths and eyes are on their breasts.

26 And there are people whose thighs and legs are like long straps because there are no bones in their thighs. And they are called 'strap-feet'. And they cast their legs upon the great pear trees that they have there and go up with their help, like a man who climbs with a rope, and eat from the fruit of the trees. And when they see a human, they jump and seize him and mount on his shoulders and twist their legs around his shoulders and strangle him.

27 And there are people, whose appearance is like that of ravens, and they throw stones and sticks directly at men. And they killed many from the army of Alexander.

28 And there are those, whose legs are like the legs of an ass, while the rest of bodily members are like those of humans.

29 And there are people whose heads are like the head of a lion, and they have scaly tails.

30 ܘܐܝܬ ܐܢܫܝܢ ܒܡܕܢܚܐ |fol. 70v| ܫܡ̈ܝܟܐ. ܘܠܐ ܐܝܬ ܠܗܘܢ ܣܦܪܐ ܥܠ ܥܠܢܐܝܬ ܘܠܐ ܟܬ̈ܒܐ ܘܠܐ ܬܠܩ̈ܐ. ܘܟܕ ܕܢܚ ܫܡܫܐ ܒܐܦ̈ܝܗܘܢ ܡܐܠܝܢ ܒܠܗ ܫ̈ܢܝܐ ܡܢ ܚܡܝܡܘܬܐ ܕܫܡܫܐ ܒܕܡܐ ܠܬܫܥ ܫ̈ܥܝܢ.

31 ܐܫܬܡܥ ܠܝ ܐܝܟ ܕܫܡܥܗ ܐ̱ܢܘܢ ܕܚܙܐ ܒܓܙܪܬܐ ܕܒܝܬ ܒܢ̈ܝܐ ܕܡܢ ܚܕܗ ܘܠܟܠ ܬܪܝܢ ܪ̈ܫܝܢ ܘܐܪ̈ܒܥ ܐܝ̈ܕܝܢ. ܘܡܢ ܚܕܗ ܘܬܠܬ ܚܕ ܦܓܪܐ ܘܚܕܐ ܪܝܫܐ. ܘܠܝܢ ܗܘܘ ܒܗ ܫ̈ܢܝܐ ܥܠ ܢܬܘܬܐ ܕܐܒܗܘܗܝ. ܘܟܕ ܡܝܬ ܚܕ ܡܢܗܘܢ ܦܫ ܒܓܘܫܡܗ ܬܠܝܐ ܒܚܪܗ ܬܠܬܐ ܝܘ̈ܡܝܢ. ܘܡܢ ܡܝܬ ܐܦ ܗ̇ܘ ܒܬܪܗ ܐܚܪܢܐ.

32 ܐܝܬ ܒܓܙܪ̈ܬܐ ܐ̈ܝܠܢܐ ܕܝܠܕܝܢ ܒܢ̈ܝܢܫܐ ܘܦ̈ܪܚܬܐ ܘܡܬܬܢܣܒܐ ܒܗܘܢ ܚܝܘܬܐ. ܘܡܬܬܥܪܐ ܐܝܠܢܐ ܕܦ̇ܘܦ̇ܘ. ܘܟܕ ܡܬܓܡܪܝܢ ܦܪܚܝܢ ܘܐܙܠܝܢ ܘܢܦܠܐ ܡܢ ܡܟܐ ܚܝܘܬܐ ܘܐܟܠܐ ܠܗܘܢ.

33 ܚܙܐ ܐܢܬܬܐ ܠܓܙܪܬ ܫܬܝܢ ܒܢ̈ܝܐ ܒܬܠܬܝܢ ܘܫܒܥ ܙܒ̈ܢܝܢ ܘܒܟܠ ܫܢܬܐ ܙܒܢܬܐ ܘܬܪ̈ܬܝܢ ܝܠܕܐ ܗܘܬ. ܐܡܪܝܢ ܗܘܘ ܕܠܓܙܪܬ ܒܓܘܪܐ ܕܒܢ̈ܝܐ. ܒܗ̇ ܕܒܓܘܪܐ ܐܢܬܘܬܗܘܢ ܫܬܝܢ ܡܩ̈ܒܪܐ.

34 ܐܢܬܬܐ ܐܚܪܬܐ ܠܓܙܪܬ ܒܣܘܪܝ ܒܢ̈ܝܐ. ܒܫܡܫܐ ܒܓܠ̈ܐ ܘܣܥܘ ܥܠܗܘܢ.

30 And there are smooth (i.e., hairless) people in the East, and they have no hair whatsoever, neither eyebrows nor eyelids. And when the sun shines upon their faces, they enter the water from the sun's heat for as long as nine hours.

31 The man called Anās told us that he saw on the island of Kīš a man who had above his breast two heads and four arms, and below his breast one body and one belly. And they were quarrelling one with another about the inheritance of their father. And when one of them died, his body remained hanging upon his companion for three days, and then that other side also died.

32 There are trees in the islands that bear humans and birds, and life is breathed into them. And it is called the 'tree of Waqwaq'. And when they fully develop, they fly away and leave. And an animal comes out of the sea and eats them.

33 A certain woman gave birth to sixty children in thirty-five pregnancies. And every year, she would miscarry once and again. They would say, 'She gave birth to a *kōr* of children', because one *kōr* contains sixty *qpīzē*.[19]

34 Another woman gave birth to twenty children in five pregnancies, and all of them lived.

[19] Both *kōr* and *qpīzā* are measures of capacity.

40 ܘܣܝܐ ܬܘܒ ܐ̈ܝܠܢܐ ܕܡܢ ܝܘܩܪܐ ܘܡܕܡܝܐ ܠܦܠܓܗ ܕܢܘܡܝܐ
ܥ̈ܡܡ ܗ̈ܘ. ܘܡܢ ܦܠܓܗ ܕܢܘܡܝܐ ܘܡܕܡܝܐ ܠܓܒ ܓܪܒܝܐ
ܘܒ̈ܢܝ ܗ̈ܘ ܘܩ̈ܠܝܡ ܗ̈ܘ. ܒܡܕܡܝܐ ܕܠܐ ܡܬܚܙܝܐ <ܗܘܐ
ܡܢܗܘܢ ܡܕܡ ܠܟܠ ܡܢ ܐܪܥܐ. ܘܟܕ ܥܒܪ ܩܠܝܠ ܡܢ>
ܦܐܪ̈ܝܗܘܢ ܘܐܟܠܘ. ܘܢܦܩܬ ܒܠܥܘܡܗܘܢ ܪܘܚܐ ܣܪܝܬܐ.
ܘܐܬܡܚܝܘ ܡܚ̈ܘܬܐ ܪܘܪ̈ܒܬܐ ܟܠ ܣܓܝܗܘܢ. ܘܟܠ
ܗܕ̈ܡܝܗܘܢ ܟܕ ܠܐ ܚܙܝܢ ܗܘܘ ܕܡܚܝܢ ܗܘܘ ܠܗܘܢ. ܘܟܡܟܡܐ
ܗܘܘ ܥܠ ܕܪܒܝܐ ܡܢ ܐ̈ܝܠܢܐ. ܫܠܘܢ ܕܐܡܪܝܢ. ܕܠܐ ܢܗܘܐ
ܒܗܘܢ ܐܝܟ ܕܡܐܬ ܐܘ ܕܢܦܠ ܡܢ ܐ̈ܝܠܢܐ ܗܠܝܢ ܡܕܡ.
ܘܐܠܐ ܟܠܗܘܢ ܡܬܬܬܘܢ.

41 ܘܐܝܬ ܗܘܐ ܬܡܢ ܦܪܚܬܐ ܕܕܡܝܐ ܠܣܚܠܐ.

42 ܘܣܝܐ ܐܠܟܣܢܕܪܘܣ ܬܪܝܢ ܐ̈ܝܠܢܐ ܪܘܪ̈ܒܐ ܘܡܡܠܠܝܢ ܗܘܘ
ܐܝܟ ܒ̈ܢܝܢܫܐ ܘܡܠܠ ܥܡܗ ܚܕ ܡܢܗܘܢ ܒܠܫܢܐ ܗܢܕܝܐ
ܘܐܚܪ̈ܢܐ ܒܠܫܢܐ ܝ̈ܘܢܝܐ. ܘܐܘܕܥܘܗܝ ܟܠ ܡܘܬܗ.
ܘܗܦܟ ܡܢ ܬܡܢ ܘܡܛܐ ܒܒܒܠ.

43 ܘܢܦܩܬ ܒܠܥܘܡܗܘܢ ܣܘܬܐ ܪܒܬܐ. ܘܐܝܬ ܗܘܬ ܠܗ̇
ܕܡܘܬܐ ܕܒܪ̈ܢܫܐ ܘܕܟܢܫܪܐ. ܘܐܝܬܘܗ̇ ܐܢܬܬܐ
ܒܪܓܠܬܐ ܘܥܕܐܘܗ̇ ܦܕܡܝܗ̇. ܘܦܩܘܡܬܗ̇ ܘܐܟܠܬܗ̇ ܐܝܟ
ܣܘܬ ܥܢܐ.

44 ܘܢܦܩܘ ܒܠܥܘܡܗܘܢ ܣ̈ܘܣܬܐ ܪܘܪ̈ܒܬܐ ܟܠ ܚܕܐ ܡܢܗܘܢ
ܡܬܚܫܒܐ ܐܝ̈ܟܢ ܐܘܪܚܗ̇.

45 ܘܣܝܘ ܦܪܣ̈ܘܕܐ |fol. 71v| ܐܝܟ ܢܡܪ̈ܐ. ܘܥܒܝ̈ܢܗܘܢ ܐܝܟ
ܥܒܐ ܕܒܠܬ̈ܐ.

B1 40c–d ܗܘܐ ܡܢܗܘܢ … ܩܠܝܠ ܡܢ] Added in the left margin by the same hand.

40 And again, he saw the trees that were grew taller from the morning until midday and grew shorter from midday until evening time. And they wasted away until nothing of them could be seen above the earth. And when they encamped (there) and plucked some of their fruit and ate them, a foul spirit went out against them. And they were afflicted with many sores on their loins and their limbs, while not seeing what struck them. And they heard a voice of thunder from among those trees, saying, 'Let no one take anything from these trees, lest anyone of you should die! And if not, all of you will die!'

41 And there was a bird there that looked like a partridge.

42 And Alexander saw two great trees that spoke like humans. And one of them talked to him in the Greek language and another in the Latin language. And they made known to him about his death. And he turned back from there and died in Babylon.

43 And a great animal went out against them, which had the appearance of both human and beast. And they brought a woman stripped naked and threw her in front of it, and it tore her apart and ate her, like a wild beast.

44 And great animals went out against them, each of them fifteen cubits long.

45 And they saw bats who were like eagles and had teeth like the teeth of dogs.

46 ܘܚܙܘ ܐܝ̈ܠܢܐ ܕܠܝܬ ܠܗ ܘܠܐ ܦܐܪ̈ܐ. ܘܦܪܫܘܬܐ ܚܕ̣ܐ ܥܠ ܪܫܗ ܕܐܝܠܢܐ ܘܠܟܠ ܡܢܗ̇ ܕܦܪܫܘܬܐ ܙܠܝܩܐ ܐܝܟ ܙܠܝܩܐ ܕܫܡܫܐ.

47 ܐܫܬܥܝܢ ܪܒܢ ܥܡܢܘܐܝܠ ܕܫܡܥ ܡܢ ܓܒܪܐ ܬܓܪܐ ܐܠܟܣܢܕܪܝܐ. ܕܐܙܠ ܠܓܙܪܬܐ ܚܕ̣ܐ ܒܝܡܐ ܘܠܐ ܡܫܟܚ ܒܪܢܫܐ ܠܡܥܠ ܠܗ̇ ܡܢ ܣܓܝܐܘܬ ܚܝ̈ܘܬܐ ܡܚܒܠܢܝ̈ܬܐ ܘܐܝܬ ܒܗ̇ ܐܝ̈ܠܢܐ ܙܘܥ̈ܪܐ. ܐܡܪ ܕܚܕ ܙܒܢ ܗܘܝܢ ܥܠ ܩܪܝܒܘܬܐ ܕܓܙܪܬܐ ܗ̇ܝ. ܐܡܪܢ ܚܕ̣ ܡܢܢ ܘܣܠܩ ܠܓܙܪܬܐ ܗ̇ܝ ܘܣܠܩ ܠܚܕ̣ ܡܢ ܐܝ̈ܠܢܐ ܕܬܡܢ. ܘܢܦܩܬ ܡܢ ܡܢܐ ܚܝܘܬܐ ܕܕܡܝܐ ܠܟܠܒܐ. ܘܕܒܩܬ ܒܪܓܠܗ ܥܠ ܚܨܗ̇. ܘܐܬܬ ܘܡܛܬ ܠܬܚܬ ܡܢ ܐܝܠܢܐ ܗܘ. ܘܢܛܪܬ ܠܗ ܕܢܚܘܬ ܙܒ̈ܢܝܢ ܣܓܝ̈ܐܢ ܘܠܐ ܢܚܬ ܓܒܪܐ ܗܘ ܡܢ ܐܝܠܢܐ. ܘܐܪܦܝܬ ܕܢܘܚ ܘܡܪܟܒܬܗ ܥܠ ܘܢܦܩܬܗ ܠܕܘܒܟܗ ܒܐܝܠܢܐ ܠܡܣܠܩ ܕܓܒܪܐ ܗܘ. ܘܟܕ ܥܒܕܬܗ ܢܟܕܘ ܗܘ ܘܐܝܠܢܐ. ܘܥܒܪܬ ܘܐܟܠܬ ܠܓܒܪܐ.

48 ܚܝܘܬܐ ܕܡܬܩܪܝܐ ܒܪ̈ܬܝܢ ܡܟܣܝܐ ܪܫܗ ܡܢ ܡܪܟܒܗ̇ ܕܐܡܗ̇. ܘܪܚܫܐ ܓܠܐ. ܘܗܦܟܐ ܘܡܚܠܐ ܪܫܗ ܠܒܪܐ ܕܐܡܗ̇. ܘܗܕܐ ܚܝܘܬܐ ܒܪ̈ܬܝܢ ܗ̣ܝ ܗ̣ܝ ܪܥܝܐ. ܘܐܡܪܝܢ ܕܐܝܬ ܒܪܫܗ ܩܪܢܐ ܚܕ̣ܐ ܐܘܪܟܗ̇ ܕܪܥܐ ܘܒܚܝܘܬܗ̇ ܐܝܟ ܓܡܠܗ ܕܒܪܢܫܐ ܘܕܚܝܘܬܐ ܘܕܦܪܫܘܬܐ ܒܝܫܐܝܬ. ܘܒܥܕܢ ܡܢܗ̇ |fol. 72r| ܘܡܬܪ̈ܐ ܥܠ̈ܐ ܡܢ ܡܐܬܝܢ ܕܫܢ̈ܝܢ. ܘܒܕܡܐ ܠܐܪܒܥܐ ܐܠܦܐ ܕܫܢ̈ܐ ܡܛܠ ܥܘܦܪܐ.

46 And they saw trees that had no fruit, and a certain bird on the top of a tree, and above the bird rays, like the rays of the sun.

47 Rabban Emmanuel told us that he heard from a man, who was a merchant from Alexandria, that there is an island in the sea, and no human is able to enter it because of the multitude of rapacious animals. And there are great trees there. He said that when they were travelling near that island, one of them dared and went up to that island, and he climbed one of the trees that are there. And an animal that looked like a dog went out from the sea, and its tail was rolled around its loins. And it came and stood under that tree and beckoned him many times to get down, but that man did not go down from the tree. And it loosened its tail and rolled it around (the tree) and started to shake its tail with the tree towards that man. And at once, both he and the tree were set on fire. And it went away and entered the sea.

48 The animal called rhinoceros brings its head forth from the womb of its mother, and feeds on dried grass and turns back and puts its head into the womb of its mother. This rhinoceros animal is, in fact, unicorn. And they say that it has on its head one horn, the length of which is one elbow, and its thickness as that of a human thigh or an animal or bird, according to nature. And they make good belts from it — from two hundred dinars and up to four thousand dinars, on account of (their) beauty.

49 ܒܝܡܐ ܕܦܘܢܛܘܣ ܐܝܬ ܢܘܢܐ ܐܘܪܟܗ ܡܐܬܝܢ ܐܡ̈ܝܢ. ܕܢܦܩ
ܡܢܗ ܒܫܢ̈ܝ ܐܠܦܐ. ܘܟܕ ܚܙܝܢ ܠܗ ܢܦܩܝܢ ܥܠ ܡܫܚܐ
ܘܫܒܩܝܢ ܠܗ ܕܢܣܩ. ܘܥܒܪ.

50 ܘܐܝܬ ܒܗ ܢܘܢܐ ܐܘܪܟܗ ܡܐܬܝܢ ܐܡ̈ܝܢ. ܘܦܬܝܗܘܢ
ܕܢܘܢܐ ܢܘܢܬܐ ܐܚܪܬܐ. ܘܦܬܝܗ ܕܐܚܪܬܐ ܐܪܒܥܐ
ܢ̈ܘܢܐ ܚܕ ܒܦܬܝܗ ܕܚܕܕ̈ܐ. ܐܝܟ ܩܠܦܐ ܕܒܝܠܐ ܚܕ ܠܓܘ
ܡܢ ܚܕ.

51 ܘܐܝܬ ܒܗ ܐܝܟ ܩܪ̈ܢܬܗ ܕܬܘܪܐ ܥܠܝܐ ܘܡܠܘܐܐ ܘܡܢ
ܥܠܘܗ ܒܥܒܕܝܢ ܣܦܝܢܐ. ܗܘ ܕܝܢ [ܡܫܟ̈ܢܐ].

52 ܘܚܙܝܢ ܒܥܪܒܐ ܐܠܦܐ ܚܕܐ ܕܢܘܢܐ ܕܒܥܝܐ ܠܥܒܪܐ ܥܠ
ܢܗܪܐ. ܘܐܠܦܐ ܐܚܪܬܐ ܡܥܒܪܐ ܠܥܢܬܐ.

53 ܘܐܝܬ ܒܝܡܐ ܕܦܘܢܛܘܣ ܢܘܢܐ ܕܫܪܐ ܘܡܬܬܪܐ ܡܢܝܐ
ܕܝܡܐ.

54 ܘܐܝܬ ܐܠܐ ܗܘ ܕܝܢ ܩ̈ܝܐ. ܥܠ ܚܕ ܡܐܐ ܘܥܣܪܝܢ ܐܡ̈ܝܢ
ܫܘܪܗ ܘܦܬܝܘܗ ܕܥܠ ܚܕ ܡܢܗܘܢ ܐܠܦ ܒܬܝܢ.

51b ܡܫܟ̈ܢܐ] ܫܟ̈ܢܐ B1

49 In the Sea of Qūlzam, there is a fish whose length is two hundred cubits. The sailors are afraid of it, and when they see it, they strike a piece of wood. And it hears the sound of wood and flees.

50 And there is in it a fish, whose length is two hundred cubits. And in the belly of this fish, there is another fish, and in the belly of this other (fish), there are four fishes, one inside of another, like the peels of onion — one inside of another.

51 And there is in it [a fish] that looks like a bull, that gives birth and suckles. And from its skin, they make shields, that is bucklers.

52 And one can see in Basra the rib of a fish, from which a bridge over the river is made, and another rib — a vestibule to a house.

53 And there is in the Sea of Qūlzam a fish that flies, and it is called 'sea-locust'.

54 And there are turtles, that is *qrāyē*,[20] and each of them is one hundred and twenty cubits in circumference. And there is one thousand offspring in the belly of each of them.

[20] Neo-Aramaic ܩܪ̈ܝܐ 'turtles'.

55 ܘܐܝܬ ܒܗ ܢܘܢܐ ܕܕܡܘܬ ܓܡ̈ܠܐ.

56 ܘܐܝܬ ܓܙܪܬܐ ܚܕܐ ܥܠ ܝܡܐ ܕܣܢܩܝܢ ܥܠ ܡܛܪܐ ܡܪܝܡܝܢ ܐ̈ܝܕܝܗܘܢ ܠܫܡܝܐ. ܘܒܥܝܢ ܡܢ ܐܠܗܐ. ܘܐܬܐ ܥܠܝܗܘܢ ܡܛܪܐ ܒܪܫܝܬܗ.

57 ܓܙܪܬܐ ܕܣܝܢܘܦ ܐܝܬܘܗܝ. ܒܗ ܡܢ ܩ̈ܕܡܝܢ ܐܫܬܟܚ ܒܚܕܐ ܡܢ ܓܙܪ̈ܬܐ ܕܒܝܢ ܩܐܡܐ ܚܕ ܪܒܐ ܘܡܓܙܪܐ ܘܡܝܬܐ. ܘܦܩܕ ܡܠܟܐ ܕܢܣܒܘܢ ܒܢ̈ܝ ܡܕܝܢܬܐ ܒܣܪܗ ܠܡܐܟܠ. ܘܫܩܠܘ ܒܢ̈ܝ ܡܕܝܢܬܐ ܬܠܬܐ ܩ̈ܕܡܝܢ ܡܢ ܒܣܪܗ ܬܪ̈ܬܝܢ ܬܩ̈ܠܬܐ. ܘܫܩܠܬ ܬܠܬܐ ܐܚܪܬܐ. ܟܐܦܐ ܕܪܫܗ ܡܝܬܐ ܕܡܠܟܐ. ܘܫܩܠܘ ܡܢ ܒܣܪܗ ܬܫܥܝܢ ܡܐ̈ܢܐ ܡܫܚܐ ܠܢܗܝܪܐ. ܕܠܝܢ ܗܘܘ ܠܡܐ̈ܢܐ ܒܫܠܝܐ |fol. 72v| ܠܒܬ̈ܝܗܘܢ ܘܡܫܚܝܢ ܗܘܘ ܡܫܚܐ.

58 ܓܙܪܬܐ ܚܕܐ ܕܡܬܩܪܝܐ ܦܪܛܢܛ ܡܫܬܡܥ ܒܗ̇ ܩܠܐ ܕܙܡܪܐ ܘܕܩ̈ܠܝܐ ܘܕܪ̈ܩܕܐ ܟܠܗ ܠܠܝܐ. ܘܐܡܪܝܢ ܐܢܫܝܢ ܡܢ ܒܢ̈ܝ ܐܬܪܐ ܗܘ ܕܡܢ ܬܡܢ ܢܦܩ ܒܪ ܐܟܣܢܝܐ ܕܗܘܐ ܐܢܛܝܦܛܪܘܦ. ܐܡܝܢ ܘܐܡܝܢ.

55 And there is in it a fish that looks like a camel.

56 And there is an island where when every day when they need rain, they raise their hands to heaven and beseech God, and the rain comes to them at once.

57 There is an island in India: on one of the days, they have found on one of the islands of Kīš a great whale, heavy and dead. And the king ordered that the people of the city should take its meat to eat. And during three days the people of the city took away two-thirds of its meat, and one third remained. The side of its head was the king's portion. And they took from its eye ninety pitchers of oil for (making) light. They were drawing the pitchers with a rope into its eyes and bringing up the oil.

58 An island called Barṭīl: the sound of singing and tambourines and timbrels is heard there all night. And the people from among the locals say that it is from there the son of perdition, who is Antichrist, shall come. So be it, Amen.

2.4. Synopsis of Recensions

RI	RII	RII	RI
I.1	II.1	II.1	I.1
I.2	II.2	II.2	I.2
I.3	II.3	II.3	I.3
I.4	II.4	II.4	I.4
I.5	II.5	II.5	I.5
I.6	II.6	II.6	I.6
I.7	II.7	II.7	I.7
I.8		II.8	I.13
I.9		II.9	I.14
I.10		II.10	I.15
I.11		II.11	I.16
I.12		II.12	I.17
I.13	II.8	II.13	I.18
I.14	II.9	II.14	I.19
I.15	II.10	II.15	I.20
I.16	II.11	II.16	I.21
I.17	II.12	II.17	I.22
I.18	II.13	II.18	I.24
I.19	II.14	II.19	I.28
I.20	II.15	II.20	I.29

I.21	II.16	II.21	I.30
I.22	II.17	II.22	I.31
I.23		II.23	I.32
I.24	II.18	II.24	I.34
I.25		II.25	I.35
I.26		II.26	I.36
I.27		II.27	I.37
I.28	II.19	II.28	I.38
I.29	II.20	II.29	
I.30	II.21	II.30	I.39
I.31	II.22	II.31	I.40
I.32	II.23	II.32	I.42
I.33		II.33	I.44
I.34	II.24	II.34	I.45
I.35	II.25	II.35	I.46
I.36	II.26	II.36	
I.37	II.27	II.37	
I.38	II.28	II.38	
I.39	II.30	II.39	I.61
I.40	II.31	II.40	I.62, I.65
I.41		II.41	
I.42	II.32	II.42	I.63
I.43		II.43	

I.44	II.33	II.44	
I.45	II.34	II.45	
I.46	II.35	II.46	
I.47		II.47	
I.48		II.48	
I.49		II.49	I.58
I.50		II.50	I.59
I.51		II.51	I.60
I.52		II.52	
I.53		II.53	
I.54	II.54	II.54	I.54
I.55	II.55	II.55	I.55
I.56		II.56	I.57
I.57	II.56	II.57	
I.58	II.49	II.58	I.64
I.59	II.50		
I.60	II.51		
I.61	II.39		
I.62	II.40		
I.63	II.42		
I.64	II.58		
I.65	II.40		

3. COMMENTARY

 https://doi.org/10.11647/OBP.0237.03

The primary objective of this section is twofold. First of all, it provides philological observations that aim at elucidating some rare, obscure, or misspelt words, especially various toponyms. In addition to that, it makes an attempt at a source-critical analysis of the extremely diverse material that was used by the compiler of the *Marvels*.

At this point, a caveat is in order. While I did my best to be as comprehensive as possible in tracing relevant parallels in the corpus of Syriac literature, the scope of Muslim sources used for this commentary is more modest. It is limited, mainly, to the most important geographical and paradoxographical compositions in Arabic (and to a certain extent in Persian) up to the time of al-Qazwīnī. The resulting parallels, thus, are by no means exhaustive, and for some of the discussed traditions or accounts more relevant material from Muslim sources could be adduced. I believe that paradoxographical works of some post-Qazwīnian writers, such as *Ḫarīdat al-ʿağāʾib wa-farīdat al- ġarāʾib* by Ibn al-Wardī,[1] as well as various later reworkings of *ʿAğāʾib al-maḫlūqāt* in Arabic and Persian, many of which are unstudied and unpublished,[2] may provide additional comparanda for some of the traditions in the *Marvels*. The same applies to the rich corpus of paradoxographical literature produced in Ottoman Turkish during the period from the fifteenth to the seventeenth century, which for the most part remains unstudied and partially unedited.[3]

[1] See Demidchik (2004, 210–19).

[2] For an overview and references to some of them, see Demidchik (2004, 49–50).

[3] For an overview, see Sariyannis (2015).

Another clarification concerns the use of al-Qazwīnī's *ʿAǧāʾib al-maḫlūqāt.* As a result of its immense popularity, the composition has a complicated textual history and is attested in at least four different recensions.[4] While a critical edition of *ʿAǧāʾib al-maḫlūqāt* is still a desideratum, anyone interested in the original text of al-Qazwīnī's work should start with consulting its text in ms. München, Bayerische StaatsBibliothek, Cod. arab. 464, that was copied in the year 1280, during the lifetime of the author,[5] as well as make use of the Cairo edition(s) and that of Fārūq Saʿd.[6] The compiler of the *Marvels,* however, was active, most likely, several centuries after al-Qazwīnī's death and, thus, if he had direct access to the text of this work, it was, probably, already in a revised and expanded form. In light of these considerations, I believe that the eclectic text published by Heinrich Ferdinand Wüstenfeld in 1848, which reflects a very late stage in the textual development of *ʿAǧāʾib al-maḫlūqāt,*[7] would serve purposes of this commentary better than the original version. Accordingly, although I habitually refer to Wüstenfeld's text as that of al-Qazwīnī, it is only for the sake of convenience, while being fully aware that some of the passages discussed might be later additions to the original composition.

---

[4] See von Hees (2002, 91–96); Ruska (1913).

[5] A digital reproduction of the manuscript is available online at https://daten.digitale-sammlungen.de/~db/0004/bsb00045957/images/

[6] Saʿd 1973. For an Italian translation of the work, based on this edition, see Bellino (2008).

[7] It reproduces the text of the fourth, most evolved, redaction of the work.

* * *

I.1 (= II.1) the city of brass in Andalus

This city should be identified with the legendary 'city of brass' (often referred to in Arabic as *madīnat al-baht*) of Muslim sources.[8] A very popular motif among Arab and Persian writers, its account was included in *One Thousand and One Nights*. While most of the Muslim sources agree in locating this city in the West, most commonly, in the region of Andalus, there is a difference of opinions as to who was its founder, Solomon or Alexander the Great. Thus, among the authors, who mention the city of brass in connection with Alexander or Ḏū l-Qarnayn, his Islamic alter ego, are Ibn al-Faqīh al-Hamaḏānī (10th c.)[9] and al-Bīrūnī (11th c.).[10]

Closer to the time of the *Marvels*, we see Zakariyā al-Qazwīnī (13th c.) including this legend into his *Āṯār al-bilād*: 'The City of Brass, also called the City of Copper, to which pertains a strange tale, very much out of the ordinary: now, I have seen a number (of writers) write about it in a certain number of writings, some of which I wrote myself, and withal it is indeed a City famous in the mentioning of it, Ibn al-Faqīh says that the Ancient Sages were of the opinion that as for the City of Brass, it was built by Dhu-l-Qarnayn, who deposited therein his treasures and their talisman which no one is able to withstand. He placed therein the

[8] For a comprehensive overview of Muslim sources, which includes original texts in Arabic and Persian, see Barry (1984). For non-Muslim medieval writers, see also Russell (1984); Ambartsumian (2013).

[9] See *Muḫtaṣar kitāb al-buldān*; ed. de Goeje (1885, 71).

[10] See *Kitāb al-ǧamāhir*; ed. Krenkow (1936, 101–102).

bahta-stone, and this is the Magnet of Man: for should a man stop facing towards it, it draws him like the magnet draws iron, nor can he separate himself from it until he dies. Now (the City) is in the wilds of Andalus...'[11]

I.2 (= II.2) the splendour of Alexandria

Popular among Muslim writers, this tradition appears in many works,[12] usually in connection with the city of Alexandria only. A close parallel is provided by the following account from Ibn Ḫordāḏbeh's *Kitāb al-masālik*: 'As for the building of Rome and Alexandria, it is said that the construction (of the latter) lasted three hundred years and that for seventy years its inhabitants would not dare go out during the day without wearing a black veil, to protect their eyes from the dazzling whiteness of its walls'.[13] It is possible that the compiler of the *Marvels*, or the source he used for this unit, misunderstood Ibn Ḫordāḏbeh's account and took the description of Alexandria to apply to Rome as well.

I.3 (= II.3) the lighthouse of Alexandria

The described monument is the famous lighthouse of Pharos in Alexandria. This tradition, which ultimately goes back to Classical sources, was popular among Muslim authors and is found in

---

[11] Ed. Wüstenfeld (1948–1949, 2:375); trans. Barry (1984, 307). Cf. also *ʿAǧāʾib al-maḫlūqāt*; ed. Wüstenfeld (1948–1949, 1:211–13).

[12] For some references, see Bellino & Mengozzi (2016, 446, nn. 93–94).

[13] Ed. de Goeje (1889, 160).

various works.[14] For a very similar account, see Ibn Ḫordāḏbeh's *Kitāb al-masālik*: 'Its unusual lighthouse is built in the sea, upon a crab of glass. Besides its own inhabitants, there are there 600 000 Jews, who are like slaves to them'.[15]

In what concerns Syriac writers before the compiler of the *Marvels*, we find this tradition included by the anonymous West Syrian author of the *Chronicle of the Year 1234* into a small section dealing with 'the marvels that are in the world': 'In the great Alexandria, then, there is a lighthouse, that is a place of observation, built on the seashore, upon the four crabs of glass'.[16]

It should be added that the noun ܛܰܠܐ 'dew' does not make much sense in the context of the description of the lighthouse, and, probably, is a result of textual corruption. Perhaps, the original reading was the noun ܬܶܠܐ 'hill'. In favour of this suggestion speaks the fact that both the Arabic and Neo-Aramaic version feature a similar alternative reading in this place: ربوة 'hill' and ܓܘܿܕܵܐ 'mountain, hill', respectively.[17]

---

[14] For references and discussion, see Behrens-Abouseif (2006); Doufikar-Aerts (2010, 186–87); Vorderstrasse (2012); Bellino & Mengozzi (2016, 446, n. 95).

[15] Ed. de Goeje (1889, 160).

[16] ܐܝܬ ܗܟܝܠ ܒܐܠܟܣܢܕܪܝܐ ܪܒܬܐ ܡܢܪܬܐ ܐܘܟܝܬ ܕܘܟܐ ܕܕܘܩܐ ܕܒܢܝܐ ܥܠ ܣܦܪ ܝܡܐ. ܥܠ ܐܪܒܥܐ ܣܪܛܢܐ ܕܙܓܘܓܝܬܐ.; ed. Chabot (1916–1937, 1:112).

[17] Bellino & Mengozzi (2016, 441, unit 3).

I.4 (= II.4) the mirror of the lighthouse of Alexandria

This tradition, which ultimately goes back to Classical sources, was popular among Muslim authors and is found in various works, where it was often transmitted together with the previous unit I.3.[18] For a similar account, see Ibn Ḫordāḏbeh's *Kitāb al-masālik*: 'A mirror that hangs on the lighthouse of Alexandria: a person sitting under it could see another person, who would be at Constantinople, notwithstanding the width of the sea between them'.[19]

Like the previous unit I.3, this tradition was included in his work by the West Syrian author of the *Chronicle of the Year 1234*: 'And on its top — a mirror, in which they see everything that happens in the sea for a hundred miles'.[20]

I.5 (= II.5) the lighthouse of brass

A very close parallel is provided by the following account from Ibn Ḫordāḏbeh's *Kitāb al-masālik*: 'The minaret (or lighthouse) of brass in the land of ʿAd, with a horseman of brass on it: during the sacred months, water flows from it, and people drink it, water with it (fields) and pour it into their cisterns. After the sacred months, this water ceases'.[21] For other attestations of this tradition in the works of Muslim writers, see *Muḫtaṣar kitāb al-buldān* of al-Hamaḏānī.[22]

---

[18] For references and discussion, see Behrens-Abouseif (2006).

[19] Ed. de Goeje (1889, 115).

[20] ܘܒܪܝܫܗ ܡܚܙܝܬܐ ܕܚܙܝܢ ܒܗ ܟܠ ܕܡܬܓܕܫ ܒܝܡܐ ܥܠ ܡܐܐ ܡ̈ܝܠܝܢ.; ed. Chabot (1916–1937, 1:112).

[21] Ed. de Goeje (1889, 116).

[22] Ed. de Goeje (1885, 72). For more references, see Bellino & Mengozzi

There is a certain ambiguity as to how better to translate in this context the Syriac noun *mnārtā*, which could refer both to 'lighthouse' and 'minaret'.[23] While in the previous two units where it also appears (i.e., I.3–4/II.3–4), the meaning 'lighthouse' fits well the context, here it is less so. In fact, the Syriac *mnārtā* in this unit preserves ambiguity of the cognate Arabic noun *manāra*, used by Ibn Ḫordāḏbeh and other Arab writers to refer to this monument, which likewise can mean both 'lighthouse' and 'minaret'.

A noteworthy linguistic aspect of this unit is that it features the Neo-Aramaic noun *spāqē* 'vessels, jars' alongside its Classical Syriac synonym *gūrnē*.[24] Perhaps, in this way, the compiler of the *Marvels* (or his source) wanted to refer to two different kinds of reservoirs for keeping water.

I.6 (= II.6) the city surrounded by seven walls

The exact source of this tradition is unclear. Among the distant parallels, one can mention the Median fortress of Ecbatana that was made of seven concentric walls, according to Herodotus (*Hist.* 1.98). Later on, in the Muslim geographical tradition, several cities are reported to have seven walls: some writers, such as

---

(2016, 446, n. 96).

[23] See Sokoloff (2009, 785).

[24] For the Neo-Aramaic *spāqā*, see Maclean (1901, 229). Cf. also the cognate verb *sapəq* 'to empty' and adjective *spiqa* 'empty' in the Urmi dialect of Neo-Aramaic; Khan (2016, 3:274, 279).

al-Mas'ūdī and al-Qazwīnī, relate that about Alexandria,[25] while others, such as al-Hamadānī,[26] about Jerusalem.

I.7 (= II.7) the wall between the Caspian and Mediterranean seas

A close parallel can be found in a brief passage dealing with the Byzantine province of Ṭāfilā, i.e. Thrace, in Ibn Ḫordāḏbeh's *Kitāb al-masālik*. Its geographical limits are described in the following way: 'Borders of this province: from the East — the gulf of the Mediterranean Sea; from the West — the wall (*al-sūr*), built from the Caspian Sea (*baḥr al-Ḫazar*) to the Mediterranean Sea (*baḥr al-Šām*), and its length is four days' journey'.[27]

The exact origins of this tradition are unclear. Bellino and Mengozzi suggest that this tradition may refer to the legendary wall built by Alexander the Great in the Caucasus to defend his realm from the barbaric nations of Gog and Magog.[28] Another possibility is that it might be a distorted echo of a description of the Great Wall of Gorgan, a Sasanian-era defence system stretching eastwards of the Caspian Sea.[29] Moreover, it might refer to

---

[25] See *Āṯār al-bilād*; ed. Wüstenfeld (1948–1949, 2:97). For additional references, see Bellino & Mengozzi (2016, 446, nn. 97–98).

[26] See *Muḫtaṣar kitāb al-buldān*; ed. de Goeje (1885, 97).

[27] Ed. de Goeje (1889, 105). For additional references, see Bellino & Mengozzi (2016, 439, n. 72).

[28] Bellino & Mengozzi (2016, 439).

[29] See Chaichian (2013); Sauer et al. (2013).

the Derbent wall, another major defensive complex from the Sasanian period, located on the other side of the Caspian Sea and stretching westwards.[30]

Both marine toponyms, i.e., the 'Sea of the Khazars' (ܝܡܐ ܕܚܙܪ) for the Caspian Sea and the 'Sea of Syria' (ܝܡܐ ܕܣܘܪܝܐ) for the Mediterranean Sea, are attested in the works of medieval Syriac authors, such as Bar ʿEbroyo (13th c.).[31] It should be added, however, that there was some confusion among Muslim geographers regarding the exact location of the 'Sea of Khazars', as a result of which this name was sometimes applied to the Black Sea.[32] This confusion can also be found in the works of Syriac Christian authors, as demonstrates the *Dictionary* of Bar Bahlūl (10th c.), who in the entry on ܦܢܛܘܣ, 'Pontus' quotes the following description of this sea by Ḥunayn Ibn Isḥāq (9th c.): بحر يقال له فنطوس وهو بحر الخزر.[33]

I.8 the city with seventy gates

The city should be identified as Memphis in Egypt.[34] For a very close parallel, see the following description from Ibn Ḫordāḏbeh's *Kitāb al-masālik*: 'Memphis — the city of Pharaoh, who lived here and made seventy gates, and made the city walls from iron and brass. There where there four rivers that flowed

---

[30] On this monument, see Gadjiev (2017).

[31] See *Candelabrum of the Sanctuary*; ed. Bakoš (1930–1933, 2:308, 312).

[32] See Takahashi (2003, 113).

[33] Ed. Duval (1888–1901, 2:1578).

[34] As has been suggested by Bellino & Mengozzi (2016, 439).

out from under his throne'.[35] This account also appears in the works of other Muslim writers.[36]

Both the Arabic and Neo-Aramaic version of this unit feature seven gates instead of seventy,[37] which is, most likely, the result of a scribal mistake. Bellino and Mengozzi raise a possibility that the opening phrase مدينة ما 'a certain city' in the Arabic version of this unit is the result of corruption of the original مدينة منف 'the city of Memphis'.[38] In light of the Syriac original text, however, this suggestion does not seem particularly likely, since مدينة ما appears to be nothing else but a faithful rendering of the phrase ܡܕܝܢܬܐ ܚܕܐ. Moreover, the authors themselves point out that the postclitic *mā* is well attested as an indefinite marker throughout the text of the Arabic version,[39] which prevents us from regarding the case of مدينة ما as exceptional.

I.9 the brass columns with chains in Egypt

A close parallel is provided by the following account from Ibn Ḫordāḏbeh's *Kitāb al-masālik*: 'There are two columns in 'Ayn

---

[35] Ed. de Goeje (1889, 161).

[36] Cf. al-Hamaḏānī, *Muḫtaṣar kitāb al-buldān*; ed. de Goeje (1885, 73).

[37] Bellino & Mengozzi (2016, 442, unit 8).

[38] Bellino & Mengozzi (2016, 449).

[39] Bellino & Mengozzi (2016, 432).

Šams in the land of Egypt. These are remains of (former) columns. On the top of each of the columns was a string of brass. From one of the tops, the water flows from under the string, which reaches only until the half of the column, not going lower. It oozes continuously, night and day. The wet part of the column is green and moist; the water does not fall to the ground. This is a work of Hūšhank'.[40]

It is noteworthy that the plural noun *qūmrē* 'chains, bonds' of the Syriac *Vorlage* is mistranslated as 'moons' in both the Arabic and Neo-Aramaic version, i.e. الاقمار and ܣܗܪ̈ܐ, respectively.[41]

I.10 the brass horseman in Andalus

The meaning of the inner-textual gloss *Qōrnetōs*, meant to explain the toponym *Andalus* in this unit, is unclear. For some reason, it has been omitted in both the Arabic and Neo-Aramaic version. Another inner-textual gloss in this unit provides us with information regarding the linguistic background of the compiler or transmitters of the *Marvels* as it explains the Classical Syriac noun *šūšmānē*, 'ants' with the Neo-Aramaic *šekwānē*.[42]

A close parallel is provided by the following account from Ibn Ḫordāḏbeh's *Kitāb al-masālik*: 'The horseman of brass in the land of Andalus: with his hands in this manner, spreading his arm as if he was saying, "There is no passage beyond me. No one can

[40] Ed. de Goeje (1889, 161).

[41] The Neo-Aramaic noun *sara* 'moon' is attested in the dialect of Urmi; see Khan (2016, 3:283).

[42] See Maclean (1901, 305); Khan (2008, 2:1406; 2016, 3:52).

enter this land because he will be devoured by ants.'"[43] For other attestations of this tradition in the works of Muslim writers, see *Kitāb al-aʿlāq an-nafīsa* of Aḥmad ibn Rustah.[44]

An interesting case of an independent reception of this literary motif among Syriac Christians can be found in the tradition of the oral circulation of the narratives from the *One Thousand and One Nights* among the speakers of Neo-Aramaic. One of the offspins of this work, recorded among the speakers of Barwar dialect, features a story about the overseas adventures of a certain king of Yemen and his son (cf. Night 503). When they arrive at an island inhabited by monkeys who are engaged in an ongoing war against wolves, the leader of the monkeys provides the king and his son with the following information regarding the limits of his domain: 'He said "The border of the monkeys is the top of the mountain there. There King Solomon has written a monument'. He said 'From here onwards is the valley of the ants (*wádit šəkwàne*)'. He said 'Everything that enters this valley will be eaten by the ants"'.[45]

I.11 the gigantic building in Egypt

This building should be identified as one of the Egyptian pyramids,[46] an unsurprisingly popular item in the descriptions of

[43] Ed. de Goeje (1889, 116).

[44] Ed. de Goeje (1892, 78).

[45] Ed. and trans. Khan (2008, 3:1614–15).

[46] As has been suggested by Bellino & Mengozzi (2016, 440).

Egypt by Muslim writers.[47] A close parallel is provided by the following account from Ibn Ḫordāḏbeh's *Kitāb al-masālik*:

> Two pyramids in Egypt: the height of each of them is 400 cubits; they become narrow with their height. They both are laid over with marble and alabaster. Their length, as well as width, is 400 royal cubits. All magic and all marvels of medicine and astronomy are engraved on them in the *musnad* script. They say that only Allah knows that they are buildings of the king Claudius Ptolemy. And it is written upon them: "I built them. The one who lays claim to the might of his kingdom, let him destroy them. And to destroy is easier than to build. (But) even the tax money of the (whole) world would not (suffice to) destroy them."[48]

I.12 the gardens of Qōnyā

The 'city of Qōnyā' is, most likely, Konya of Central Anatolia, known in antiquity as Iconium, which served as the capital of the Seljuk Sultanate of Rūm.[49] The story, which is explicitly introduced as a part of oral tradition, refers, perhaps, to the famous gardens of Meram, located in the southern suburbs of Konya, whose history can be traced back to the high days of the Seljuk rule over the city.[50]

[47] On pyramids in Arabic sources, see Fodor (1970); Pettigrew (2004); Cooperson (2010).

[48] Ed. de Goeje (1889, 159).

[49] On the city's history during the Islamic period, see Goodwin (1986).

[50] See Redford (2000, 63–65).

The noun *yatīrūtā* 'abundance' in the description of how the gardens' owner came in possession of his fortune seems to be a result of textual corruption of the original *yārtūtā* 'inheritance'. In favour of this suggestion speaks the corresponding reading *al-wirṯ* 'inheritance' in unit 12 of the Arabic version.[51]

The ethnic identity of the unnamed owner of the gardens is described with the adjective *rhūmāyā*, literally 'Roman'. In the context of the medieval Middle East, however, it could be also translated as 'Greek' or even as 'Byzantine'.[52]

The identity of Joseph, the transmitter of the story, as well as that of his brother Mār ʿAbdīšōʿ of Elam (apparently a bishop), is unclear. In the Neo-Aramaic version (as well as in the Arabic one), the latter is referred to as 'Mār ʿAbdīšōʿ, metropolitan of Elam' (ܡܪܝ ܥܒܕܝܫܘܥ ܡܝܛܪܢ ܕܥܝܠܡ).[53] At the moment, it is impossible to ascertain whether he should be identified with the East Syrian bishop and hymnographer, bearing the same name, who was active during the 13th century.[54]

I.13 (= II.8) the river Bāeṭlas

The name of the river is spelt as *Baʾṭlas* in II.8, and as *Bāṭlās* in the Neo-Aramaic version.[55] While I have not been able to find a close

---

[51] Bellino & Mengozzi (2016, 443).

[52] On the range of meanings conveyed by this ethnonym, see Payne Smith (1879–1901, 2:3831–32, as well as discussion in (Tannous 2018b).

[53] Bellino & Mengozzi (2016, 443).

[54] For the little that is known about this obscure figure, see Burkitt (1928, 269–70). See also discussion in Bellino & Mengozzi (2016, 435, n. 56).

[55] Bellino & Mengozzi (2016, 443).

parallel to this tradition in Arabic and Persian geographical works, it is possible to regard it as a later modification of a somewhat similar account that appears in the Syriac *Book of Natural Beings*: 'They say that in the inner Spain there is a river called Baṭes, which pours its waters into the sea during the first six hours of the day, while they follow their natural order. And during the other six hours, its waters are stopped in their source, and the whole riverbed appears dry'.[56] This account also appears in Bar ʿEbroyo's *Candelabrum of the Sanctuary*, in almost the same form.[57]

I.14 (= II.9) the Sea of Reeds

For a very similar account, see the section on the Sea of Reeds in the Syriac *Book of Natural Beings*: 'And if it happens that some animal or human falls into it, — as long as he is alive, he floats upon the water and does not sink to the depth. But if he dies, or some corpse falls into it, he sinks to the depth at once'.[58] Its origins go back to the Greco-Roman geographical tradition of Late Antiquity, as one can judge from the following sentence in the description of the Dead Sea by Julius Africanus (3rd c.): 'Corpses

[56] ܒܐܣܦܢܝܐ ܓܘܝܬܐ ܐܡܪܝܢ ܕܐܝܬ ܢܗܪܐ ܕܫܡܗ ܒܛܝܣ. ܕܫܬ ܫ̈ܥܐ ܩܕܡܝܬܐ ܕܝܘܡܐ ܫܕܐ ܡ̈ܝܘܗܝ ܒܝܡܐ ܟܕ ܢܛܪܝܢ ܒܛܟܣܐ ܕܟܝܢܗܘܢ. ܘܒܫܠܡ ܫܬ ܫ̈ܥܐ ܐܚܪ̈ܢܝܬܐ ܡܬܟܠܝܢ ܡ̈ܝܘܗܝ ܒܡܒ̈ܘܥܝܗܘܢ. ܘܟܠܗ ܫܠܝܚܗ ܡܬܚܙܝܐ ܝܒܝܫܐ; ed. Ahrens (1892, 46 [Syr.]).

[57] See ed. Bakoš (1930–1933, 2:319–20).

[58] ܘܐܢ ܓܕܫ ܘܢܦܠ ܒܗ ܚܝܘܬܐ ܡܕܡ ܐܘ ܒܪܢܫܐ ܟܡܐ ܕܚܝ ܗܘ ܠܥܠ ܛܐܦ ܘܠܐ ܢܚܬ ܠܥܘܡܩܐ. ܐܢ ܕܝܢ ܢܡܘܬ ܐܘ ܫܠܕܐ ܡܕܡ ܬܦܘܠ ܒܗ ܡܢ ܫܥܬܗ ܠܥܘܡܩܐ ܡܬܛܒܥ ܠܗ; ed. Ahrens (1892, 48 [Syr.]).

are carried beneath its depths, but the living would not easily even dip under it'.[59]

It should be pointed out that the toponym 'Sea of Reeds' (ܝܡܐ ܕܣܘܦ), derived in its turn from the biblical יַם סוּף,[60] could refer to two different locations in Syriac sources. Thus, some writers, like the author of the *Book of Natural Beings*, quoted above, identify it with the 'Dead Sea' (ܝܡܐ ܡܝܬܐ).[61] On the other hand, Bar Bahlūl in his *Dictionary* explains it as the sea that the Israelites crossed during their exodus from Egypt, while giving the 'Red Sea' (ܝܡܐ ܣܘܡܩܐ) as its alternative name.[62] It is noteworthy that the authors of both the Arabic and Neo-Aramaic versions of the *Marvels* follow the latter understanding of this toponym, as they translate it as البحر الأحمر and ܝܲܡܵܐ ܣܘܼܡܵܩܵܐ, respectively.[63]

I.15 (= II.10) the place ʾEwrīqōs

The roots of this tradition in Syriac literature could be traced back to the following passage in the Syriac version of Pseudo-Nonnos' scholia on the homilies of Gregory of Nazianzus: 'Now the Euripos (ܐܘܪܝܦܘܣ) is a region of the sea between the island of Boiotia and Attica which changes (direction) seven times in a

[59] Ed. Wallraff et al. (2007, 61).

[60] Cf. the Peshitta version of Exod. 10.19, 13.18 *et passim*.

[61] Ed. Ahrens (1892, 48 [Syr.]).

[62] See the entry ܝܡܐ; ed. Duval (1888–1901, 1:846). Cf. Bar ʿEbroyo's *Candelabrum of the Sanctuary*; ed. Bakoš (1930–1933, 2:309–10). See also discussion by Takahashi (2003, 107–108).

[63] Bellino & Mengozzi (2016, 443, unit 14).

day. Now it changes in that the water in this part escapes and as it were is sucked up and again vomited forth, and the water again fills up as it was (before). This happens, as they say, seven times a day'.[64] Later, Bar Bahlūl includes a brief reference to this toponym into his *Dictionary*.[65] In the process of its reception and transmission by Syriac writers, this tradition was further modified, as one can see from the following description in the Syriac *Book of Natural Beings*: 'About the sea of ʾĀrōpōs. There is a rock in the sea called ʾĀrōpōs that goes up and down ten times during a day. It, then, goes down for five hundred cubits at one time, until the sea bottom shows up, and goes up in the (same) manner'.[66] Our passage, apparently, reflects one of such later reworkings of the original tradition, during which, among other things, the toponym 'Euripos' was changed into 'Euriqos' as a result of confusion between the letters *Pē* and *Qōp*.

I.16 (= II.11) the river in Syria

The river described in this unit is very similar to that of unit I.19, with the only significant difference being that I.16 does not specify on which day of the week it flows. For a very similar account, see the Syriac *Book of Natural Beings*: 'On the border of Syria, between ʿĪqā and Deʾōpāsās, there is a river that on one day out of seven flows well with plentiful and mighty waters. And during

[64] *Scholia to 'Invective I'* 34; ed. Brock (1971, 229–230 [Syr.], 98 [trans.]).

[65] See the entry ܐܘܪܝܦܘܣ; ed. Duval (1888–1901, 1:92).

[66] ܥܠ ܐܪ̈ܘܦܘܦܘܣ ܝܡܐ. ܐܝܬ ܟܐܦܐ ܚܕܐ ܒܝܡܐ ܕܡܬܩܪܝܐ ܐܪܘܦܘܣ ܕܣܠܩܐ ܘܢܚܬܐ ܒܝܘܡܐ ܚܕ ܘܢܚܬܐ. ܢܚܬܐ ܕܝܢ ܐܝܟ ܚܡܫ ܡܐܐ ܐܡ̈ܝܢ ܒܚܕ ܙܒܢ: ܥܕܡܐ ܕܡܬܚܙܝܐ ܐܪܥܗ ܕܝܡܐ ܘܣܠܩܐ ܒܗ ܒܕܡܘܬܐ; ed. Ahrens (1892, 49 [Syr.]).

those six days, its flow stops and ceases completely. And it always observes this law: it flows on the day of Sabbath'.[67] The ultimate source of this tradition is, most likely, the following description of a river that the Roman emperor Titus saw in Syria, provided by Josephus (*Bell.* 7.5.1): 'It runs between Arcea (Ἀρκέας) ... and Raphanea (Ῥαφαναίας), and has an astonishing peculiarity. For, when it flows, it is a copious stream with a current far from sluggish; then all at once its sources fail, and for the space of six days it presents the spectacle of a dry bed; again, as though no change had occurred, it pours forth on the seventh day just as before. And it has always been observed to keep strictly to this order; whence they have called it the Sabbatical river, so naming it after the sacred seventh day of the Jews'.[68] In the Muslim tradition of paradoxography, a similar river is described in *ʿAǧāʾib al-maḫlūqāt* of al-Qazwīnī, who, however, locates it in the 'land of Slavs'.[69]

I.17 (=II.12) the well flowing with water, salt and naphtha

Establishing the original form of the toponym poses a certain difficulty, as it is spelt differently across the manuscripts: *Knīgar* in

[67] ܒܬܘܚܡܐ ܕܣܘܪܝܐ ܒܝܬ ܚܘܡܐ ܠܐܘܩܝܢܘܣ ܐܝܬ ܢܗܪܐ ܕܪܕܐ ܠܫܒܬܐ ܘܩܐܡ ܟܠܗ ܗܠܝܢ ܘܡܫܬܐ ܡܕܪܐ ܥܒܪ. ܘܥܡܠܝܢ ܥܠܬܐ ܢܩܘܡ ܠܚܕܐ ܡܛܠ ܘܡܥܡܪܐ ܪܕܝܗ. ܘܠܗܢܐ ܢܡܘܣܐ ܒܟܠܙܒܢ ܢܛܪ ܗܘ: ܡܪܕܝܬܗ ܒܝܘܡܐ ܕܫܒܬܐ ܚܕ.; ed. Ahrens (1892, 49–50 [Syr.]).

[68] Ed. Thackeray et al. (1926–1965, 3:534–35). On the transmission of Josephus' works in Syriac, see Minov (2019, 112–14).

[69] Ed. Wüstenfeld (1848–1849, 1:182).

V and L,[70] *Kānīlāz* in B1. Both the Arabic and Neo-Aramaic versions omit it, featuring the generic 'a country' instead. Since none of these variants is attested as a recognizable toponym in Syriac or other sources that were available to me, perhaps, it should be emended to ܟܫܓܪ *Kašgar,*[71] a city in Central Asia.

Another noteworthy aspect of this unit is that it features several non-standard spellings. Thus, the Classical Syriac noun for 'pool' ܩܒܝܐ, *qebyā* is spelt as ܩܘܝܐ, *qawyā* in V. Another spelling variant of this noun, found in this unit in V and B1 of II.12, is ܩܘܬܐ, *qewtā,* which, however, might be the result of a scribal mistake. In addition to that, we come across the spelling ܢܘܛܐ, *nūṭā* for 'naphtha' in B1 of II.12, which is a phonetic spelling of the East Syrian pronunciation of ܢܦܛܐ.[72] In fact, both these cases of phonetic spelling could be due to the influence of Neo-Aramaic orthography. Thus, Maclean's *Dictionary* gives the forms ܩܘܝܐ, *qewyā* for the former, and ܢܘܛܐ, *nūṭā* for the latter.[73]

I.18 (= II.13) the red spring in Pūštīdar

The toponym *Pūštīdar* (spelt as *Pūštīdārā* in L, *Pūštī* in II.13, and *Pūštīdār* in the Neo-Aramaic version[74]) is, most likely, of an Iranian origin. Bellino and Mengozzi explain it by referring to the

[70] In L the reading ܟܥܫܓܪ is also possible.

[71] For attestation in Syriac sources, see Payne Smith (1879–1901, 1:1842).

[72] See Nöldeke (2001, 15, n. 3).

[73] Maclean (1901, 272 and 210, respectively).

[74] Bellino & Mengozzi (2016, 444, unit 18).

Persian compound *pušt dār* 'prop, thick clothing, propped'.[75] Perhaps, it should be identified with the toponym *Pušt-ī Dār*, mentioned by the Qajar official Mirza Mohib ʿAli Khan Nizam al-Mulk in his treatise on the disputed borderlands between the Ottoman Empire and Qajar Iran.[76]

This tradition, which does not seem to be attested in the major Arabic and Persian paradoxographical and geographical works, could be a part of the local folklore of Kurdistan that might have reached the compiler of the *Marvels* by way of oral transmission. Remarkably, it features an explicitly Christian element: the last sentence of the unit mentions *ḥnānā* (lit. 'grace, mercy'), a kind of contact relic typical for the Syriac Christian tradition. It consists of a mixture of blessed oil, water, and dust from the tombs of saints, and was used mostly for the purposes of healing.[77] In both the Arabic and Neo-Aramaic versions, this understanding of *ḥnānā* in our passage is made unambiguous through the addition of a gloss that explains it to be 'the dust of blessing' (تراب البركة / ܕܘܩܐ ܕܒܘܪܟܬܐ).[78] Perhaps, the addressee of this gloss was Eduard Sachau, the Western scholar, on whose behalf these two versions were produced, and who was not expected to know what *ḥnānā* is.

---

[75] Bellino & Mengozzi (2016, 448, n. 101).

[76] See Zoroufi (1968, 89).

[77] See Jullien & Jullien (2010).

[78] Bellino & Mengozzi (2016, 444, unit 18).

The mention of *ḥnānā* in this context, however, poses some questions, since as far as we know, it was not a necessary condition for this substance to have red colour, not to speak of the fact that it was supposed to be produced in an ecclesiastical setting. A possible explanation of this oddity might be that the original form of this tradition, before its integration into the *Marvels*, featured not *ḥnānā*, but another similar-sounding word, that is *henna* (Arab. *ḥinnāʾ*, Pers. *ḥinā*, Neo-Aramaic *xənna*),[79] a plant-based reddish dye popular through the Middle East, where it was and is still used for temporary tattoos and hair colouring.[80] The East Syrian Christians of Northern Mesopotamia were no strangers to this practice and used *henna* for dyeing the hair and hands, especially at weddings.[81] Given the reddish colour of *henna*, this substance would make better sense in the context of this unit. Taking into consideration a possibility of the oral transmission of this tradition, it is conceivable that the compiler of the *Marvels* or subsequent copyists of the work might have changed the original *henna* to *ḥnānā*, whether intentionally or by accident.

I.19 (= II.14) the river flowing on Sabbath

The river described in this unit is very similar to that of unit I.16, with the only significant difference being that I.19 says explicitly on which day of the week it flows. For a very similar account, see the Syriac *Book of Natural Beings*: 'And moreover, in Spain, there

---

[79] For Neo-Aramaic, see Maclean (1901, 102); Khan (2016, 3:328).

[80] See Colin (1986).

[81] For examples, see Khan (2016, 3:328, 4:311).

is another river, whose flow is withheld during six days, and on Sabbath, it flows'.[82] This river should not be confused with the river Sambation of Jewish sources, on which see the next unit.

I.20 (= II.15) the river of sand

For a very similar account, see the Syriac *Book of Natural Beings*: 'On the river of sand: It is told about this river that it flows not with water, but with dry sand. And it makes a loud sound and flows with great vehemence and frightening force. And it cannot be crossed on a ship or on foot. And its flow stops on the day of Sabbath and until the sunset. The sand, which is in it, appears solid as the dry land'.[83] An almost identical account is found in Bar ʿEbroyo's *Candelabrum of the Sanctuary*.[84] In Syriac sources, this river is also mentioned in the prayer of Cyriacus in the *Martyrdom of Cyriacus and Julitta*.[85]

This river should be identified with the famous river Sambation of late antique and medieval Jewish sources, which was

---

[82] ܘܒܗ̇ ܬܘܒ ܒܐܣܦܢܝܐ ܐܝܬ ܢܗܪܐ ܐܚܪܢܐ ܕܫܬܐ ܝܘ̈ܡܝܢ ܟܠܝܐ ܡܪܕܝܬܗ ܘܒܫܒܬܐ ܪܕܐ; ed. Ahrens (1892, 46 [Syr.]).

[83] ܥܠ ܢܗܪܐ ܕܚܠܐ. ܡܬܐܡܪ ܕܝܢ ܥܠ ܢܗܪܐ ܗܢܐ ܕܠܘ ܡ̈ܝܐ ܐܝܟ ܡܪܕܝܬܗ. ܐܠܐ ܚܠܐ ܝܒܝܫܐ. ܘܡܫܡܥ ܩܠܐ. ܘܒܚܝܠܐ ܡܫܚܠܦܐ ܘܒܥܘܫܢܐ ܕܚܝܠܐ ܪܕܐ. ܘܠܐ ܒܐܠܦܐ ܡܬܥܒܪ ܒܗ ܘܠܐ ܒܪܓܠ. ܘܒܝܘܡܐ ܕܫܒܬܐ ܟܠܝܐ ܡܪܕܝܬܗ ܘܥܕܡܐ ܕܥܪܒ ܫܡܫܐ. ܡܬܚܙܐ ܠܗ ܚܠܐ ܕܒܓܘܗ ܐܝܟ ܝܒܝܫܬܐ ܐܪܥܐ ܡܩܝܡܬܐ.; ed. Ahrens (1892, 46–47 [Syr.]).

[84] ܘܡܬܐܡܪ ܥܠ ܢܗܪܐ ܚܕ ܕܠܘ ܡ̈ܝܐ ܗܘ ܡܪܕܝܬܗ. ܐܠܐ ܚܠܐ ܝܒܝܫܐ ܘܒܚܝܠܐ ܚܣܝܢܐ ܪܕܐ ܘܠܐ ܒܐܠܦܐ ܡܬܥܒܪ ܐܦܠܐ ܒܪܓܠ. ܘܒܝܘܡܐ ܕܫܒܬܐ ܟܠܝܐ ܡܪܕܝܬܗ. ܘܒܪܡܫܐ ܕܒܬܪ ܫܒܬܐ. ܡܬܚܙܐ ܠܗ ܚܠܐ ܕܒܓܘܗ ܐܝܟ ܝܒܝܫܬܐ ܐܪܥܐ ܡܩܝܡܬܐ.; ed. Bakoš (1930–1933, 2:320).

[85] See ed. Bedjan (1890–1897, 3:276).

thought to flow during six days of the week, but stand still on Sabbath.[86] The 'river of sand' (Arab. *wādī al-raml*) that stops on Sabbath was also a popular motif among Arab geographers.[87] Some of them, like Abū Ḥāmid al-Ġarnāṭī (12th c.),[88] situated this river in the West. It is this element, absent from the Syriac parallels quoted above, that brings the compiler of the *Marvels* close to the Muslim geographical tradition in this particular case.

I.21 (= II.16) the raining place Maṭlāyā

A very close parallel is provided by the following account from Ibn Ḫordāḏbeh's *Kitāb al-masālik*: 'In the land of Romans, on the sea of Khazars, there is a city called al-Mustaṭila. It rains there continuously during winter as well as during summer so that its inhabitants can neither beat nor winnow their grain. They pile it in sheaves in their houses. Then, they take a certain quantity of ears, according to their need, rub them in their hands, after which they grind it and bake it'.[89]

I.22 (= II.17) the rain in Hejaz

A close parallel is provided by the following account from Ibn Ḫordāḏbeh's *Kitāb al-masālik*: 'The people of the Hejaz and Yemen (*al-Yaman*) are under the rain during the whole summer,

[86] See Pennacchietti (1998, 30–33); Rothkoff (2007).

[87] See Doufikar-Aerts (2010, 181–83).

[88] See his *Tuḥfat al-albāb*; ed. Ferrand (1925, 48).

[89] Ed. de Goeje (1889, 156). See also comments in Bellino & Mengozzi (2016, 441).

and they gather harvest during the winter. In Sanaa and neighbouring countries, it rains during the whole of June, July, August, and a part of September, from midday until sunset'.[90]

It is noteworthy that the toponym *Taymnā*, 'the South' of the Syriac *Vorlage* is rendered as التيمى 'Tayma' (i.e. the large oasis of Tayma in north-west Arabia) in the Arabic version, whereas in the Neo-Aramaic version it is changed into the generic ܦܩܥܬܐ 'the plain'.

I.23 the river in Azerbaijan

For a very similar account, compare the entry on the 'river of Azerbaijan' (نهر اذربيجان) in al-Qazwīnī's *ʿAǧāʾib al-maḫlūqāt*: 'Muḥammad ibn Zakariyyāʾ al-Rāzī, who got the report from Abū al-Qāsim al-Ǧayhānī, the author of *al-Masālik wa-l-mamālik al-šarqiyya*, related that in Azerbaijan there is a river whose waters flow, turn into stones and become slabs of rock used for building'.[91]

I.24 (= II.18) the fount near the city of ʿAmas

This and three following units (i.e., I.25–27) comprise a distinctive group of traditions since all of them are connected with the region of *Bēt Dlīǧ / Bēt Dlīš*. This toponym refers, most certainly,

---

[90] Ed. de Goeje (1889, 156).

[91] Ed. Wüstenfeld (1848–1849, 1:176). Al-Qazwīnī reports a very similar tradition in connection with the 'fount of Azerbaijan' (عين اذربيجان); ed. Wüstenfeld (1848–1849, 1:189).

to Bitlis (Kurd. *Bidlīs*; Arm. *Baghaghesh / Baghesh*), a city in eastern Turkey and the capital of Bitlis Province.[92] Located in the valley of the Bitlis River, 15 km south-west of Lake Van, this city stood on an important road that connected the Armenian plateau with the Mesopotamian plain. The capital of a Kurdish Muslim principality from the 13th to the 19th century, Bitlis was also home to a large Armenian community.[93]

The exact location of the town *ʿAmas*,[94] mentioned in this unit is unclear. From the location of the fount on the 'sea-shore', it could be deduced that the town was situated somewhere not far from the south-western shores of Lake Van. Perhaps, it should be identified with Himis (Arm. *Khums*, modern *Emek Köy*), a village in the Kardshkan district, located ca. 10 km south of the southern shore of the lake.[95] The description of the fount fits well the geological profile of the area around Lake Van, characterized by hydrothermal activity.

There seem to be no close parallels to this tradition in the major Arabic and Persian paradoxographical and geographical works. It might well have reached the compiler of the *Marvels* by way of oral transmission.

---

[92] See Sinclair (1987–1990, 1:297–311); Hewsen (2001).

[93] See Sinclair (2001); Thomson (2001).

[94] Spelled as *ʿAms* in II.18. In the Neo-Aramaic and Arabic versions, it is spelled as *ʿAmās* and *ʿAmmās*, respectively; Bellino & Mengozzi (2016, 445).

[95] See Sinclair (1987–1990, 1:226, 229).

I.25 the mountain fount of Pānōr

The toponym *Ḥizān* in this unit refers, most likely, to Hizan (Kurd. *Xīzan*), a town and a district in Bitlis Province of Turkey, located about 40 km south-east of the city of Bitlis.[96] The toponym *Pānōr* should be identified with the Panor mountain pass, located about halfway between Bitlis and Hizan.[97] As for the toponym *Ṭāṭīq*, it should be identified, most probably, with the small plain to the left of the river Kocaçay, in the vicinity of the modern villages Yolcular and Dereağzi. According to Sinclair, this area was called Tatik or Dadig during the Medieval period.[98]

Similarly to I.24, this tradition does not seem to be attested in the major Arabic and Persian paradoxographical and geographical works. It might well have reached the compiler of the *Marvels* by way of oral transmission.

I.26 the sweet-water fount in Lake Van

The toponym *Ṭāṭōn* in this unit refers, most certainly, to the modern Tatvan (Kurd. *Tetwan*; Arm. *Datvan*), a coastal town on the western shore of Lake Van.[99] In the early modern Muslim sources, it appears as *Tātwān*, as in *Sharafnama* of Sharaf al-Din Bidlisi

---

[96] See Sinclair (1987–1990, 1:230–34).

[97] See Sinclair (1987–1990, 1:230–31), as well as the map following p. 326.

[98] Sinclair (1987–1990, 1:230). Cf. *Sharafnama* of Sharaf al-Din Bidlisi, where it is mentioned several times as *Tātīk*; ed. Véliaminof-Zernof (1860–1862, 1:213, 432).

[99] See Sinclair (1987–1990, 1:274).

(16th c.),[100] or as *Taḥt-ı Van*, as in the *Seyahatname* of Evliya Çelebi (17th c.).[101]

Similarly to I.24 and I.25, this tradition does not seem to be attested in the major Arabic and Persian paradoxographical and geographical works. It might well have reached the compiler of the *Marvels* by way of oral transmission.

I.27 the river island in Ṭārōn

The toponym *Ṭārōn* is of Armenian origin and refers to the region of Taron, located to the north-west of Bitlis, that forms a part of the Muş province of modern Turkey.[102] It is not clear whether the river, described in this unit, should be identified with the modern Murat river (Arm. *Aratsani*), the major watercourse of the region.

It might be noted that while the majority of the Christian population of Taron was constituted by Armenians, there was also a recognizable East Syrian presence in the region. To that bears witness the existence of a bishopric that included this region, as one can conclude from the mention of 'Mār Ḥnānīšōʿ bishop of Rustāqā, Ṭārōn, and Ūrmī' in the colophon of an East Syrian manuscript, produced in the year 1577.[103]

Similarly to I.24–26, this tradition does not seem to be attested in the major Arabic and Persian paradoxographical and geographical works and might have reached the compiler of the

[100] Ed. Véliaminof-Zernof (1860–1862, 1:349).

[101] Ed. Dankoff (1990, 60, 198).

[102] See Sinclair (1987–1990, 1:291–96); Hewsen (2001).

[103] See Wilmshurst (2000, 417).

Marvels by way of oral transmission. Given the prominence of Friday as a beneficial day in this account, it is possible that it originated in a Muslim milieu.

I.28 (= II.19) the long-eared people

The motif of people with ears large enough to cover themselves is attested across many ancient cultures, including the Greco-Roman world.[104] Thus, the Greek historian Ctesias in his description of India, mentions the nation of Otoliknoi, who 'have huge ears which they use to cover themselves like an umbrella'.[105] This monstrous race appears in the works of Muslim writers as well, where they are often identified with one of the mythic nations associated with Gog and Magog and called Mansak or Manšak. For an example, cf. the following description from al-Qazwīnī's *ʿAǧāʾib al-maḫlūqāt*:

> To these [living creatures] also belong peoples called Mansak. They live in an eastern direction near Gog and Magog, look like human beings but have ears like those of an elephant. Each ear is like a garment. When they go to sleep, they lie down on one ear and cover themselves with the other.[106]

---

[104] For an overview, see Kirtley (1963).

[105] Trans. Nichols (2011, 80).

[106] Ed. Wüstenfeld (1848–1849, 1:448); trans. van Donzel & Schmidt (2009, 66).

A remarkable aspect of this unit is that it features the only explicit inner-textual gloss in Persian in our work. In the concluding sentence, the 'Persian' name for the long-eared people is provided, transliterated into Syriac as *gālīm gōš* (*ǧālīm ǧūš* in L). This loan-word reflects a singular form of the New Persian collective compound noun گلیم گوشان, *gilīm-gošān*, literally 'carpet-eared ones' or 'blanket-eared ones',[107] used to refer to the mythological long-eared people in Classical Persian sources. For instance, *gilīm gošān* are mentioned in one of the poems of Manuchehri Damghani (11th c.).[108]

It is unclear whether the inclusion of this gloss should be ascribed to the compiler of the *Marvels* or, perhaps, to the literary (or oral) Muslim source that he might have used for this tradition. In what concerns the latter scenario, it should be pointed out that a very similar gloss with the Persian name is added to al-Qazwīnī's description of the long-eared people, quoted above, in some copies of *ʿAǧāʾib al-maḫlūqāt*, such as the one found in ms. London, British Library, Or. 14140 (early 14th c.), fol. 131v: ويقال لهم كليم كوشان.[109]

[107] See Steingass (1892, 1096).

[108] Ed. de Biberstein-Kazimirski (1886, 181 [Pers.]).

[109] For the image of this folio, see Carboni (2015, 90, fig. 3.34). The whole manuscript is also available online: https://www.qdl.qa/en/archive/81055/vdc_100023586788.0x000001.

I.29 (= II.20) the dog-people of Karnāš

Some late antique Syriac works, such as the *Chronicle of Pseudo-Zachariah Rhetor* (6th c.), contain brief references to the legendary 'dog-men' (ܟܠܒ ܒܢ̈ܝܢ),[110] which go back to Greco-Roman tradition. Moreover, the dog-men play a central role in a metrical homily on Apostle Andrew, ascribed to Ephrem, where God sends the apostle to evangelise 'the country of dogs' (ܐܬܪܐ ܕܟܠܒܐ).[111] Yet, none of these or other ancient and medieval Syriac compositions seem to contain an account comparable to that of this unit.

It seems more likely that this tradition reached the compiler of the *Marvels* through Muslim sources.[112] While I have not been able so far to identify the toponym *Karnāš* and find a close parallel to this account, I believe that its origins should be sought among stories similar to the following account from the anonymous Persian composition *ʿAǧāʾib al-dunyā* (13th c.):

> There is a people in the islands of Kūhra (کوهره) and Bārīk (باریك), whose men wear garments (made) of tree bark, whereas their women go around naked. They use swords as weapons and eat human flesh. When they catch a man, they hand him over to the women, before eating him, so that they (i.e., the women) would become pregnant from him and give birth to beautiful children, because they

---

[110] Ed. Brooks (1919–1924, 2:214); see also translation and comments in Greatrex et al. (2011, 451).

[111] Edited by van Esbroeck (1998, 93–105).

[112] For some references, see Bellino & Mengozzi (2016, 434, n. 54).

> themselves are ugly. They have prolonged faces, like dogs.[113]

I.30 (= II.21) the sheep-tailed people of Arabia

These creatures should be identified, most likely, with *nasnās/nisnās* (pl. *nasānis*), the legendary wild human-like creatures of Arabic and Persian Muslim sources.[114] Thought to be the descendants of the ancient Arab tribe of ʿAd, cursed by God, or the product of crossbreeding between humans and animals, they were often located in the region of Yemen and said to be hunted by local Arabs for food. For examples, see accounts found in the anonymous *Kitāb ġarāʾib al-funūn wa-mulaḥ al-ʿuyūn* (11th c.)[115] and *Ṭabāʾiʿ al-ḥayawān* of al-Marwazī (12th c.).[116]

I.31 (= II.22) the scorpion-legged people

It seems likely that this unit is derived from the description of the men with scorpion legs in the following passage from the Syriac version of the *Alexander Romance* (III.7):

> and we saw too wolves and leopards and panthers and beasts with scorpions' tails, and elephants, and wild bulls, and ox-elephants, and men with six hands apiece; and we

---

[113] Ed. Smirnova (1993, 410, fol. 135b).

[114] See Viré (1986, 133–34); Kruk (1995, 33–34); El-Zein (2009, 142–43).

[115] Ed. Rapoport & Savage-Smith (2014, 512–13).

[116] Ed. Minorsky (1942, 59–60).

saw men with scorpions' legs and teeth like dogs and faces like women.[117]

I.32 (= II.23) the island of cannibals

The cannibal inhabitants of distant lands were one of the most common topoi of Muslim paradoxographical and geographical works.[118] References to various islands inhabited by cannibals are found in the earliest specimen of Arabic travel writing, such as *Aḫbār al-ṣīn wa-l-hind* by Abū Zayd al-Sīrāfī (9th c.),[119] and *ʿAǧāʾib al-hind* by Buzurg Ibn Šahriyār (10th c.).[120] For parallels to the notion of eating humans alive, cf. the anonymous *Kitāb ġarāʾib al-funūn wa-mulaḥ al-ʿuyūn* (11th c.): 'The island of al-Dāsbī. Its inhabitants are of the Zanj race, with pepper-like hair. When a foreigner falls in their hands, they eat him alive. They devour human flesh like dogs'.[121]

The name of the island in this unit varies somewhat across the manuscripts: *Klāmīs* in V and *Balōs* in L and B1 of II.23. It is the latter variant, however, that should be recognized as the orig-

117 ܘܚܙܝܢ ܕܐܒ̈ܐ ܘܢܡܪ̈ܐ ܘܦܠܛܘܪ ܘܣܩܘ̈ܬܐ ܕܕܘ̈ܒܐ ܒܡܪ̈ܟܐ. ܘܦܝܠܐ ܕܬܘܪ̈ܐ ܕܒܪܐ. ܘܬܘܪ̈ܝ ܦܝܠܐ. ܘܟܒ̈ܪܐ ܕܥܒܕ ܥܡ ܐܢ̈ܫܐ. ܘܚܙܝܢ ܥܩܪ̈ܒܝ ܪ̈ܓܠܐ. ܘܫ̈ܢܝܢ ܟܠ̈ܒܐ. ܘܦܪ̈ܨܘܦ ܢܫ̈ܐ.; ed. Budge (1889, 174–75 [Syr.], 98 [trans.]). I have modified the translation of Budge, who prefers to read ܥܩܪ̈ܒܝ ܪ̈ܓܠܐ as ܥܩ̈ܝܡܝ ܪ̈ܓܠܐ, and translates them, correspondingly, as 'men with twisted legs'.

118 For general discussion, see Szombathy (2015).

119 Ed. Mackintosh-Smith & Montgomery (2014, 27).

120 Trans. Freeman-Grenville (1981, 73–74).

121 Ed. Rapoport & Savage-Smith (2014, 482).

inal form, since it reflects the well-attested in Arabic sources toponym, *Bālūs,* one of the most famous islands of cannibals in Muslim literature. For example, see the following account from Ibn Ḫordāḏbeh's *Kitāb al-masālik*: 'To the left, at the distance of two days journey from it, there is the island of Bālūs, whose inhabitants are cannibals'.[122] Cf. also al-Marwazī's notice: 'The inhabitants of Bālūs are cannibals'.[123] According to Minorsky, this island should be identified with the port on the south-western coast of Sumatra.[124]

I.33 the tree climbers of Serendib

The toponym *Serendib* (spelt in V as *Sarndīb*), referring to the modern island of Sri Lanka, is attested in the works of some medieval Syriac authors, such as Bar ʿEbroyo (13th c.).[125] The island is also mentioned in unit I.51.

A close parallel is provided by the following description of the inhabitants of the island of al-Rāmī, located not far from Serendib, from Ibn Ḫordāḏbeh's *Kitāb al-masālik*: 'And they climb trees with their hands (only), without putting their feet on them'.[126] According to Minorsky, this island should be identified with Sumatra.[127] The identification of it as Serendib in the *Mar-*

---

[122] Ed. de Goeje (1889, 66).

[123] *Ṭabāʾiʿ al-ḥayawān*; ed. Minorsky (1942, 49* [Arab.], 59 [trans.]).

[124] Minorsky (1970, 187).

[125] See *Candelabrum of the Sanctuary*; ed. Bakoš (1930–1933, 2:310, 314).

[126] Ed. de Goeje (1889, 65).

[127] Minorsky 1970, p. 187, n. 5.

vels could be a result of the reliance of its compiler on some geographical work that placed the island of al-Rāmī not far from Serendib. For example, the author of the Persian geographical treatise *Ḥudūd al-ʿālam* (10th c.) describes this island as located 'in the region of Sarandīb'.[128]

I.34 (= II.24) the people with dog teeth

Although some Muslim writers also refer to people having dog teeth,[129] given the mention of Alexander in this unit, it seems more likely that this tradition derives from the following account in the Syriac version of the *Alexander Romance* (III.7), describing various monstrous races that the king and his men met during their march from the Caspian gates to India: 'and we saw men with scorpions' legs and teeth like dogs and faces like women'.[130]

I.35 (= II.25) the headless people

While descriptions of the race of men without heads are found in works of several Muslim writers,[131] it seems more likely that this report is derived from the following account from the Syriac version of the *Alexander Romance* (III.7):

---

[128] Trans. Minorsky (1970, 57).

[129] Cf. the description of Gog and Magog in al-Qazwīnī's *ʿAǧāʾib al-maḫlūqāt*; ed. Wüstenfeld (1848–1849, 1:448).

[130] ܘܚܙܝܢ ܓܒܪ̈ܝܢ ܕܪ̈ܓܠܐ. ܘܫܢ̈ܝܢ ܕܟܠ̈ܒܐ. ܘܦܪ̈ܨܘܦ ܢܫ̈ܐ.; ed. Budge (1889, 174–75 [Syr.], 98 [trans. (modified)]).

[131] Cf. the description of the inhabitants of the island of Ǧāba in al-Qazwīnī's *ʿAǧāʾib al-maḫlūqāt*; ed. Wüstenfeld (1848–1849, 1:112).

> Then we departed thence through fear, and came to a certain place. And the people who were in that place had no head at all, but they had eyes and a mouth in their breasts, and they spoke like men, and used to gather mushrooms from the ground and eat them. Now each mushroom weighed twenty pounds. And those men were like children in their minds, and in their way of life they were very simple.[132]

I.36 (= II.26) the strap-feet people

These mythological anthropoid creatures appear already in Greco-Roman sources, where they are often referred to as Ἱμαντόποδες / *Himantopodes* and located in Africa or India.[133] Later on, one finds them mentioned in the works of various Muslim authors.[134] To Syriac Christians these creatures were known from the Syriac version of the *Alexander Romance* (III.7), where they are said to attack Alexander's troops: 'And we departed thence and arrived at the country of the people whose feet are twisted; and when they saw us, they began to throw stones, and they threw accurately and aimed at us'.[135]

---

132 ܬܘܒ ܡܢ ܕܚܠܬܐ ܡܢ ܬܡܢ ܐܫܩܠܢ. ܘܠܕܘܟܬܐ ܚܕܐ ܐܬܝܢ. ܘܒܢܝܢܫܐ ܕܒܗ̇ ܕܘܟܬܐ ܟܠ ܟܠܗ ܪܫܐ ܠܝܬ ܗܘܐ ܠܗܘܢ. ܐܠܐ ܥܝܢܐ ܘܦܘܡܐ ܒܚܕܝܗܘܢ ܐܝܬ ܗܘܐ ܠܗܘܢ. ܘܐܝܟ ܒܢܝܢܫܐ ܡܡܠܠܝܢ ܗܘܘ. ܘܡܠܩܛܝܢ ܗܘܘ ܟܡ̈ܐܐ ܡܢ ܐܪܥܐ ܘܐܟܠܝܢ ܗܘܘ. ܘܟܠ ܟܡܐܐ ܥܣܪܝܢ ܠܝܛܪ̈ܝܢ ܬܩܠ ܗܘܐ. ܘܗ̇ܢܘܢ ܒܢܝܢܫܐ ܪ̈ܥܝܢܗܘܢ ܐܝܟ ܪ̈ܥܝܐ ܕܛܠܝܐ ܐܝܬܘܗܝ ܗܘܐ. ܘܒܕܘܒܪ̈ܝܗܘܢ ܣܓܝ ܒܪܝܪܝܢ ܗܘܘ.; ed. Budge (1889, 179–80 [Syr.], 100–101 [trans.]).

133 Cf. Pliny, *Nat. Hist.* 5.8.46; Strabo, *Geogr.* 2.1.9; Pomponius Mela, *Chor.* 3.103; Pseudo-Callisthenes, *Alexander Romance* 3.28.

134 For Persian and some Arabic sources, see Aʿlam (1996).

135 ܘܡܢ ܬܡܢ ܐܫܩܠܢ. ܘܠܐܬܪܐ ܕܒܢ̈ܝܫ ܪ̈ܓܠܐ ܡܦܬܠܝܢ. ܘܟܕ ܚܙܘ ܠܢ ܫܪܝܘ ܠܡܫܕܝܐ

While in this case it is difficult to establish exact source used by the compiler of the *Marvels*, one can point out a passage from al-Qazwīnī's *ʿAǧāʾib al-maḫlūqāt*, which has many common elements with our unit. In this passage, al-Qazwīnī quotes at length an account of a seafarer named Yaʿqūb ibn Isḥāq al-Sarrāǧ about his adventures on the island of Saksar.[136] After he manages to escape the cannibalistic dog-headed people, after whom the island is named, Yaʿqūb wanders into a grove of fruit trees. There he is ambushed and enslaved by one of the people living in this part of the island, who mounts on Yaʿqūb's shoulders. Twisting his feet around his victim's neck, the soft-legged man forces Yaʿqūb to carry him around the fruit trees, so that he might pick fruits from them. It is only with great difficulty that Yaʿqūb manages to get rid of his captor.

I.37 (= II.27) the raven-like people

This account is most likely derived from the following passage from the Syriac version of the *Alexander Romance* (III.7), which describes an attack of the raven-like people against Alexander's troops:

> and within the wood there were wild men, whose faces resembled ravens, and they held missiles in their hands, and their clothing was of skins. When they saw us, they cast missiles at my troops and slew some of them; and I commanded my troops to shout and to charge them at full

ܒܐ̈ܟܐ. ܘܬܪܥܝܬܐ ܥܕܝܢ ܗܘܘ ܘܚܫܝܢ ܗܘܘ ܠܗ.; ed. Budge (1889, 177–78 [Syr.], 99 [trans.]).

[136] See Wüstenfeld (1848–1849, 1:121–22).

speed; and when we had done this, we slew six hundred and thirty-three of them, and they slew of my horsemen one hundred and sixty-seven.[137]

I.38 (= II.28) the ass-legged people

This report is most likely derived from a brief description from the Syriac version of the *Alexander Romance* (III.7), which concludes the passage describing the attack by the strap-feet people, quoted above in I.36, with the following statement: 'and there were some among them with asses' legs'.[138]

I.39 (= II.30) the hairless people

The exact origin of this account is unclear.

I.40 (= II.31) the conjoined twins from the island of Kīš

The exact origin of this account is unclear. The story finds distant parallels among expressions of the general interest in the cases of conjoined twins, exhibited by not a few Muslim men of letters. For examples, see al-Bīrūnī, *Kitāb al-āṯār al-bāqiyah;*[139] al-Qazwīnī,

[137] ܘܒܬܪܗ ܒܢ̈ܝܢܫܐ ܒܪ̈ܢܝܐ ܐܝܬ ܗܘܐ. ܕܪܓܠܐ ܗܘܐ ܦܪ̈ܣܬܗܘܢ ܠܚܒ̈ܠܐ. ܘܐܪܕܘ̈ܗܘܢ ܥܪ̈ܕܬܐ ܐܣܝܪܝܢ ܗܘܘ. ܘܐܬܬܘܝܘ ܗܘܬ ܬܟܣܬܗܘܢ ܕܪ̈ܟܒܐ. ܟܕ ܕܝܢ ܚܙܘ ܠܝ. ܪ̈ܕܝܬܐ ܥܠ ܣܠܩܬܝ، ܥܪܘ. ܘܠܐܪ̈ܥܐ ܡܚܝܘܗܝ ܡܛܠܬ. ܘܠܣܠܩܬܝ، ܦܩܕܬ ܠܦܪ̈ܫܐ. ܘܒܪܗܛܐ ܚܠܝܨܘܗܝ ܠܡܐܙܠ. ܘܟܕ ܗܟܢ ܥܒܕܢ. ܩܛܠܢ ܡܢܗܘܢ ܫܬܡܐܐ ܘܬܠܬܝܢ ܘܬܠܬܐ. ܘܩܛܠܘ ܡܢ ܦܪ̈ܫܐ ܕܝܠܝ. ܡܐܐ ܘܫܬܝܢ ܘܫܒܥܐ.; ed. Budge (1889, 176 [Syr.], 99 [trans.]).

[138] ܘܐܦ ܕܪ̈ܓܠ ܚܡܪ̈ܐ ܐܝܬ ܗܘܘ ܒܗܘܢ.; ed. Budge (1889, 178 [Syr.], 99 [trans.]).

[139] Sachau (1879, 93).

ʿAǧāʾib al-maḫlūqāt;[140] the anonymous Persian *ʿAǧāʾib al-dunyā*;[141] Ḥamdallāh Mustawfī Qazwīnī (14th c.), *Nuzhat al-qulūb*.[142]

The toponym *Kīš* (also mentioned in unit II.57) is well-known and refers to the island located in the lower Persian Gulf.[143] Situated half-way between Siraf and Hormuz, its port was one of the major emporiums of the Gulf in medieval times.[144] The location of this story, as well as the fact that the narrator reports hearing it from a certain Anās, probably a Muslim, makes it plausible to suggest that it originated and/or circulated as a part of the folklore of Muslim traders and seamen of the Persian Gulf.

I.41 the old man in the sea

The exact origin of this account is unclear. Likewise, the toponym *Myaṭāl* (*Mīṭālaṭ* in L) is not immediately recognizable. Since the narrator reports that he heard this story from a certain Christian clergyman Qūryāqōs, a citizen of Mosul and merchant, it is possible that it originated and/or circulated as a part of the folklore of Muslim traders and seamen of the Persian Gulf and the Indian Ocean. Perhaps, the mysterious 'old man' could be related to the figure of the 'old man of the sea' (Arab. *šayḫ al-baḥr*), a malevolent protagonist who plays a major role in the fifth voyage of Sindbad the Sailor, included in the *One Thousand and One*

---

140 Wüstenfeld (1848–1849, 1:12, 451).

141 Smirnova (1993, 477).

142 Le Strange (1919, 274–75).

143 See Potts (2004).

144 See Kauz (2006).

Nights.[145] Moreover, Muslim paradoxographical and geographical works contain a number of accounts about seafarers meeting people in the middle of the ocean.[146]

I.42 (= II.32) the tree of Waqwaq

The legendary island or archipelago of Waqwaq, located sometimes in the sea of China and sometimes in the Indian Ocean, was one of the most popular topoi of the Muslim paradoxographical imagination.[147] A number of accounts, dealing with this island, feature descriptions of a miraculous tree bearing fruits that resemble human or animal shapes, or are actual living beings (often women).[148] While the exact origin of the account in our unit is difficult to establish, one can cite as a relatively early parallel the following report from *ʿAǧāʾib al-hind* of Buzurg Ibn Šahriyār:

---

[145] On the complicated textual tradition of the cycle of Sindbad and influence of *ʿaǧāʾib* literature on this work, see Bellino (2015).

[146] Cf. Ibn Ḫordāḏbeh, *Kitāb al-masālik*; ed. de Goeje (1889, 65); the anonymous *Kitāb ġarāʾib al-funūn wa-mulaḥ al-ʿuyūn*; ed. Rapoport & Savage-Smith (2014, 512); the anonymous Persian *ʿAǧāʾib al-dunyā*; ed. Smirnova (1993, 441–42).

[147] For references and discussion, see Ferrand et al. (2002); Toorawa (2000).

[148] See articles in Bacqué-Grammont et al. (2007). To the sources discussed in this volume one might also add accounts from the anonymous *Kitāb ġarāʾib al-funūn wa-mulaḥ al-ʿuyūn*; ed. Rapoport & Savage-Smith (2014, 519), and the anonymous Persian *ʿAǧāʾib al-dunyā*; ed. Smirnova (1993, 342).

> Muhammad b. Babishad told me that, according to what he had learnt from men who had been to the Waqwaq country, there is a large tree there, with round leaves, or sometimes oblong, which bears a fruit like a marrow, only larger, and looking somewhat like a human being. When the wind blows, a voice comes out of it. The inside is full of air, like the fruit of the *ushar*. If one picks it, the air escapes at once, and it is nothing but skin. When he saw this fruit, a sailor was pleased by it, and cut one off to take it away. It burst immediately, and all that remained in the man's hands was like a dead crow.[149]

I.43 the woman pregnant for two years

While the exact origin of this tradition is difficult to establish, mention of the cities of Baghdad and Tus points to a Muslim milieu. Moreover, its content is in line with discussions of the extraordinary cases of long periods of gestation found in the works of some Muslim physicians.[150] For a close parallel, cf. ʿArīb ibn Saʿīd al-Qurṭubī (10th c.), *Kitāb ḫalq al-ǧanīn*: 'a tradition reports that al-Ḍaḥḥāk ibn Muzāḥim stayed sixteen months in the womb and that at birth he had teeth'.[151] As for the length of the pregnancy in our account, it evokes the views held by some Muslim writers who claimed that gestation could last as long as two years.[152]

---

[149] Trans. Freeman-Grenville (1981, 39).

[150] For references and discussion, see Kueny (2013, 189–90).

[151] Ed. Jahier & Noureddine (1956, 33).

[152] For references and discussion, see Verskin (2020, 72–73).

I.44 (= II.33) the woman who gave birth to sixty children

The story finds parallels among expressions of the general interest in extraordinary cases of multiple pregnancies exhibited by some Muslim physicians.[153] For a very close parallel, see the following account by ʿAlī al-Ṭabarī (9th c.), *Firdaws al-ḥikma*:

> More than one woman told me that in our times a certain black woman gave birth to sixty children. And they used to say that she gave birth to a *kor* of children because one *kor* is equal to sixty *qafīz*. And this was in thirty-five pregnancies or more, and she produced more twins than that. And she would miscarry once or twice in a year.[154]

Of the two measures of capacity that are mentioned in this account, i.e., *kōr* and *qpīzā*,[155] the latter (spelt, in its plural form, as *qpīsē* in V and L, and as *qpīzē* in B1) is a unit of weight equivalent to about 64 lbs., and has an Iranian etymology.[156] It is well attested both in Classical Arabic and New Persian as *qafīz* (or *kafīz*).

I.45 (= II.34) the woman who gave birth to twenty children

This tradition probably belongs to the same source as the previous unit. For close parallels in Muslim sources, see the recurring mentions of the case of a woman giving birth to twenty children, as in the following passage from *Firdaws al-ḥikma* of ʿAlī al-

---

[153] For references and discussion, see Kueny (2013, 187).

[154] Ed. Siddiqi (1928, 37).

[155] See Sokoloff (2009, 612, 1391).

[156] See Ciancaglini (2008, 250).

Ṭabarī: 'another woman gave birth to twenty children in four pregnancies, five children in every pregnancy, and they (all) lived'.[157] For similar accounts, see also ʿArīb ibn Saʿīd al-Qurṭubī, *Kitāb ḫalq al-ǧanīn*;[158] Ibn Qayyīm al-Ǧawzīyyah (14th c.), *Tibyān fī aqsām al-Qurʾān*.[159] This tradition ultimately goes back to Aristotle, who, in one of his works, mentions 'a certain woman who had twenty children at four births; each time she had five, and most of them grew up'.[160]

I.46 (= II.35) the woman pregnant with seven children

While the immediate source of this account is unclear, the compiler of the *Marvels* likely derived it from the same source as the three previous units. The mention of the 'Frankish man' (*Prangāyā*) as a protagonist points at its origins during the Crusades or post-Crusader period.

I.47 the child suckled by the dead woman

The primary aim of this grotesque account is to promote the notion of Syriac as the primeval language, an important expression of Syriac Christian identity, roots of which can be traced back to the pre-Islamic period.[161] While it seems to be implied already in

[157] Ed. Siddiqi (1928, 37).

[158] Ed. Jahier & Noureddine (1956, 27).

[159] Ed. al-Ḥarastānī & al-Zaġlī (1994, 305).

[160] *Hist. anim.* 7.4; trans. Thompson (1910, sect. 584b).

[161] On development of this notion in Late Antiquity, see Rubin (1998); Moss (2010).

the discussion of biblical names based on Syriac etymologies by Theodoret of Cyrus (5th c.), this idea finds fully articulated expression only in Pseudo-Ephrem's *Cave of Treasures* (ca. 6th c.), whose author claims that before the destruction of the tower of Babel all people spoke Syriac and that all languages in the world are derived from Syriac.[162] These and some additional expressions of Syriac primacy continued to circulate among Syriac Christians during the medieval period.

With this story, the compiler of the *Marvels* introduces what seems to be a unique and novel argument in favour of the primacy of Syriac. Its line of argumentation is akin to the one found in an account from Herodotus' *Histories* that describes a linguistic experiment, supposedly conducted in ancient Egypt during the reign of Psammetichus.[163] Driven by the desire to establish what nation is oldest in the world, this king ordered that a couple of new-born children should be brought up without a person speaking with them. When the children grew up, the first sound they had uttered was 'bekos' (βεκός), which was interpreted by the king's counsellors as the Phrygian word for 'bread'. According to Herodotus, it is as a result of this experiment that the Egyptians conceded the honour of being the oldest nation to the Phrygians.

As for its possible antecedents, I have as yet been unable to discover any close analogues of this story in Muslim or other sources from the medieval Islamicate world. There are, however, several literary works that share with our account the motif of

---

[162] *Cave* 24.9–11; see also Minov (2013, 165–75).

[163] *Hist.* 2.2; ed. Godley (1926–1930, 1:274–77. For an analysis of this story, see Gera (2003, 68–111).

breastfeeding corpse, which, apparently, originated in the Muslim literary *imaginaire* before the time of the composition of the *Marvels*. One such example of miraculous nursing is found in the Judeo-Arabic version of the popular medieval Arabic frontier epic *Sīrat Dhāt al-Himma*. There, the recently-born hero Junduba is found in the desert by his adoptive father prince Dārim, suckling the breast of his murdered mother: 'He (i.e., Dārim) saw the princess Arbāb, left behind and slain, and this newborn was suckling from her. The milk was pouring out in excess, by the power of the Possessor of Power [...], and his mother was nursing him, though she was dead at his side'.[164]

Another narrative that bears witness to this motif is the story of Meyyitzâde from the *Seyahatname* of the famous Ottoman traveller Evliya Çelebi (17th c.).[165] It appears as an etiological account in the context of the description of the tomb, located in the Kasımpaşa neighbourhood of Istambul, which was named after this person, i.e., *Kabr-i Meyyitzâde*.[166] According to Çelebi, the father of Meyyitzâde left his pregnant wife at home when he set out on a military campaign with Sultan Mehmed Khan III in the year 1595–96. When upon his return, he learned that his wife had died, he ordered her grave to be opened, at which point they found inside the child alive, suckling the right breast of his dead mother, whose body had not rotten (*vâlidesinin sağ memesin emer,*

---

[164] Trans. from Schine (2019, 182).

[165] Ed. Dankoff et al. (1996, 198). I thank Aslı Niyazioğlu for drawing my attention to this parallel.

[166] On this monument, see Crane (2000, 367).

aslâ çürümemiş). In the aftermath of this miraculous event, the boy was given the name Meyyitzâde 'the son of the corpse'.

I.48 the martyrdom of the ape's son

This unit provides us with the only instance when the compiler of the *Marvels* explicitly mentions his written source. The reference to 'the book of Mār Basil' most likely points to the erotapocritic composition known as the *Questions of Basil and Gregory*, which is attested both in Syriac and Arabic.[167] And indeed, an account almost identical to that of our unit is found in some textual witnesses of the Arabic version of the *Questions*. Since the only existing edition of this work by Ǧirǧis Bey Yaʿqūb is a rare book in Western libraries, I offer below the complete Arabic text and English translation of the story, based on one of the earliest textual witnesses of the *Questions*, i.e., ms. Monastery of St. Catherine, Sinai, Ar. 481 (1091), fols. 307v–308r.[168]

---

[167] On the Syriac version, which is still unpublished, see Baumstark (1922, 79–80), who gives a list of its manuscripts in n. 1. The full text of the Arabic version was published from an unspecified manuscript by Bey Yaʿqūb (1920, 94–155). I thank Barbara Roggema for providing me with a copy of this rare edition. For a recent discussion of the Arabic version that includes an inventory of its manuscripts, see Roggema (2019).

[168] I am most grateful to Alice Croq, who is currently preparing an edition of the Arabic version of the *Questions*, for letting me publish here the Arabic text and English translation of this passage prepared by her. Except for a few minor variants, this text is identical with that of Question 70 in Bey Yaʿqūb (1920, 126–27).

مسله احد وسبعين قال غريغوريوس ما تقول في مولود ولد له وجهان واربع ارجل وفيه شبه من الحيوان يجب ان يعمد ام لا؟

اجاب باسيليوس ما ينبغي ان يعمد ولكن يستبقا منجل تسبيح الله واعلم انه كان في قلونيه المدينة قرد ضاجع امراه نصرانيّه كان بولص الرسول قد اعمدها فولدت من ذلك القرد ذكرا كان صورته قرد وانسان من صدره الي رجليه قردا وعنقه ووجهه انسانا وكان يتكلم مثل انسان وكان يدخل الي الكنيسه ويسمع الكتب المقدسّه ويتعلّم فلمّا صار ابن عشرين سنه كان يطلب ويحرص ان يعمد فاجتمع من اجله سنوذس اي مجمع وكان الريس عليه تيموثاوس تلميذ بولص فجري بينهم خلفا في ذلك فمنهم من كان يقول نعم ومنهم من يقول لا فوثب ذيونيسيوس اسقف اثينا فقال امّا انا فلا ادخل الاعضا النجسه الحيوانيّه في ما المعموديه المقدّسه واجتمع راي الجماعه ورسموا تلك السنوذس ان لا يعمد انسان مختلف الخلقه فلما دخل طربيوس[169] الملك الكافر الي قلونيه المدينه والزمهم بالذبايح للاصنام جا هذا مسرعا فوقف قدّام الملك وقال له امّا انا فاني نصراني وان ذلك الملك اجاز عليه اصنافا من العقوبات فلم ينتقل عن امانته بل كان وهو يعذب[170] يصيح ويقول انا نصراني فامر الملك ان يطرح في اناء مملو زفت

[169] طرنيوس in Bey Yaʿqūb's edition.

[170] يعمد in the manuscript is a corruption; the reading of Bey Yaʿqūb's edition should be preferred.

وكبريت وحين طرحوه فيه صرخ وقال هذا السفل يكون معموديّتي يا مسيح الله فبعد موته قال تيطوس الاسقف بالحقيقه ان جسده يقوم يوم القيامه.

Question seventy-one. Gregory said: 'What do you say about someone who was born with two faces or four legs and has something similar to an animal, — should he be baptized or not?'

Basil answered: 'It is not right to baptize him, but he should be allowed to live for the glorification of God. Know that in the city of Callinicum, there was an ape who had slept with a Christian woman. The apostle Paul had baptized her, and from this ape, she gave birth to a male child whose appearance was like that of a human and an ape: from his chest to his feet he was an ape, and his neck and face were human. He spoke like a human being, and he went to the church and listened to the Holy Scriptures and learned. When he reached the age of twenty, he asked and strove to be baptized. A synod, that is to say, a council, was gathered on his account, and it was presided over by Timothy, the disciple of Paul. They disagreed on this matter: some of them were saying "yes" and others "no". And Dionysius, the bishop of Athens, got up and said, "As for me, I am not going to let impure animal limbs enter the waters of holy baptism!" And the assembly agreed with his opinion, and this synod laid down a rule that no human being of a different appearance should be baptized. And when the infidel king Ṭarabiyūs came to the city of Callinicum, he requested

> from them to sacrifice to pagan idols. This one (i.e., the boy) came quickly and stood in front of the king and said to him, "As for me, I am a Christian". And this king had him suffer several kinds of punishments, but he did not deny his faith, and moreover, as he was tortured, he shouted and said, "I am Christian!" The king, then, ordered that he should be thrown into a reservoir[171] filled with pitch and brimstone. When they threw him into it, he shouted and said, "May this reservoir be my baptism, O Christ God!" After his death, Titus the bishop said, "Truly, his body will rise up at the resurrection"'.

As one can see, except for minor differences, the two versions of this story, that of the *Marvels* and that of the *Questions*, present basically the same narrative. The absence in the text of the former of such details as the mention of Paul baptising the woman, of Paul's disciple Timothy presiding over the council, and of the bishop Titus in the concluding sentence, brings us to the conclusion that the narrative of the *Marvels* is a slightly abbreviated version of the more extensive original version of the *Questions*. Unfortunately, given the absence of a critical edition of either version of the *Questions*, i.e., Syriac and Arabic, it is difficult to say anything certain as to when precisely and in which milieu this story originated, nor whether the compiler of the *Marvels* relied on Syriac or Arabic text in this specific case.

---

171 سفل in the manuscript, but it is better to adopt the reading of Bey Yaʿqūb's edition, i.e., اناء.

In what concerns the message of the story, it resorts to grotesque imagery in order to tackle important issues related to the problem of communal identity by stressing the paramount significance of baptism as the primary marker of belonging to the Christian community. The notion of baptism of blood is crucial for unpacking the meaning of this narrative. Rooted in the deep symbolic connection between the sacrament of baptism and martyrdom, the understanding of martyrdom as the second baptism, or even as a last-resort substitute for proper baptism, had developed among Christians already during Late Antiquity.[172] In the Syriac milieu, this notion is attested in some hagiographic works, such as the *Martyrdom of Āzād,* whose author describes the martyrs as 'baptized in a second baptism' (ܥܡ̈ܝܕܝܢ ܒܡܥܡܘܕܝܬܐ ܕܬܪܬܝܢ),[173] as well as in canonical compositions, such as the *Canons of Hippolytus* and the *Testament of Our Lord,* claiming that if a catechumen is martyred before having been baptized, he or she should nevertheless be regarded as having successfully accomplished this sacrament with his/her blood.[174]

I.49 the child raised by a dog

The story presented in this unit is, most likely, one of the later variants of a very similar account of the curious event, also said to have taken place in the city of Basra in the aftermath of a

---

[172] See Jeanes (1993).

[173] Ed. Bedjan (1890–1897, 2:251).

[174] See Bradshaw et al. (2002, 103).

plague, which was included by al-Jāḥiẓ (9th c.) into his *Kitāb al-ḥayawān*:

> The learned men of Basra claimed, and Abū ʿUbayda al-Naḥwī, Abū l-Yaqẓān Suḥaym b. Ḥafṣ, Abū l-Ḥasan al-Madāʾinī mentioned, (who knew it) from Muḥammad b. Ḥafṣ, (who knew it from) from Maslama b. Muḥārib: A certain house having been ravaged by the plague, the neighbours were convinced that there was no one left alive in it. Now there was a baby in that house, not yet weaned nor able to stand upright: it crawled on all fours. One of the neighbours who had survived went and shut the door of the house. Some months later, one of the family's heirs came to the house; he opened the door and went inside into the courtyard, and was amazed to find a baby playing with the puppies of a bitch that had belonged to the owners of the house. He was dumbfounded. A few moments later the bitch appeared: when the baby saw her, it crawled over to her and began to suck her dugs, which the animal offered to it. The baby, left alone and forgotten in the house, must have felt hungry, and seeing the puppies being suckled by their mother, have crawled over to the bitch, which obligingly placed herself so as to allow it to suck. Having once given it suck, she continued in the same way, and the baby likewise.[175]

Al-Jāḥiẓ brings this story as confirmation of the 'divine direction' that guides all created beings by instilling in them 'innate knowledge' for the best course of action.

---

175 Ed. Hārūn (1965–1969, 2:155–56); trans. (augmented) Pellat (1969, 143).

I.50 the plague in Basra

While the exact origin of this tradition is difficult to establish, the mention of the city of Basra points to a Muslim milieu. Tracing its origins is made difficult by the fact that there were quite a few outbreaks of epidemics that afflicted the city during the medieval period. Thus, in addition to the obvious case of the Black Death (1346–1353), one comes across references to plagues that devastated Basra during the years 688–689, 955, and 1436.[176]

I.51 the buffalos of Serendib

The toponym *Serendib* (spelled in V as *Sarnādīb*), referring to the modern island of Sri Lanka, is attested in the works of some medieval Syriac authors, such as Bar ʿEbroyo (13th c.).[177] The island is also mentioned in unit I.33. The plural noun ܓܡܫ̈ܐ 'buffalo bulls', vocalized in V as *gamešē*, should probably be understood not as a misspelt form of the Classical Syriac *gāmūšē*,[178] but rather as a variant spelling of its Neo-Aramaic cognate *gāmīšē*.[179]

For a very close parallel, cf. the following passage from the description of the island of Rāmī in Ibn Ḫordāḏbeh's *Kitāb al-masālik*: 'After Serendib, there is the island of Rāmī. ... And on it,

---

[176] See Ashtor (1976, 87, 170, 278).

[177] See *Candelabrum of the Sanctuary*; ed. Bakoš (1930–1933, 2:310, 314).

[178] See Payne Smith (1879–1901, 1:741–42); Ciancaglini (2008, 137).

[179] See Maclean (1901, 52), who lists the alternative spelling ܓܵܡܝܼܫ̈ on p. 53.

there are buffaloes without tails (جواميس لا اذناب)'.[180] This tradition is also attested in al-Qazwīnī's *ʿAǧāʾib al-maḫlūqāt*, although without mention of Serendib.[181]

I.52 the mountain of snakes

It is possible that this report is derived from the following description from one of the offshoots of the Syriac *Alexander Romance* known as the *Exploits of Alexander*:

> and beyond the nation of the Mnīnē there are no human beings but only terrible mountains and hills and valleys and plains and horrible caves, in which are serpents and adders and vipers, so that men cannot go thither without being immediately devoured by the serpents, for the lands are waste, and there is nothing there save desolation.[182]

I.53 the wolf and leopard

This report is almost certainly derived from the following passage from the Syriac version of the *Alexander Romance* (III.7): 'and we

---

[180] Ed. de Goeje (1889, 61). For a discussion of various locations of this island, sometimes identified with Sumatra, in the works of Arab geographers, see Carboni (2015, 354, n. 52).

[181] Ed. Wüstenfeld (1848–1849, 1:108).

[182] ܘܠܒܪ ܡܢ ܥܡܐ ܕܡܢܝ̈ܢܐ ܠܝܬ ܒܢܝ̈ܢܫܐ ܐܠܐ ܐܢ ܛܘܪ̈ܐ ܕܚܝ̈ܠܐ. ܘܪ̈ܡܬܐ ܘܢ̈ܚܠܐ ܘܦܩ̈ܥܬܐ ܘܡܥ̈ܪܐ ܕܚܝ̈ܠܐ. ܕܐܝܬ ܒܗܘܢ ܚܘ̈ܘܬܐ ܘܐܦ̈ܥܐ ܘܐܟ̈ܕܢܐ. ܕܒܢ̈ܝܢܫܐ ܠܬܡܢ ܠܐ ܐܙܠܝܢ. ܕܠܐ ܡܚܕܐ ܐܟܠܝܢ ܠܗܘܢ ܚܘ̈ܘܬܐ. ܡܛܠ ܕܐܪ̈ܥܬܐ ܚܪ̈ܒܐ ܐܢܝܢ. ܘܡܕܡ ܠܝܬ ܬܡܢ. ܐܠܐ ܐܢ ܚܘܪܒܐ.; ed. Budge (1889, 265–66 [Syr.], 152 [trans.]).

saw too wolves and leopards and panthers and beasts with scorpions' tails'.[183]

I.54 (= II.54) the sea turtles

Similarly to unit I.10, this narrative features an inner-textual gloss that explains the Classical Syriac noun *gālē* 'turtles' with the Neo-Aramaic *qrāyē*.[184]

A close parallel is provided by the following account from the description of the inhabitants of the part of the 'Great Eastern Sea' close to the port of Aden in Ibn Ḫordāḏbeh's *Kitāb al-masālik*: 'And there are in it (i.e., the sea) turtles (*salāḥif*). One such turtle is twenty cubits in circumference, and it has about a thousand eggs in its belly. And their shell makes a good shield'.[185] This passage also appears in al-Qazwīnī's *ʿAǧāʾib al-maḫlūqāt*[186] in a form closer to that of our unit, that is, without the last sentence.

I.55 (= II.55) the camel-fish

This unit most likely comes from the same source as the previous one. For a very close parallel, cf. the following passage from the description of the inhabitants of the 'Great Eastern Sea' in Ibn

---

183 ܘܚܙܝܢ ܕܐܒ̈ܐ ܘܢܡܪ̈ܐ ܘܦܗܠܘܬܪ ܘܚܝ̈ܘܬܐ ܕܕܘܢܒ̈ܝ ܥܩܪ̈ܒܐ.; ed. Budge (1889, 174 [Syr.], 98 [trans.]).

184 See Maclean (1901, 284), under ܩܪܐ; Khan (2016, 3:54).

185 Ed. de Goeje (1889, 61).

186 Ed. Wüstenfeld (1848–1849, 1:109).

Ḫordāḏbeh's *Kitāb al-masālik*: 'There is also a fish that looks like a camel (سمك على خلقة الجمل)'.[187]

I.56 the islands of life and death

The exact origin of this account is unclear.

I.57 (= II.56) the island of prayers for rain

The exact origin of this account is unclear.

I.58 (= II.49) the giant fish and sailors

The hydronym 'the sea of Qūlzam' (also mentioned in unit II.53) is a calque from the Arabic *baḥr al-Qulzum* of Muslim sources, which was applied sometimes to the Red Sea as a whole and sometimes only to the Gulf of Suez because the port known as Qulzum (from Greek Κλύσμα) was located on its western banks.[188] An alternative Syriac name for the Read Sea, i.e. ܝܡܐ ܣܘܦܐ, is found in works of medieval authors, such as Bar ʿEbroyo.[189]

Two main elements of this description are found in an account by Buzurg Ibn Šahriyār (10th c.), who relates how Ahmad b. Hilal, a ruler of Oman, came across a whale 'more than 200 cubits long' that was stranded ashore, while supplementing it with the following information: 'Ismailawayh the shipmaster told me that this fish abounds in the Sea of Zanj and in the Great Sea

[187] Ed. de Goeje (1889, 61).

[188] See Becker & Beckingham (1986).

[189] See *Candelabrum of the Sanctuary*; ed. Bakoš (1930–1933, 2:309–10).

of Samarqand. It is called a *Wal*. It likes wrecking ships. If it attacks a ship, [the sailors] strike pieces of wood against one another, and shout and beat drums'.[190]

I.59 (= II.50) the big fish with smaller fish inside

Compare a very similar description of a whale from Abū Zayd al-Sīrāfī's *Aḫbār al-ṣīn wa-l-hind*:

> In this sea there is also a kind of fish that reaches twenty cubits in length. We caught one of these and split open its belly. Inside it was another fish of the same genus. We took this second fish out then split its belly open too-and there inside it was yet another fish of the same type! All of them were alive and flapping about, and they all resembled each other in form.[191]

Cf. also the description of different kinds of fish by Ibn Ḫordāḏbeh.[192]

---

[190] *ʿAǧāʾib al-hind* 9; trans. Freeman-Grenville (1981, 9–10). This description might, in its turn, be based on a similar account of Abū Zayd al-Sīrāfī, *Aḫbār al-ṣīn wa-l-hind* I.1.1; ed. Mackintosh-Smith & Montgomery (2014, 34–35), beginning of which is lost. This tradition is found in many later geographical and zoological works. Cf. also Ibn Ḫordāḏbeh, *Kitāb al-masālik*; ed. de Goeje (1889, 61); Ḥamdāllah al-Mustawfī al-Qazwīnī, *Nuzhat al-qulūb*; trans. Stephenson (1928, 58).

[191] Ed. Mackintosh-Smith & Montgomery (2014, 22–23). Cf. also Buzurg Ibn Šahriyār, *ʿAǧāʾib al-hind* 11; trans. Freeman-Grenville (1981, 11); Ibn Ḫordāḏbeh, *Kitāb al-masālik*; ed. de Goeje (1889, 61).

[192] Ed. de Goeje (1889, 61).

I.60 (= II.51) the bull-fish

This unit most likely comes from the same source as units I.54 and I.55. For a very close parallel, cf. the following passage from the description of the inhabitants of the 'Great Eastern Sea' in Ibn Ḫordāḏbeh's *Kitāb al-masālik*: 'There is (also) a fish that looks like cattle (*al-baqar*), which gives birth and suckles. And they make shields from its skin'.[193]

I.61 (= II.39) Alexander and the two talking birds

This account is most likely derived from the following episode from the Syriac version of the *Alexander Romance* (III.7), which takes place when Alexander and his troops arrive at a place called Obarkia:

> And on the seventh day we saw two birds, the bodies of which were very large, and their faces were like the face of a man; and suddenly one of them said in the Greek language, "O Alexander, thou art treading the land of the gods;" and again it said to me in the same language, "Alexander, the victory over Darius and the subjection of king Porus are enough for thee."[194]

---

[193] Ed. de Goeje (1889, 61).

[194] ܘܒܝܘܡܐ ܕܫܒܥܐ ܚܙܝܢ ܬܪ̈ܬܝܢ ܦܪ̈ܚܝܢ. ܕܪ̈ܘܪܒܝܢ ܓܘܫ̈ܡܝܗܘܢ ܛܒ. ܘܦܪ̈ܨܘܦܝܗܘܢ ܐܝܟ ܦܪ̈ܨܘܦ ܒܢܝ̈ܢܫܐ. ܘܡܚܕܐ ܚܕܐ ܡܢܗܝܢ ܒܠܫܢܐ ܝܘܢܝܐ ܐܡܪܐ ܗܘܬ. ܐܠܟܣܢܕܪܐ. ܐܪܥܐ ܕܐܠܗ̈ܐ ܕܐܫ ܐܢܬ. ܘܬܘܒ ܒܗ ܒܠܫܢܐ ܐܡܪܬ ܠܝ. ܐܠܟܣܢܕܪܘܣ ܣܦܩ ܠܟ ܙܟܘܬܐ ܕܗܘܝ ܕܪܝܘܫ ܘܫܘܥܒܕܗ ܕܦܘܪ ܡܠܟܐ.; ed. Budge (1889, 180 [Syr.], 101 [trans.]).

I.62 (= II.40) Alexander and the two growing trees

See commentary on unit II.40 below.

I.63 (= II.42) Alexander and the two talking trees

It is most likely that this unit presents in a very abbreviated and somewhat reworked form the extended account from the Syriac version of the *Alexander Romance* (III.7), in which the king during his journey through India comes across the sacred garden with the two trees, the male tree of the sun and the female tree of the moon, which can talk; when Alexander asks them about his future, both trees inform him (one of them in the Greek language) that he will die at Babylon.[195]

It should be noted that the version of unit II.42 adds in the concluding sentence that Alexander died 'in Babylon', which, perhaps, reflects better the original version of the *Marvels*. Babylon as the place of Alexander's death is mentioned in some other Syriac sources.[196]

I.64 (= II.58) the island of the Antichrist

This account reflects the belief, widespread among Muslims, that al-Daǧǧāl, the False Messiah of Islamic apocalypticism, is restrained by being chained to a mountain on an island, from which he eventually shall emerge at the time of eschatological consummation.[197] A close parallel is provided by the following

---

[195] Ed. Budge (1889, 185–89 [Syr.], 104–106 [trans.]).

[196] Cf. the short *Life of Alexander*; ed. de Lagarde (1858, 207).

[197] See Cook (2002, 117–20).

account from Ibn Ḫordāḏbeh's *Kitāb al-masālik*: 'And the king of Zābağ is called Maharāğ. And in his kingdom, there is an island called Barṭāīl (برطايل), from where the sound (of musical instruments) and drum beating are heard every night. And mariners say that the Deceiver (الدجال) is there'.[198] A very similar description of the island of al-Daǧǧāl appears in al-Qazwīnī's *ʿAǧāʾib al-maḫlūqāt,*[199] as well as in the works of several other Muslim writers.[200] It has been suggested by Minorsky that this island might be identified with Bali.[201]

I.65 (= II.40) Alexander and the two growing trees

See commentary on II.40.

II.29 the people with lions' heads and scaly tales

This account is most likely derived from the following passage from the Syriac version of the *Alexander Romance* (III.7): 'We set out again from thence and came to another place where there were men with lion's heads and scaly tails'.[202]

---

[198] Ed. de Goeje (1889, 68).

[199] Ed. Wüstenfeld (1848–1849, 1:111).

[200] Cf. *Kitāb ġarāʾib al-funūn wa-mulaḥ al-ʿuyūn*; ed. Rapoport & Savage-Smith (2014, 480); Šaraf al-Zamān Ṭāhir al-Marwazī, *Ṭabāʾiʿ al-ḥayawān*; ed. Minorsky (1942, 38* [Arab.], 50 [trans.]).

[201] Minorsky (1942, 152).

[202] ܘܡܢ ܬܡܢ ܬܘܒ ܐܙܠܢ ܘܠܐܬܪܐ ܕܡܘܬܒܐ ܐܚܪܢ. ܘܐܝܬ ܗܘܐ ܒܢ̈ܝܢܫܐ ܕܪ̈ܫܝܗܘܢ ܐܪܝܐ ܘܕܘ̈ܢܒܝܗܘܢ ܠܚܠܝܬܐ.; ed. Budge (1889, 178 [Syr.], 100 [trans.]).

II.36 the woman giving birth to the lizard-like child

The toponym *Bēt Sasē* does not seem to be attested in any other Syriac sources. While the immediate origin of this story is unclear, it finds parallels among the expressions of general interest in extraordinary cases of congenital disorders exhibited by some Syriac Christian writers, as well as by Muslim paradoxographers. Thus, a somewhat similar account is found in the excerpt from a West Syrian chronicle, preserved in ms. Berlin, Sachau 315 (Berlin Syr. 167), fol. 65r, which opens with the following report: 'In the year 1344 of the Greeks, which is the year 423 of the Arabs, a certain woman in the city of Bagdad gave birth to a likeness of a snake of short stature that had a head, mouth, and neck like those of a human being, but no arms and legs'.[203]

As for Muslim writers, in the part of the introduction to al-Qazwīnī's *ʿAǧāʾib al-maḫlūqāt* that elucidates the category of 'strange', the author notes among other examples such a group of natural phenomena as 'the birth of animals of strange appearance (تولد حيوان غريب الشكل)', within which he lists several cases of birth defects among humans, including that of a woman from the region of Balkh who gave birth to a child that looked like a *nasnās*.[204]

---

[203] ܒܫܢܬ ܐܫܡܕ ܕܝܘ̈ܢܝܐ ܕܗܝ ܫܢܬ ܬܟܓ ܕܛܝ̈ܝܐ ܐܢܬܬܐ ܚܕܐ ܒܒܓܕܕ ܡܕܝܢܬܐ ܝܠܕܬ ܕܡܘܬܐ ܕܚܘܝܐ. ܟܪܝܐ ܩܘܡܬܐ. ܕܐܝܬ ܠܗ ܪܫܐ ܕܒܪܢܫܐ ܘܦܘܡܐ ܘܨܘܪܐ. ܕܠܐ ܐܝ̈ܕܝܐ ܘܕܠܐ ܪ̈ܓܠܐ.; Sachau (1899, 2:525).

[204] Ed. Wüstenfeld (1848–1849, 1:12). On *nasnās*, see the commentary to unit I.30 above. For a discussion of Muslim views regarding the causes of birth defects, see Kueny (2013, 181–82).

II.37 the horned serpents

This unit is most likely derived from the following passage from the Syriac version of the *Alexander Romance* (III.7): 'And in the midst of the phalanx there sprang up snakes with horns on their heads, some red and some white, and they bit and killed a number of the men'.[205]

II.38 the animal bigger than an elephant

It is most likely that this report is an abbreviated form of the following account from the Syriac version of the *Alexander Romance* (III.7):

> After the moon had set and it was dark, an animal which was bigger in its body than an elephant and which they call *Mašqlat* in the language of the country, came into the ditch and wished to spring upon us, but I straightway called out to my troops to take courage and stand ready. Now the longing and desire of the animal was to enter the ditch and to kill men, and suddenly it rushed into the ditch and killed twenty-six men, and amid loud noises and struggles it too perished by the hands of my troops; and after it was dead, we with three hundred men dragged it with great toil from the ditch and lifted it out.[206]

---

[205] ܐܦ ܚܘ̈ܘܬܐ ܘܩܪ̈ܢܬܐ ܒܪ̈ܝܫܝܗܘܢ ܐܝܬ ܗܘܐ ܕܣܘ̈ܡܩܝܢ. ܘܐܝܬ ܗܘܐ ܕܚܘ̈ܪܝܢ. ܡܢ ܡܨܥܬ ܦܠܓܐ ܣܠܩܘ ܗܘܘ. ܘܠܣܓܝܐܐ ܕܒ̈ܢܝܢܫܐ ܢܟܬܘ ܗܘܘ ܘܩܛܠܘ.; ed. Budge (1889, 174 [Syr.], 97 [trans.]).

[206] ܘܡܢ ܒܬܪ ܕܣܗܪܐ ܥܪܒ ܘܚܫܘܟܐ ܗܘܐ. ܚܝܘܬܐ ܚܕܐ ܕܒܦܓܪܗ̇ ܡܢ ܦܝܠܐ ܪܒܝܐ ܗܘܬ. ܡܫܩܠܬ ܒܠܫܢܗ ܕܐܬܪܐ ܗܘ ܩܪܝܢ ܠܗ̇. ܠܓܘ ܚܪܝܬܐ ܐܬܬ ܘܪܓܬ ܕܥܠܝܢ ܬܫܘܪ. ܘܗܘ ܒܥܕܢܐ ܠܚܝ̈ܠܘܬܝ، ܩܥܝܬ. ܕܐܬܠܒܒܘ ܘܡܛܝܒܘܬܐ ܠܡܩܡܘ. ܗ̇ܝ ܕܝܢ ܪܓܬܗ̇ ܘܪ̈ܓܝܓܬܗ̇ ܗܘܬ ܗܘܐ. ܕܠܚܪܝܬܐ ܬܐܬܐ. ܘܠܐܢܫܐ ܬܩܛܘܠ. ܘܡܢ ܫܠܝܐ ܠܓܘ

II.40 (= I.62 and I.65) Alexander and the growing trees

It is most likely that this story is a somewhat modified form of the following account from the Syriac version of the *Alexander Romance* (III.7):

> And upon the bank of the river there was a tree, which grew and increased from dawn until the sixth hour, and from the sixth hour until evening it diminished in height until there was nothing to be seen of it. Its smell was very pleasant, and I gave orders to gather some of its leaves and fruit, when suddenly an evil wind burst forth upon my troops and distressed them pitilessly; and we heard the sound of violent blows, and swellings and weals appeared upon the back of my troops; and after this we heard a voice from heaven like the sound of thunder which spake thus: "Let no man cut ought from this tree, neither let him approach it, for if ye approach it, all your troops will die."[207]

It should be noted that this unit also appears in Recension I, although in a very reduced form, in two almost identical units, I.62

ܚܐܪܬܐ ܪܗܛܬ. ܘܒܣܘܢܝ ܘܥܒܪܬ ܠܒܢ̈ܝܢ ܡܛܠܬ. ܘܒܩܠܐ ܚܫܝܟܐ ܘܒܬܠܬܠܬܐ ܐܘܦ ܐܦ ܗ̇ܘ ܡܢ ܐ̈ܘܪܚܐ ܣܠܩܬ ܐܟܒܪܬ. ܘܡܢ ܟܠܗ̇ ܕܡܫܝܚܬܬ ܒܡܡܠܐ ܡܫܝܚܐܐ ܒܬܠܬܠܬܐ ܠܒܢ̈ܝܢ ܦܠܓܗ̇ ܡܢ ܚܐܪܬܐ ܠܟܠ ܘܐܣܩܡ.; ed. Budge (1889, 175 [Syr.], 98 [trans.]).

207 ܘܥܠ ܣܦܪ ܢܗܪܐ ܗ̇ܘ ܐܝܠܢܐ ܚܕ ܐܝܬ ܗܘܐ. ܘܡܢ ܨܦܪܐ ܘܥܕܡܐ ܠܫܬ ܫܥ̈ܝܢ ܡܪܒܐ ܪܒܐ ܗܘܐ. ܘܡܢ ܫܬ ܫܥ̈ܝܢ ܘܥܕܡܐ ܠܪܡܫܐ ܡܢ ܪܘܡܗ ܒܨܪ ܗܘܐ. ܥܕܡܐ ܕܡܕܡ ܡܕܡ ܠܐ ܡܬܚܙܝܐ ܗܘܐ. ܘܪܝܚܗ ܛܒ ܒܣܝܡ ܗܘܐ. ܘܡܢ ܛܪ̈ܦܘܗܝ ܘܡܢ ܦܐܪ̈ܘܗܝ ܦܩܕܬ ܠܡܩܛܦ. ܘܡܢ ܥܠܠܐ ܪܘܚܐ ܒܝܫܬܐ ܒܫܠܝܘܬ ܢܦܩܬ. ܘܕܠܐ ܚܘܣ ܐܠܝܨܬ ܐܢܘܢ. ܘܩܠܐ ܕܡܚܘ̈ܬܐ ܚܣܝ̈ܢܬܐ ܫܡܥܢ. ܘܡܚܒ̈ܠܐ ܘܥܘ̈ܡܬܬܐ ܥܠ ܚܨ ܚܝ̈ܠܘܬܝ ܡܬܚܙܝܢ ܗܘܘ. ܘܒܬܪܟܢ ܩܠܐ ܡܢ ܫܡܝܐ ܫܡܥܢ. ܐܝܟ ܩܠܐ ܕܪܥܡܐ ܘܗܟܢܐ ܐܡܪ ܗܘܐ. ܕܐܢܫ ܡܢ ܐܝܠܢܐ ܗܢܐ ܠܐ ܢܦܣܘܩ. ܐܦܠܐ ܢܬܩܪܒ ܠܗ. ܡܛܠ ܕܐܢ ܡܬܩܪܒܝܬܘܢ ܠܗ; ܚܝ̈ܠܘܬܟܘܢ ܟܠܗܘܢ ܡܝܬܝܢ. ed. Budge (1889, 178 [Syr.], 100 [trans.]).

and I.65. One should perhaps take it as an indication that Recension II better preserves the part of the original version of the *Marvels* that was derived from the *Alexander Romance.*

II.41 the partridge-looking bird

This unit is most likely derived from the following passage from the Syriac version of the *Alexander Romance* (III.7), which follows the preceding account of the trees: 'And there were birds too which were like partridges'.[208]

II.43 the half-human animal attacking Alexander's troops

It is most likely that this report is an abbreviated form of the following account from the Syriac version of the *Alexander Romance* (III.7):

> At the ninth hour of the day, behold a creature half beast half man, which in its body was (like) a wild boar reared upright; and it was not at all afraid of us. I commanded my troops to catch it, and when they drew near to it, it was not at all afraid and did not run away from them. Then I ordered a naked woman to go towards it, that we might easily seize it; but when the woman went up to it, the beast took hold of the woman and rent her, and began to devour her. When we saw this, we went against it at full speed, and smote it and killed it.[209]

---

[208] ܘܐܝܬ ܗܘܐ ܬܘܒ ܦܪ̈ܚܬܐ ܕܕܡ̈ܝܢ ܗܘܘ ܠܣܟ̈ܠܐ. ed. Budge (1889, 178–79 [Syr.], 100 [trans.]).

[209] ܘܒܫܥܐ ܬܫܥ ܫ̈ܥܝܢ ܕܐܝܡܡܐ. ܗܐ ܚܝܘܬ ܒܦܠܓ ܚܝܘܐ. ܕܒܦܓܪܗ ܐܝܟ ܚܙܝܪ ܒܪܐ ܙܩܝܦ ܗܘܐ. ܘܡܕܡ ܒܡܕܡ ܠܐ ܐܬܬܙܝܥܬ. ܘܦܩܕܬ ܠܚܝܠܘܬܝ ܕܢܐܚܕܘܢܝܗ̇. ܘܟܕ ܚܝܠܘܬܝ

II.44 the great animals attacking Alexander's troops

This unit is most likely derived from the following passage from the Syriac version of the *Alexander Romance* (III.7):

> Then we set out from thence and came to a place amid groves of trees which were large, and in these woods there were wild beasts like the wild asses of our own country. Each of them was fifteen cubits in length, and as they were not dangerous, my troops killed a number of them and ate them.[210]

II.45 the threatening bats

This report is almost certainly derived from the following passage from the Syriac version of the *Alexander Romance* (III.7): 'and we saw bats which were as big as vultures, and their teeth were like those of men'.[211]

ܠܘܬܗ ܐܬܦܢܝܢܢ. ܟܕܒܝܢ ܠܐ ܐܬܬܪܝܚܬ. ܘܟܕ ܡܬܒܥܝܢܢ ܠܐ ܚܙܝܬ. ܘܗܕܝܢ ܦܩܕܬ ܕܐܢܬܬܐ ܚܕܐ ܒܬܘܠܬܐ ܚܠܦܘܗܝ ܬܬܐܬܐ. ܘܕܠܐܠܘܬ ܠܟܠܗܘܢ. ܘܟܕ ܐܬܬܐ ܠܘܬܗ ܐܢܠܬ. ܫܘܬܐ ܗܝ ܠܐܢܬܬܐ ܐܚܝܕܬܗ. ܘܥܪܩܬ ܠܡܐܟܠ ܡܢܗ. ܘܟܕ ܚܙܝܢ ܒܢܝܗܝܠܐ ܚܠܦܘܗܝ ܐܢܠܝܢ. ܘܡܚܝܢܢ ܘܩܛܠܢܗ.; ed. Budge (1889, 177 [Syr.], 99 [trans.]).

210 ܬܘܒ ܡܢ ܬܡܢ ܐܫܬܠܡ ܘܠܐܬܪܐ ܚܕ ܒܝܬ ܥܒܐ ܕܐܝܠܢܐ ܕܫܩܝܠ ܪ̈ܘܪܒܝܢ ܗܘܘ ܐܬܝܢ. ܘܒܓܘ ܗܘ ܥܒܐ ܚܝܘܬܐ ܐܝܬ ܗܘ̈ܝ. ܐܝܟ ܥܪ̈ܕܐ ܕܒܪܝܬܐ ܕܐܬܪܢ ܕܝܠܢ. ܘܐܘܪܟܐ ܚܕܐ ܚܕܐ ܡܢܗܘܢ ܚܡܫܬܥܣܪܐ ܐܡ̈ܝܢ. ܘܠܐ ܡܚܒܠܢܝܬܐ ܐܝܬܝܗܝܢ ܗܘ̈ܝ. ܚܝܠܘܬܐ ܕܝܠܝ ܩܛܠܘ ܡܢܗܘܢ ܣܓܝܐܐ ܘܐܟܠܘ.; ed. Budge (1889, 180 [Syr.], 101 [trans.]).

211 ܘܚܙܝܢ ܦ̈ܪܚܕܘܕܐ ܕܪܘܪ̈ܒܝܢ ܐܝܟ ܢܫ̈ܪܐ. ܘܫܢ̈ܝܗܘܢ ܐܝܟ ܕܒ̈ܢܝܢܫܐ.; ed. Budge (1889, 176 [Syr.], 98 [trans. (modified)]).

II.46 the bird on a tree-top

This unit is most likely derived from the following passage from the Syriac version of the *Alexander Romance* (III.7):

> And from thence we set out and came to a certain place which was waste; and in the midst of that place there was a bird sitting upon a tree without leaves and without fruit, and it had upon its head something like the rays of the sun, and they called the bird the 'palm bird' (phoenix).[212]

II.47 the dog-like animal on the island

The exact origin of this account is unclear. Since the narrator reports that he heard this story from a certain Christian clergyman called Emmanuel, who in his turn had heard it from a certain merchant from Egypt, it is possible that it originated and/or circulated as a part of the folklore of Muslim traders and seamen of the Persian Gulf and the Indian Ocean.

II.48 the rhinoceros

The text refers to the rhinoceros using the noun *karkdānā*, which is derived from the usual Arabic term for this animal, i.e., *karkadan*, in its own turn a loan from the New Persian *kargadan*.[213] In the following inner-textual gloss, the compiler of the *Marvels*

[212] ܘܡܢ ܬܡܢ ܐܫܩܠܢ ܘܠܕܘܟܬܐ ܚܕܐ ܐܬܝܢ. ܘܕܘܟܬܐ ܗܝ ܚܪܒܐ ܗܘܬ. ܘܡܨܥܬܗ ܗܝ ܕܘܟܬܐ ܦܪܚܬܐ ܚܕܐ ܥܠ ܐܝܠܢܐ ܚܕ. ܕܠܐ ܦܐܖ̈ܐ ܘܠܐ ܛܖ̈ܦܐ ܐܝܬ ܗܘܐ ܒܗ ܝܬܒܐ ܗܘܬ. ܘܥܠ ܪܫܗ ܒܕܡܘܬ ܙܠܝܩܐ ܕܫܡܫܐ ܐܝܬ ܗܘܐ. ܘܦܪܚܬܐ ܕܬܡܖ̈ܐ ܩܪܝܢ ܗܘܘ ܠܗ.; ed. Budge (1889, 180 [Syr.], 101 [trans.]).

[213] See Sokoloff (2009, 654); Ciancaglini (2008, 198).

also identifies this animal as *raymā*. The noun *raymā* is attested already in the Peshitta version of the Old Testament, where it is used to render the Hebrew רְאֵם 'wild ox' (cf. Deut. 33.17; Ps. 29.6; 92.11; Job 39.9). As one can infer from such phrases as ܩܪ̈ܢܬܐ ܕܪ̈ܝܡܐ (Deut. 33.17) and ܩܪ̈ܢܬܝ ܐܝܟ ܕܪ̈ܝܡܐ (Ps. 92.11), during this early period speakers of Syriac regarded this animal as having more than one horn. At some point, however, the noun came to be used to refer to an animal that had only one horn, often assumed to be the unicorn of Greco-Roman sources, but sometimes also the rhinoceros.[214] One observes this semantic shift in the entry on ܪܝܡܐ in the *Dictionary* of Bar Bahlūl, who quotes the description of this animal by Ḥnanīšōʿ bar Sarošway (9th c.): 'In its body, it looks like a big and strong deer. And it has one horn in the middle of its head. And it is very tall and powerful'.[215] In this entry, Bar Bahlūl also quotes Moses ibn Ḥunayn, who provides several Arabic synonyms of *raymā*, such as الحريش, الريم, and, notably, الكركدن 'rhinoceros'.

As for the source-critical evaluation of the description of the rhinoceros presented in this unit, its two main elements are well attested in the Muslim tradition of zoological and geographical writing. Thus, already al-Jāḥiẓ in his *Kitāb al-ḥayawān* refers,

---

[214] This semantic shift might have taken place due to the influence of the Septuagint tradition, where Hebrew רְאֵם is consistently rendered as μονόκερως. Cf. also the chapter on *raymā* in the Syriac *Book of Natural Beings*; ed. Ahrens (1892, 14–15 [Syr.]), which is derived from the description of μονοκέρωτος 'unicorn' in the Greek version of *Physiologus*; cf. ed. Sbordone (1936, 78–82).

[215] Ed. Duval (1888–1901, 2:1898–99).

although with some reservations, to a belief held by Indians that the young of the rhinoceros can graze upon the surrounding vegetation by putting their heads out of their mothers' wombs.[216] One comes across several later Arab writers, who also find this tradition problematic.[217]

The other detail, that is, the report that the horn of rhinoceros is used to make exquisite and expensive belts, is likewise well represented in Muslim sources. The closest to the text of this unit among them is perhaps the following passage from the description of the country of Qāmirūn, situated between India and China, in Ibn Ḫordāḏbeh's *Kitāb al-masālik*:

> And there are rhinoceros (الكركدن) here, who have on their forehead a horn, one elbow (ذراع) long and two handfuls (قبضتان) thick. This horn is covered with images from beginning to end. And if it is cut, you can see images, white on jet-like black, of humans or an animal, or a fish, or a peacock, or some other bird. And the inhabitants of China make from them belts that cost from three hundred dinars up to three or even four thousand dinars.[218]

---

216 Ed. Hārūn (1965–1969, 7:123–24).

217 Cf. polemic against the report of al-Jāḥiẓ in al-Mas'ūdī's *Murūğ al-ḏahab*; ed. de Meynard et al. (1966–1979, 1:215), or Abū Ḥāmid al-Ġarnāṭī, *Tuḥfat al-albāb*; ed. Ferrand (1925, 109–110). For a discussion, see Ettinghausen (1950, 15–16).

218 Ed. de Goeje (1889, 67–68).

Similar accounts of the use of rhinoceros' horn can be found, with some variations, in the works of many other Arab and Persian writers.[219]

II.52 the bridge and vestibule made from the rib of a fish

While the exact origin of this tradition is not clear, the mention of the city of Basra (see also units I.49, I.50) points to a Muslim milieu. For a close parallel, cf. Buzurg Ibn Šahriyār's *ʿAǧāʾib al-hind*:

> Abu Muhammad al-Hasan b. Amr told me: With my own eyes I have seen the side of a fish that a shipmaster brought us. He had cut a piece that measured five cubits on the side where the bone is thick; and then put it over a brook like a bridge, by the gate of a garden that we had in an island. The remaining portion was about twenty cubits long.[220]

Similar accounts are found in works by later Muslim authors.[221]

---

[219] Cf. Abū Zayd al-Sīrāfī, *Aḫbār al-ṣīn wa-l-hind*; ed. Mackintosh-Smith & Montgomery (2014, 40–43); Muḥammad al-Idrīsī (12th c.), *Nuzhat al-muštāq fī iḫtirāq al-āfāq*; trans. Ahmad (1960, 30); Ḥamdāllah al-Mustawfī al-Qazwīnī, *Nuzhat al-qulūb*; trans. Stephenson (1928, 28). For a discussion, see Ettinghausen (1950, 53–55, 101–104).

[220] Trans. Freeman-Grenville (1981, 21).

[221] Cf. al-Qazwīnī, *ʿAǧāʾib al-maḫlūqāt*; ed. Wüstenfeld (1848–1849, 1:141); Ḥamdāllah al-Mustawfī al-Qazwīnī, *Nuzhat al-qulūb*, on *Qusṭā* fish; trans. Stephenson (1928, 57).

II.53 the fish called 'sea-locust'

The reference is most likely to the flying fish (Exocoetidae family). Compare the following passage from Abū Zayd al-Sīrāfī's *Aḫbār al-ṣīn wa-l-hind*: 'They have also reported that in a certain part of the sea there are small flying fish that fly over the surface of the water, called 'water locusts' (جراد الماء)'.[222]

II.57 the whale stranded ashore

The toponym *Kīš* is well known and refers to the island located in the lower Persian Gulf.[223] Similarly to the story in unit I.40/II.31 that also mentions this island, this account might have originated and/or circulated as a part of the folklore of Muslim traders and seamen of the Persian Gulf. A similar story is found in *ʿAǧāʾib al-hind* by Buzurg Ibn Šahriyār, who relates how Ahmad b. Hilal, a ruler of Oman, came across a whale stranded ashore, and had 'the fat from its eyes' extracted.[224] One comes across mentions of 'oil' (ܡܫܚܐ) being extracted from whale eyes in some medieval Syriac works, such as the *Book of Natural Beings*[225] and the *Dictionary* of Bar Bahlūl.[226]

[222] Ed. Mackintosh-Smith & Montgomery (2014, 34–35).

[223] For references, see the commentary to unit I.40 above.

[224] Trans. Freeman-Grenville (1981, 9). Cf. also Abū Zayd al-Sīrāfī, *Aḫbār al-ṣīn wa-l-hind* II.16.1; ed. Mackintosh-Smith & Montgomery (2014, 126–27).

[225] Ed. Ahrens (1892, 53 [Syr.]).

[226] See the entry ܡܐܠܘܣ; ed. Duval (1888–1901, 2:1691).

4. INDEXES

 https://doi.org/10.11647/OBP.0237.04

4.1. Index of toponyms

Alexandria	I.2/II.2, I.3/II.3, I.4/II.4, II.47
ʿAmas / ʿAms	I.24/II.18
Andalus	I.1/II.1, I.10
Azerbaijan	I.23
Babylon	II.42
Baghdad	I.43
Balōs	II.23
Baqāwās (i.e. Waqwaq)	I.42
Barṭīl	I.64/II.58
Basra	I.49, I.50, II.52
Bāṭlas	I.13/II.8
Bēt Dlīğ / Bēt Dlīš (i.e. Bitlis)	I.24/II.18, I.25, I.26, I.27
Bēt Sasē	II.36
Callinicum	I.48
Constantinople	I.4/II.4
Corinth (?)	I.10
Egypt	I.9, I.11
ʾEwrīqōs	I.15/II.10
Hejaz	I.22/II.17
Ḥīzān	I.25
India	I.57, II.57
Kānīlāz (= Knīgar)	II.12
Karnāš	I.29/II.20
Kīš	I.40/II.31, II.57

Klāmīs (= Balōs)	I.32
Knīgar (= Kānīlāz)	I.17
Maṭlāyā	I.21/II.16
Myaṭāl	I.41
Pānōr	I.25
Persia	II.15
Puštīdar / Pūštī	I.18/II.13
Qātāğ	I.25
Qōnyā (i.e. Konya)	I.12
River of Sin	I.27
Rome	I.2/II.2
Sabbatical river	II.14
Sea of Khazars (i.e. the Caspian Sea)	I.7/II.7, I.21/II.16
Sea of Qūlzam (i.e. the Red Sea)	I.58/II.50, II.53
Sea of Reeds (i.e. the Dead Sea)	I.14/II.9
Sea of Syria (i.e. the Mediterranean Sea)	I.7/II.7
Serendib (i.e. Sri Lanka)	I.33, I.51
Spārē	I.19/II.14
Syria	I.16
Ṭāṭīq	I.25
Ṭāṭōn	I.26
Ṭōs (i.e. Tus)	I.43
Waqwaq	II.32

4.2. Index of ethnonyms, demonyms, and personal names

ʿAbdīšōʿ of Elam	I.12
Adam	I.47
Alexander (the Great)	I.1, I.31/II.22, I.34/II.24, I.37/II.27, I.53, I.61/II.39, I.62, I.63/II.42, I.65, II.37
Anās	I.40/II.31
Arabs	I.30/II.21
Aramaic	I.47
Basil (the Great)	I.48
Dionysios, bishop of Athens	I.48
Emmanuel, Rabban	II.47
Frankish	I.46/II.35
Greek	I.12 (lit. 'Roman'), I.63
Jews	I.3/II.3
Latin	I.63
Quryāqos, priest of Mosul	I.41, I.47
Romans	I.21/II.16
Syriac	I.47
Tiberius, king	I.48

5. BIBLIOGRAPHY

Primary sources

Ahmad, S. Maqbul. 1960. *India and the Neighbouring Territories in the Kitāb nuzhat al-mushtāq fī'khtirāq al-ʾāfāq of al-Sharīf al-Idrīsī: A Translation with Commentary of the Passages Relating to India, Pakistan, Ceylon, Parts of Afghanistan, and the Andaman, Nicobar, and Maldive Islands, etc.* Publication of the De Goeje Fund 20. Leiden: Brill.

Ahrens, Karl. 1892. *Das 'Buch der Naturgegenstände'* Kiel: C.F. Haeseler.

Bakoš, Ján. 1930–1933. *Le Candélabre du Sanctuaire de Grégoire Abouʾlfaradj dit Barhebrœus, I–II.* 2 vols. Patrologia Orientalis 22.4, 24.3. Paris: Firmin-Didot.

Bedjan, Paul. 1890–1897. *Acta martyrum et sanctorum.* 7 vols. Paris–Leipzig: Otto Harrassowitz.

Bellino, Francesca. 2008. *Zakariyyāʾ ibn Muḥammad al-Qazwīnī. Le meraviglie del creato e le stranezze degli esseri.* Islamica 5. Milano: Mondadori.

Bey Yaʿqūb, Ğirğis. 1920. *Rasāʾil dīniyya qadīma.* al-Qāhirah: Maṭbaʿa al-Muqtaṭaf wa-l-Muqaṭṭam.

Brock, Sebastian P. 1971. *The Syriac Version of the Pseudo-Nonnos Mythological Scholia.* University of Cambridge Oriental Publications 20. London: Cambridge University Press.

Brooks, Ernest W. 1919–1924. *Historia ecclesiastica Zachariae Rhetori vulgo adscripta.* 4 vols. CSCO Syr. III.5–6. Louvain: Typographeo Reipublicae.

Budge, Ernest A.W. 1889. *The History of Alexander the Great, being the Syriac Version of the Pseudo-Callisthenes*. Cambridge: Cambridge University Press.

Chabot, Jean Baptiste. 1916–1937. *Anonymi auctoris Chronicon ad annum Christi 1234 pertinens*. 3 vols. CSCO 81, 82, 109, Syr. 36, 37, 56. Paris: Typographeo Reipublicae.

Dankoff, Robert. 1990. *Evliya Çelebi in Bitlis: The Relevant Section of the Seyahatname, Edited with Translation, Commentary, and Introduction*. Evliya Çelebi's Book of Travels 2. Leiden: Brill.

Dankoff, Robert, Seyit Ali Kahraman, and Yücel Dağli. 1996. *Evliya Çelebi Seyahatnâmesi: Topkapı Sarayı Bağdat 304 yazmasının transkripsiyonu, dizini. I. Kitap*. İstanbul: Yapı Kredi Yayınları Ltd..

de Biberstein-Kazimirski, Albert. 1886. *Menoutchehri, poète persan du 11ème siècle de notre ère (du 5ième de l'hégire). Texte, traduction, notes et introduction historique*. Paris: Klincksieck.

de Goeje, Michael J. 1885. *Compendium libri Kitâb al-Boldân auctore Ibn al-Faqîh al-Hamadhânî*. Bibliotheca geographorum Arabicorum 5. Leiden: Brill.

———. 1889. *Kitâb al-Masâlik wa'l-Mamâlik (Liber Viarum et Regnorum) auctore Abu'l-Kâsim Obaidallah ibn Abdallah Ibn Khordâdhbeh et excerpta e Kitâb al-Kharâdj auctore Kodâma ibn Djaʿfar*. Bibliotheca geographorum Arabicorum 6. Leiden: Brill.

———. 1892. *Kitâb al Aʿlâk an-nafîsa VII, auctore Abû Alî Ahmed ibn Omar ibn Rosteh, et Kitâb al-Boldân, auctore Ahmed ibn abî Jakûb ibn Wâdhih al-Kâtib al-Jakûbî.* Bibliotheca geographorum Arabicorum 7. Leiden: Brill.

de Lagarde, Paul A. 1858. *Analecta syriaca.* Leipzig: B.G. Teubner.

de Meynard, Charles B., Pavet de Courteille, and Charles Pellat. 1966–1979. *Masʿūdī. Les prairies d'or.* 7 vols. Publications de l'Université Libanaise, Section des études historiques 11. 2nd rev. ed. Beirut: Publications de l'Université Libanaise.

Dodge, Bayard. 1970. *The Fihrist of al-Nadīm: A Tenth-Century Survey of Muslim Culture.* 2 vols. Records of Civilization: Sources and Studies 83. New York: Columbia University Press.

Duval, Rubens. 1888–1901. *Lexicon syriacum auctore Hassano bar Bahlule.* 3 vols. Collection orientale 15–17. Paris: Typographeo Reipublicae.

Ferrand, Gabriel. 1925. 'Le *Tuḥfat al-albāb* de Abū Ḥāmid al-Andalusī al-Ġarnāṭī, édité d'après les mss. 2167, 2168, 2170 de la Bibliothèque Nationale et le ms. d'Alger'. *Journal Asiatique* 207: 1–148, 193–304.

Flügel, Gustav. 1871–1872. *Kitâb al-Fihrist.* 2 vols. Leipzig: F.C.W. Vogel.

Freeman-Grenville, Greville S.P. 1981. *Captain Buzurg ibn Shahriyar of Ramhormuz. The Book of the Wonders of India: Mainland, Sea and Islands.* London: East-West Publications.

Godley, Alfred D. 1926–1930. *Herodotus.* 4 vols. Loeb Classical Library. 2nd rev. ed. London: William Heinemann / Cambridge, MA: Harvard University Press.

Gottheil, Richard J.H. 1888. 'A Syriac Fragment'. *Hebraica* 4 (4): 206–215.

Greatrex, Geoffrey, Robert R. Phenix, Cornelia B. Horn, Sebastian P. Brock, and Witold Witakowski. 2011. *The Chronicle of Pseudo-Zachariah Rhetor: Church and War in Late Antiquity*. Translated Texts for Historians 55. Liverpool: Liverpool University Press.

al-Ḥarastānī, ʿIṣām Fāris, and Muḥammad Ibrāhīm al-Zaġlī. 1994. *al-Tibyān fī aqsām al-Qurʾān li-Šams al-Dīn Muḥammad ibn Abī Bakr al-maʿrūf bi-Ibn Qayyim al-Ğawzīyyah*. Beirut: Muʾassasat al-Risālah.

Hārūn, ʿAbd al-Salām Muḥammad. 1965–1969. *Abū ʿUthmān ʿAmr ibn Baḥr al-Jāḥiẓ. Kitāb al-ḥayawān*. 8 vols. Maktabat al-Jāḥiẓ, al-Kitāb 1. 2nd ed. al-Qāhirah: Muṣṭafā al-Bābī al-Ḥalabī.

Jahier, Henri, and Abdelkader Noureddine. 1956. *ʿArib ibn Saʿid al-Katib al-Qurtʾubi. Le Livre de la génération du fœtus et le traitement des femmes enceintes et des nouveaux-nés*. Publications de la Faculté mixte de médecine et de pharmacie d'Alger 3. Algiers: Librairie Ferraris.

Jubūri, Kāmil Salmān, and Mahdi al-Najm. 2010. *Masālik al-ʾabṣār fī mamālik al-ʾamṣār by Šahābuddīn Ibn Faḍlullāh al-ʿUmari*. 27 vols. Beirut: Dar al-Kotob al-Ilmiyah.

Krenkow, Fritz. 1936. *Kitāb al-ğamāhir fī maʿrifat al-ğawāhir min taṣnīf Abī al-Rīḥān Muḥammad ibn Aḥmad al-Bīrūnī*. Hyderabad: Maṭbaʿat Ğamʿīyat Dāʾirat al-Maʿārif al-ʿUthmānīyah.

Le Strange, Guy. 1919. *The Geographical Part of the Nuzhat-al-Qulūb Composed by Ḥamd-Āllah Mustawfī of Qazwīn in 740 (1340)*. E.J.W. Gibb Memorial Series 23.2. Leiden: Brill.

Mackintosh-Smith, Tim, and James E. Montgomery. 2014. *Two Arabic Travel Books: Abū Zayd al-Sīrāfī. Accounts of China and India; Aḥmad Ibn Faḍlān. Mission to the Volga*. Library of Arabic Literature. New York: New York University Press.

Minorsky, Vladimir. 1942. *Sharaf al-Zamān Ṭāhir Marvazī on China, the Turks, and India: Arabic Text (circa A.D. 1120), with an English Translation and Commentary*. James G. Forlong Fund 22. London: The Royal Asiatic Society.

———. 1970. *Ḥudūd al-ʿĀlam, 'The Regions of the World': A Persian Geography, 372 A.H.–982 A.D.* E.J.W. Gibb Memorial Series NS 11. 2nd ed. London: Luzac & Company.

Nichols, Andrew G. 2011. *Ctesias on India and Fragments of His Minor Works: Introduction, Translation and Commentary*. London: Bloomsbury Academic.

Pellat, Charles. 1969. *The Life and Works of Jāḥiẓ: Translations of Selected Texts*. Islamic World. London: Routledge & Kegan Paul.

Rapoport, Yossef, and Emilie Savage-Smith. 2014. *An Eleventh-Century Egyptian Guide to the Universe: The Book of Curiosities*. Islamic Philosophy, Theology and Science: Texts and Studies 87. Leiden: Brill.

Sachau, Eduard. 1879. *The Chronology of Ancient Nations: An English Version of the Arabic Text of the Athâr-ul-bâkiya of Albîrûnî or 'Vestiges of the Past'*. London: W.H. Allen & Co.

Saʿd, Fārūq. 1973. *ʿAǧāʾib al-maḫlūqāt wa-ġarāʾib al-mawǧūdāt tālīf Zakarīyā al-Qazwīnī*. Beirut: Dār al-Āfāq al-Ǧadīdah.

Sayyid, Ayman Fuād. 2009. *The Fihrist of al-Nadīm, Abul-Farağ Muḥammad ibn Isḥāq, Composed at 377 AH.* 4 vols. London: Al-Furqan Islamic Heritage Foundation.

Sbordone, Francesco. 1936. *Physiologus*. Milan: In aedibus societatis 'Dante Alighieri–Albrighi, Segati et C.'.

Siddiqi, Muḥammad Zubair. 1928. *Firdausuʾl-Ḥikmat or Paradise of Wisdom of ʿAlī b. Rabban-al-Ṭabarī*. Berlin: Sonne.

Smirnova, Lidiya P. 1993. *ʿAǧāʾib al-dunyā (Chudesa mira)*. Pamyatniki pis'mennosti Vostoka 83. Moscow: Vostochnaya literatura.

Stephenson, John. 1928. *The Zoological Section of the Nuzhatu-l-qulūb of Ḥamdullāh al-Mustaufī al-Qazwīnī*. Oriental Translation Fund NS 30. London: Royal Asiatic Society.

Thackeray, Henry S.J., Ralph Marcus, Allen Wikgren, and Louis H. Feldman. 1926–1965. *Josephus*. 10 vols. The Loeb Classical Library. London: William Heinemann.

Thompson, D'Arcy Wentworth. 1910. *The Works of Aristotle Translated into English. Volume 4: Historia animalium*. Oxford: Clarendon Press.

van Esbroeck, Michel. 1998. 'Actes syriaques d'André attribués à Éphrem'. In *Symposium Syriacum VII: Uppsala University, Department of Asian and African Languages, 11–14 August 1996*, edited by René Lavenant, 85–105. Orientalia Christiana Analecta 256. Rome: Pontificio Istituto Orientale.

Véliaminof-Zernof, Vladimir V. 1860–1862. *Scheref-nameh, ou, Histoire des Kourdes par Scheref, Prince de Bidlis: publiée pour la première fois, traduite et annotée*. 2 vols. Saint Petersburg: Commissionaires de l'Académie Impériale des Sciences.

Wallraff, Martin, Umberto Roberto, Karl Pinggéra, and William Adler. 2007. *Iulius Africanus Chronographiae: The Extant Fragments*. Die griechischen christlichen Schriftsteller der ersten Jahrhunderte NF 15. Berlin: Walter de Gruyter.

Wüstenfeld, Heinrich F. 1848–1849. *Zakarija Ben Muhammed Ben Mahmud el-Cazwini's Kosmographie*. 2 vols. Göttingen: Dieterichsche Buchhandlung.

Secondary literature

Aᶜlam, Hūšang. 1996. 'Davāl-pā(y)'. In *Encyclopaedia Iranica*, edited by Ehsan Yarshater, vol. 7, 128–29. London: Routledge & Kegan Paul.

Ambartsumian, Artur A. 2013. '"Mednaya krepost"' v pekhleviyskoy traditsii'. In *Commentationes Iranicae: Sbornik statey k 90-letiyu Vladimira Aronovicha Livshitsa*, edited by Sergey R. Tokhtasyev and Pavel B. Lurye, 229–48. Saint Petersburg: Nestor-Istoriya.

Ashtor, Eliyahu. 1976. *A Social and Economic History of the Near East in the Middle Ages*. Berkeley, CA: University of California Press.

Bacqué-Grammont, Jean-Louis, Michele Bernardini, and Luca Berardi, eds. 2007. *L'arbre anthropogène du waqwaq, les femmes-fruits et les îles des femmes: recherches sur un mythe à large diffusion dans le temps et l'espace*. "l'Orientale", Dipartimento di Studi Asiatici, Institut Français d'Études Anatoliennes Georges Dumézil, Series minor 72. Naples: Università degli Studi di Napoli "L'Orientale".

Barry, Michael A. 1984. *The Tale of the City of Brass: An Introductory Study*. MA thesis. McGill University, Montreal.

Baumstark, Anton. 1922. *Geschichte der syrischen Literatur, mit Ausschluss der christlich-palästinensischen Texte*. Bonn: A. Marcus und E. Weber.

Becker, Carl H., and Charles G. Beckingham. 1986. 'Baḥr al-Ḳulzum'. In *The Encyclopaedia of Islam: New Edition,* 1: 931–33. Leiden: Brill.

Behrens-Abouseif, Doris. 2006. 'The Islamic History of the Lighthouse of Alexandria'. *Muqarnas* 23: 1–14.

Bellino, Francesca. 2015. 'I Sette Viaggi di Sindbād il marinaio: romanzo arabo nelle *Mille e Una Notte*'. In *Paradossi delle Notti: Dieci studi su Le Mille e Una Notte,* edited by Leonardo Capezzone and Elisabetta Benigni, 101–29. Nuova Collana Orientale 1. Pisa: Fabrizio Serra.

———. 2019. 'I viaggi di Sindbād tra Oriente e Occidente, medioevo e modernità: materiali inediti e nuove prospettive di ricerca'. In *Linee storiografiche e nuove prospettive di ricerca: XI Colloquio Internazionale Medioevo romanzo e orientale, Roma, 27–28 febbraio 2018,* edited by Francesca Bellino et al., 141–67. Medioevo Romanzo e Orientale, Colloqui 16. Soveria Mannelli, Catanzaro: Rubbettino.

Bellino, Francesca, and Mengozzi, Alessandro. 2016. 'Geographical *ʿaǧāʾib* in a Neo-Aramaic Manuscript of the London Sachau Collection'. *Le Muséon* 129 (3–4): 423–56.

Bosworth, Clifford E., and Iraj Afshar. 1985. 'ʿAjāʾeb al-Maḵlūqāt'. In *Encyclopaedia Iranica,* edited by Ehsan Yarshater, vol. 1, 696–99. London: Routledge & Kegan Paul.

Bradshaw, Paul F., Maxwell E. Johnson, and L. Edward Phillips. 2002. *The Apostolic Tradition: A Commentary*. Hermeneia. Minneapolis, MN: Fortress Press.

Braida, Emanuela. 2016. 'Christian Arabic and Garšūnī Versions of *Sindbad the Sailor*: An Overview'. *Polish Journal of the Arts and Culture* NS 3 (1): 7–28.

Brock, Sebastian P. 2011. 'Alexander Cycle'. In *Gorgias Encyclopedic Dictionary of the Syriac Heritage*, edited by Sebastian P. Brock et al., 16. Piscataway, NJ: Gorgias Press.

Burkitt, Francis C. 1928. 'The MSS. of "Narsai on the Mysteries"'. *Journal of Theological Studies* OS 29 [115]: 269–75.

Carboni, Stefano 2015. *The Wonders of Creation and the Singularities of Painting: A Study of the Ilkhanid London Qazvīnī*. Edinburgh Studies in Islamic Art. Edinburgh: Edinburgh University Press.

Chaichian, Mohammad A. 2013. 'Red Snake: The Great Wall of Gorgan, Iran'. In Idem, *Empires and Walls: Globalization, Migration, and Colonial Domination*, 53–89. Studies in Critical Social Sciences 62. Leiden: Brill.

Ciancaglini, Claudia A. 2008. *Iranian Loanwords in Syriac*. Beiträge zu Iranistik 28. Wiesbaden: Ludwig Reichert.

Colin, Georges Séraphin. 1986. 'Ḥinnāʾ'. In *The Encyclopaedia of Islam: New Edition*, 3: 461. Leiden: Brill.

Cook, David. 2002. *Studies in Muslim Apocalyptic*. Studies in Late Antiquity and Early Islam 21. Princeton, NJ: Darwin Press.

Cooperson, Michael. 2010. 'Al-Maʾmūn, the Pyramids and the Hieroglyphs'. In *ʿAbbasid Studies II: Occasional Papers of the School of ʿAbbasid Studies, Leuven, 28 June—1 July 2004*, edited by John Nawas, 165–90. Orientalia Lovaniensia Analecta 177. Leuven: Peeters.

Crane, Howard. 2000. *The Garden of the Mosques: Hafiz Hüseyin al-Ayvansarayî's Guide to the Muslim Monuments of Ottoman Istanbul*. Studies in Islamic Art and Architecture 8. Leiden: Brill.

Demidchik, Vladimir P. 2004. *Mir chudes v arabskoy literature XIII–XIV vv.: Zakariya al-Kazvini i zhanr mirabiliy*. Moscow: Vostochnaya literatura.

Doufikar-Aerts, Faustina. 2010. *Alexander Magnus Arabicus: A Survey of the Alexander Tradition through Seven Centuries: from Pseudo-Callisthenes to Ṣūrī*. Mediaevalia Groningana, New Series 10. Paris: Peeters.

———. 2016. 'A Hero Without Borders: 2 Alexander the Great in the Syriac and Arabic Tradition'. In *Fictional Storytelling in the Medieval Eastern Mediterranean and Beyond*, edited by Carolina Cupane and Bettina Krönung, 190–209. Brill's Companions to the Byzantine World 1. Leiden: Brill.

Dubler, César E. 1986. 'ʿAdjāʾib'. In *The Encyclopaedia of Islam: New Edition*, 1: 203–204. Leiden: Brill.

El-Zein, Amira. 2009. *Islam, Arabs, and the Intelligent World of the Jinn*. Contemporary Issues in the Middle East. Syracuse, NY: Syracuse University Press.

Ettinghausen, Richard. 1950. *Studies in Muslim Iconography, I. The Unicorn*. Freer Gallery of Art Occasional Papers 1/3. Washington, D.C.: Smithsonian Institution.

Ferrand, Gabriel, Greville S.P. Freeman-Grenville, Shawkat M. Toorawa, Gerald R. Tibbetts, and François Viré. 2002.

'Wāḳwāḳ'. In *The Encyclopaedia of Islam: New Edition*, 11: 103–109. Leiden: Brill.

Fodor, Alexander. 1970. 'The Origins of the Arabic Legends of the Pyramids'. *Acta Orientalia Academiae Scientiarum Hungaricae* 23 (3): 335–363.

Gadjiev, Murtazali. 2017. 'Dagh Bary'. In *Encyclopædia Iranica*, online edition; available at http://www.iranicaonline.org/articles/dagh-bary (accessed on 11 June 2020).

Gera, Deborah L. 2003. *Ancient Greek Ideas on Speech, Language, and Civilization*. Oxford: Oxford University Press.

Gero, Stephen. 1993. 'The Legend of Alexander the Great in the Christian Orient'. *Bulletin of the John Rylands University Library of Manchester* 75/1: 3–9.

Goodwin, Godfrey. 1986. 'Konya'. In *The Encyclopaedia of Islam: New Edition*, 5: 253–56. Leiden: Brill.

Griffith, Sidney H. 1999. 'The Monk in the Emir's *Majlis*: Reflections on a Popular Genre of Christian Literary Apologetics in Arabic in the Early Islamic Period'. In *The Majlis: Interreligious Encounters in Medieval Islam*, edited by Hava Lazarus-Yafeh et al., 13–65. Studies in Arabic Language and Literature. Wiesbaden: Harrassowitz Verlag.

———. 2007. *The Church in the Shadow of the Mosque: Christians and Muslims in the World of Islam*. Jews, Christians, and Muslims from the Ancient to the Modern World. Princeton, NJ: Princeton University Press.

Hewsen, Robert H. 2001. 'The Historical Geography of Baghesh/Bitlis and Taron/Mush'. In *Armenian Baghesh/Bitlis and Taron/Mush*, edited by Richard G. Hovannisian, 41–69.

UCLA Armenian History and Culture Series: Historic Armenian Cities and Provinces 2. Costa Mesa, CA: Mazda Publishers.

Jeanes, Gordon. 1993. 'Baptism Portrayed as Martyrdom in the Early Church'. *Studia Liturgica* 23: 158–76.

Jullien, Christelle, and Florence Jullien. 2010. 'Du *ḥnana* ou la bénédiction contestée'. In *Sur les pas des Araméens chrétiens: Mélanges offerts à Alain Desreumaux*, edited by Françoise Briquel-Chatonnet and Muriel Debié, 333–48. Cahiers d'études syriaques 1. Paris: Geuthner.

Katsumata, Naoya. 2002. 'The Style of the "Maqama": Arabic, Persian, Hebrew, Syriac'. *Arabic and Middle Eastern Literatures* 5 (2): 117–137.

Kauz, Ralph. 2006. 'The Maritime Trade of Kish during the Mongol Period'. In *Beyond the Legacy of Genghis Khan*, edited by Linda Komaroff, 51–67. Islamic History and Civilization 64. Leiden: Brill.

Khan, Geoffrey. 2008. *The Neo-Aramaic Dialect of Barwar*. 3 vols. Handbook of Oriental Studies, Section 1: The Near and Middle East 96. Leiden: Brill.

———. 2016. *The Neo-Aramaic Dialect of the Assyrian Christians of Urmi*. 4 vols. Studies in Semitic Languages and Linguistics 86. Leiden: Brill.

Kim, Susan M. 2017. '*Letter of Alexander to Aristotle*'. In *The Encyclopedia of Medieval Literature in Britain*, 4 vols., edited by Siân Echard and Robert A. Rouse, vol. 3, 1174–75. Wiley-Blackwell Encyclopedia of Literature. Chichester, West Sussex: Wiley Blackwell.

Kirtley, Bacil F. 1963. 'The Ear-Sleepers: Some Permutations of a Traveler's Tale'. *Journal of American Folklore* 76/300: 119–130.

Kotar, Peter. 2013. *Der syrische Alexanderroman: Eine Untersuchung über die Beziehungen des syrischen zum griechischen Alexanderroman des Pseudo-Kallisthenes*. Schriften zur Kulturgeschichte 28. Hamburg: Kovac.

Kruk, Remke. 1995. 'Traditional Islamic Views of Apes and Monkeys'. In *Ape, Man, Apeman: Changing Views since 1600. Evaluative Proceedings of the Symposium Ape, Man, Apeman: Changing Views Since 1660, Leiden, the Netherlands, 28 June—1 July, 1993*, edited by Raymond Corbey and Bert Theunissen, 29–41. Leiden: Department of Prehistory, Leiden University.

Kueny, Kathryn M. 2013. *Conceiving Identities: Maternity in Medieval Muslim Discourse and Practice*. Albany, NY: State University of New York Press.

Lazarus-Yafeh, Hava, Mark R. Cohen, Sasson Somekh, and Sidney H. Griffith, eds. 1999. *The Majlis: Interreligious Encounters in Medieval Islam*. Studies in Arabic Language and Literature. Wiesbaden: Harrassowitz Verlag.

Maclean, Arthur J. 1901. *A Dictionary of the Dialects of Vernacular Syriac as Spoken by the Eastern Syrians of Kurdistan, Northwest Persia, and the Plain of Moṣul, with Illustrations from the Dialects of the Jews of Zakhu and Azerbaijan, and of the Western Syrians of Ṭur ʿAbdin and Maʿlula*. Oxford: Clarendon Press.

Margoliouth, George. 1899. *Descriptive List of Syriac and Karshuni Mss. in the British Museum Acquired since 1873*. London: British Museum.

Mengozzi, Alessandro. 2014. 'Persische Lyrik in syrischem Gewand: Vierzeiler aus dem Buch des Khamis bar Qardaḥe (Ende 13. Jh.)'. In *Geschichte, Theologie und Kultur des syrischen Christentums: Beiträge zum 7. Deutschen Syrologie-Symposium in Göttingen, Dezember 2011*, edited by Martin Tamcke and Sven Grebenstein, 155–76. Göttinger Orientforschungen: Reihe 1, Syriaca 46. Wiesbaden: Harrassowitz Verlag.

———. Forthcoming. 'D'Ahiqar au tapis volant du roi Salomon, des mirabilia géographiques à Sindbad le marin en araméen moderne: adab et recherche orientaliste à la fin du XIXème siècle'. In *L'adab, toujours recommencé / Re-Begun Adab: 'Origins'. Transmissions and Metamorphoses*, edited by Francesca Bellino, Catherina Mayeur-Jaouen, and Luca Patrizi. Leiden: Brill.

Minov, Sergey. 2013. 'The *Cave of Treasures* and the Formation of Syriac Christian Identity in Late Antique Mesopotamia: Between Tradition and Innovation'. In *Between Personal and Institutional Religion: Self, Doctrine, and Practice in Late Antique Eastern Christianity*, edited by Brouria Bitton-Ashkelony and Lorenzo Perrone, 155–94. Cultural Encounters in Late Antiquity and the Middle Ages 15. Turnhout: Brepols.

———. 2019. 'Syriac'. In *A Guide to Early Jewish Texts and Traditions in Christian Transmission*, edited by Alexander Kulik et al., 95–137. New York: Oxford University Press.

Moss, Yonatan. 2010. 'The Language of Paradise: Hebrew or Syriac? Linguistic Speculations and Linguistic Realities in Late Antiquity'. In *Paradise in Antiquity: Jewish and Christian Views*, edited by Markus Bockmuehl and Guy G. Stroumsa, 120–37. Cambridge: Cambridge University Press.

Murre-van den Berg, Hendrika L. 2015. *Scribes and Scriptures: The Church of the East in the Eastern Ottoman Provinces (1500–1850)*. Eastern Christian Studies 21. Louvain: Peeters.

Nawotka, Krzysztof. 2017. *The Alexander Romance by Ps.-Callisthenes: A Historical Commentary*. Mnemosyne Supplements 399. Leiden: Brill.

———. 2018. 'Syriac and Persian Versions of the *Alexander Romance*'. In *Brill's Companion to the Reception of Alexander the Great*, edited by Kenneth R. Moore, 525–42. Brill's Companions to Classical Reception 14. Leiden: Brill.

Nöldeke, Theodor. 2001. *Compendious Syriac Grammar*. Trans. by James A. Crichton. Winona Lake, IN: Eisenbrauns.

Payne Smith, Robert. 1879–1901. *Thesaurus Syriacus*. 2 vols. Oxford: Clarendon Press.

Pennacchietti, Fabrizio A. 1998. 'Stranga, Ammorrus e Sambatiòn: storie di fiumi intermittenti'. *Rivista degli Studi Orientali* 72: 23–40.

Pettigrew, Mark F. 2004. *The Wonders of the Ancients: Arab-Islamic Representations of Ancient Egypt*. PhD dissertation. Berkeley: The University of California.

Potts, Daniel T. 2004. 'Kish Island'. In *Encyclopædia Iranica*, online edition; available at http://www.iranicaonline.org/articles/kish-island (accessed on 22 June 2020).

Redford, Scott. 2000. *Landscape and the State in Medieval Anatolia: Seljuk Gardens and Pavilions of Alanya, Turkey*. BAR International Series 893. Oxford: Archaeopress.

Rodinson, Maxime. 1978. 'La place du merveilleux et de l'étrange dans la conscience du monde musulman médiéval'. In *L'Étrange et le Merveilleux dans l'Islam médiéval. Actes du colloque tenu au Collège de France à Paris, en mars 1974*, 167–87. Paris: Editions J.A..

Roggema, Barbara H. 2019. 'Christian-Muslim-Jewish Relations in Patristic Literature: The Arabic *Questions and Answers of Basil and Gregory*'. In *Heirs of the Apostles: Studies on Arabic Christianity in Honor of Sidney H. Griffith*, edited by David Bertaina et al., 395–414. Arabic Christianity 1. Leiden: Brill.

Ron-Gilboa, Guy. 2017. *The ʿAǧāʾib Theme in Four Medieval Works*. PhD dissertation. The Hebrew University of Jerusalem [in Hebrew].

Rothkoff, Aaron. 2007. 'Sambatyon'. In *Encyclopaedia Judaica: Second Edition*. 22 vols., edited by Fred Skolnik and Michael Berenbaum, 17:743–44. Detroit, MI: Thomson Gale.

Rubin, Milka. 1998. 'The Language of Creation or the Primordial Language: A Case of Cultural Polemics in Antiquity'. *Journal of Jewish Studies* 49 (2): 306–33.

Ruska, Julius. 1913. 'Ḳazwīnīstudien'. *Der Islam* 4: 14–66, 236–62.

Russell, James R. 1984. 'The Tale of the Bronze City in Armenian'. In *Medieval Armenian Culture: Proceedings of the Third Dr. H. Markarian Conference on Armenian Culture*, edited by

Thomas J. Samuelian and Michael E. Stone, 250–61. University of Pennsylvania Armenian Texts and Studies 6. Chico, CA: Scholars Press.

Sachau, Eduard. 1899. *Verzeichniss der syrischen Handschriften der Königlichen Bibliothek zu Berlin.* 2 vols. Die Handschriften-Verzeichnisse der Königlichen Bibliothek zu Berlin 23. Berlin: A. Asher & Co.

Sariyannis, Marinos. 2015. '*Ajāʾib ve gharāʾib*: Ottoman Collections of *Mirabilia* and Perceptions of the Supernatural'. *Der Islam* 92 (2): 442–467.

Sauer, Eberhard W., Hamid Omrani Rekavandi, and Tony J. Wilkinson, eds. 2013. *Persia's Imperial Power in Late Antiquity: The Great Wall of Gorgan and the Frontier Landscapes of Sasanian Iran.* British Institute of Persian Studies Archaeological Monographs Series 2. Oxford: Oxbow.

Sauget, Joseph M. 1981. *Un cas très curieux de restauration de manuscrit: le* Borgia syriaque 39. *Étude codicologique et analyse du contenu.* Studi e Testi 292. Vatican City: Biblioteca Apostolica Vaticana.

Schine, Rachel. 2019. 'Nourishing the Noble: Breastfeeding and Hero-Making in Medieval Arabic Popular Literature'. *Al-ʿUṣūr al-Wusṭā* 27: 165–200.

Sinclair, Thomas A. 1987–1990. *Eastern Turkey: An Architectural and Archaeological Survey.* 4 vols. London: Pindar Press.

———. 2001. 'The Armenians and the Kurdish Emirs of Bitlis under the Kara Koyunlu'. In *Armenian Baghesh/Bitlis and Taron/Mush,* edited by Richard G. Hovannisian, 155–74.

UCLA Armenian History and Culture Series: Historic Armenian Cities and Provinces 2. Costa Mesa, CA: Mazda Publishers.

Sokoloff, Michael. 2009. *A Syriac Lexicon: A Translation from the Latin, Correction, Expansion, and Update of C. Brockelmann's Lexicon Syriacum*. Winona Lake, IN: Eisenbrauns / Piscataway, NJ: Gorgias Press.

Steingass, Francis J. 1892. *A Comprehensive Persian-English Dictionary, Including the Arabic Words and Phrases to be met with in Persian Literature*. London: Routledge & Kegan Paul.

Stoneman, Richard. 2017. 'Alexander the Great and the End of Time: The Syriac Contribution to the Development of the *Alexander Romance*'. In *Syriac in Its Multi-Cultural Context: First International Syriac Studies Symposium, Mardin Artuklu University, Institute of Living Languages, 20–22 April 2012, Mardin*, edited by Herman G.B. Teule et al., 39–46 Eastern Christian Studies 23. Leuven: Peeters.

Szombathy, Zoltán. 2015. 'Eating People is Wrong: Some Eyewitness Reports of Cannibalism in Arabic Sources'. In *Violence in Islamic Thought from the Qurʾān to the Mongols*, edited by Robert Gleave and István T. Kristó-Nagy, 200–24. Legitimate and Illegitimate Violence in Islamic Thought 1. Edinburgh: Edinburgh University Press.

Takahashi, Hidemi. 2002. 'The Greco-Syriac and Arabic Sources of Barhebraeus' Mineralogy and Meteorology in *Candelabrum of the Sanctuary*, Base II'. *Islamic Studies* 41 (2): 215–69.

———. 2003. 'Observations on Bar 'Ebroyo's Marine Geography'. *Hugoye: Journal of Syriac Studies* 6 (1): 77–130.

———. 2004. *Aristotelian Meteorology in Syriac: Barhebraeus, Butyrum Sapientiae, Books of Mineralogy and Meteorology*. Aristoteles Semitico-Latinus 15. Leiden: Brill.

———. 2006. 'Fakhr al-Dīn al-Rāzī, Qazwīnī and Bar Shakko'. *The Harp* 19: 365–380.

Tannous, Jack. 2018a. *The Making of the Medieval Middle East: Religion, Society, and Simple Believers*. Princeton, NJ: Princeton University Press.

———. 2018b. 'Romanness in the Syriac East'. In *Transformations of Romanness: Early Medieval Regions and Identities*, edited by Walter Pohl et al., 457–80. Millennium Studies 71. Berlin: Walter de Gruyter.

Taylor, David G.K. 2010. '"Your Sweet Saliva is the Living Wine": Drink, Desire, and Devotion in the Syriac Wine Songs of Khāmīs Bar Qardāhē'. In *The Syriac Renaissance*, edited by Herman G.B. Teule et al., 31–52. Eastern Christian Studies 9. Leuven: Peeters.

Thomson, Robert W. 2001. 'Bitlis and Armenian Histories'. In *Armenian Baghesh/Bitlis and Taron/Mush*, edited by Richard G. Hovannisian, 105–17. UCLA Armenian History and Culture Series: Historic Armenian Cities and Provinces 2. Costa Mesa, CA: Mazda Publishers.

Toorawa, Shawkat M. 2000. 'Wâq al-wâq: Fabulous, Fabular, Indian Ocean (?) Island(s) ...'. *Emergences: Journal for the Study of Media & Composite Cultures* 10 (2): 387–402.

van Donzel, Emeri, and Andrea B. Schmidt. 2009. *Gog and Magog in Early Syriac and Islamic Sources: Sallam's Quest for Alexander's Wall.* Brill's Inner Asian Library 22. Leiden: Brill.

Verskin, Sara. 2020. *Barren Women: Religion and Medicine in the Medieval Middle East.* Islam – Thought, Culture, and Society 2. Berlin: Walter de Gruyter.

Viré, François. 1986. 'Ḳird'. In *The Encyclopaedia of Islam: New Edition*, 5: 131–34. Leiden: Brill.

von Hees, Syrinx. 2002. *Enzyklopädie als Spiegel des Weltbildes: Qazwinis Wunder der Schöpfung – eine Naturkunde des 13. Jahrhunderts.* Diskurse der Arabistik 4. Wiesbaden: Harrassowitz Verlag.

———. 2005. 'The Astonishing: A Critique and Re-Reading of ʿAǧāʾib Literature'. *Middle Eastern Literatures* 8 (2): 101–120.

Vorderstrasse, Tasha. 2012. 'Descriptions of the Pharos of Alexandria in Islamic and Chinese Sources: Collective Memory and Textual Transmission'. In *The Lineaments of Islam: Studies in Honor of Fred McGraw Donner*, edited by Paul M. Cobb, 457–81. Islamic History and Civilization 95. Leiden: Brill.

Wilmshurst, David. 2000. *The Ecclesiastical Organisation of the Church of the East, 1318–1913.* CSCO 582, Subs. 104. Louvain: Peeters.

Wright, William. 1901. *A Catalogue of the Syriac Manuscripts Preserved in the Library of the University of Cambridge.* 2 vols. Cambridge: Cambridge University Press.

Younansardaroud, Helen. 2010. 'Eine syrisch-christliche Maqāme aus dem 19. Jahrhundert'. In *Akten des 5. Symposiums zur*

Sprache, Geschichte, Theologie und Gegenwartslage der syrischen Kirchen (V. Deutsche Syrologentagung), Berlin 14.–15. Juli 2006, edited by Rainer M. Voigt, 299–304. Semitica et Semitohamitica Berolinensia 9. Aachen: Shaker Verlag.

Zoroufi, Mohammad. 1968. *Die Resāle des Moheb ʿAlī Hān Nāzim Al-Mulk über die osmanisch-iranische Grenze (um 1850)*. Inaugural-Dissertation zur Erlangung der Doctorwürde der philosophischen Fakultät. Ludwig-Maximilians-Universität, Munich.

Zuwiyya, Zachary D., ed. 2011. *A Companion to Alexander Literature in the Middle Ages*. Brill's Companions to the Christian Tradition 29. Leiden: Brill.

6. Appendix: Manuscript Facsimiles

B1 – Berlin, Staatsbibliothek zu Berlin, Orient. quart. 802 (Berlin Syr. 59), fols. 68v–72v

© Staatsbibliothek zu Berlin – Preussischer Kulturbesitz, Orientabteilung. The images are in public domain and can be accessed online at http://resolver.staatsbibliothek-berlin.de/SBB0001DF2700000000

B2 – Berlin, Staatsbibliothek zu Berlin, Sachau 118 (Berlin Syr. 86), fols. 7r–8v

© Staatsbibliothek zu Berlin – Preussischer Kulturbesitz, Orientabteilung. The images are in public domain and can be accessed online at http://resolver.staatsbibliothek-berlin.de/SBB0001E67500000000

https://doi.org/10.11647/OBP.0237.05

B1 fol. 68v

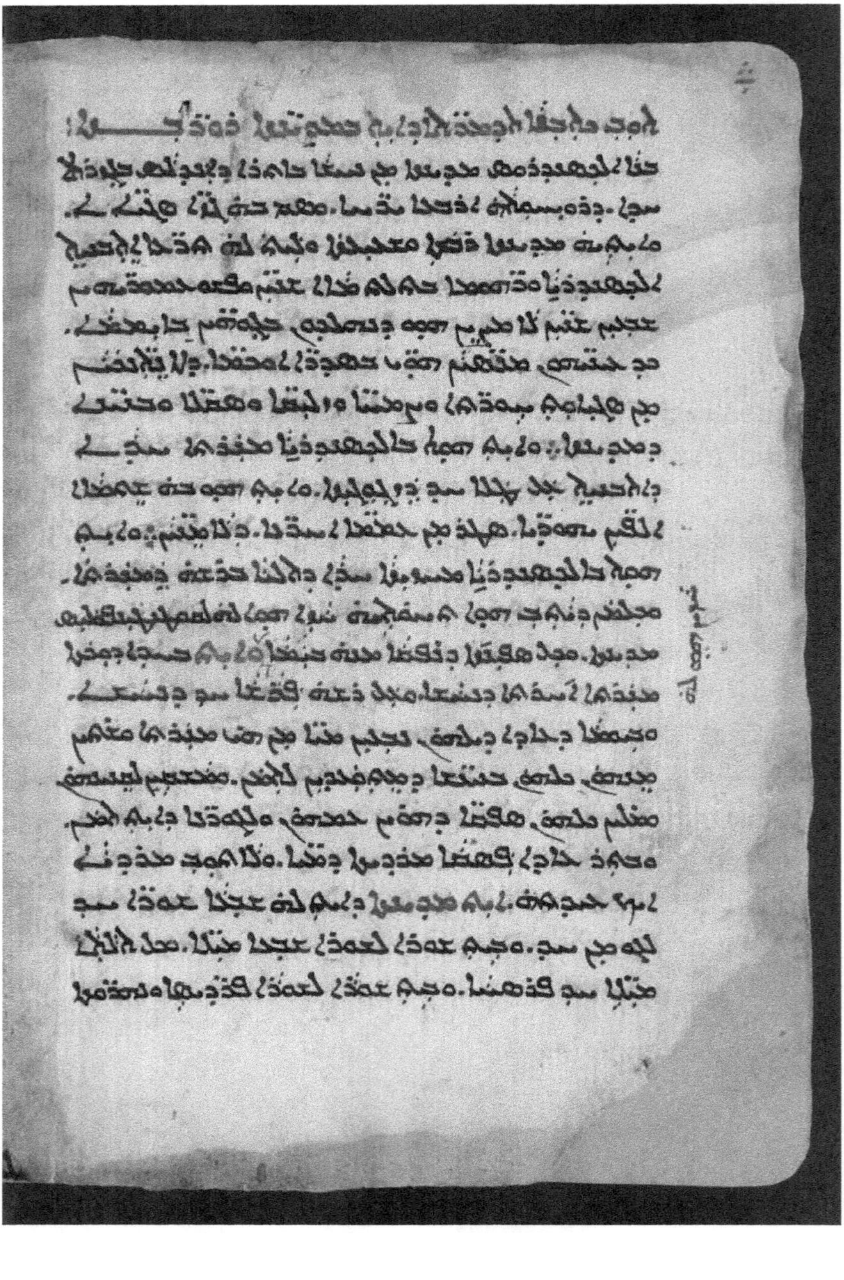

B1 fol. 69r

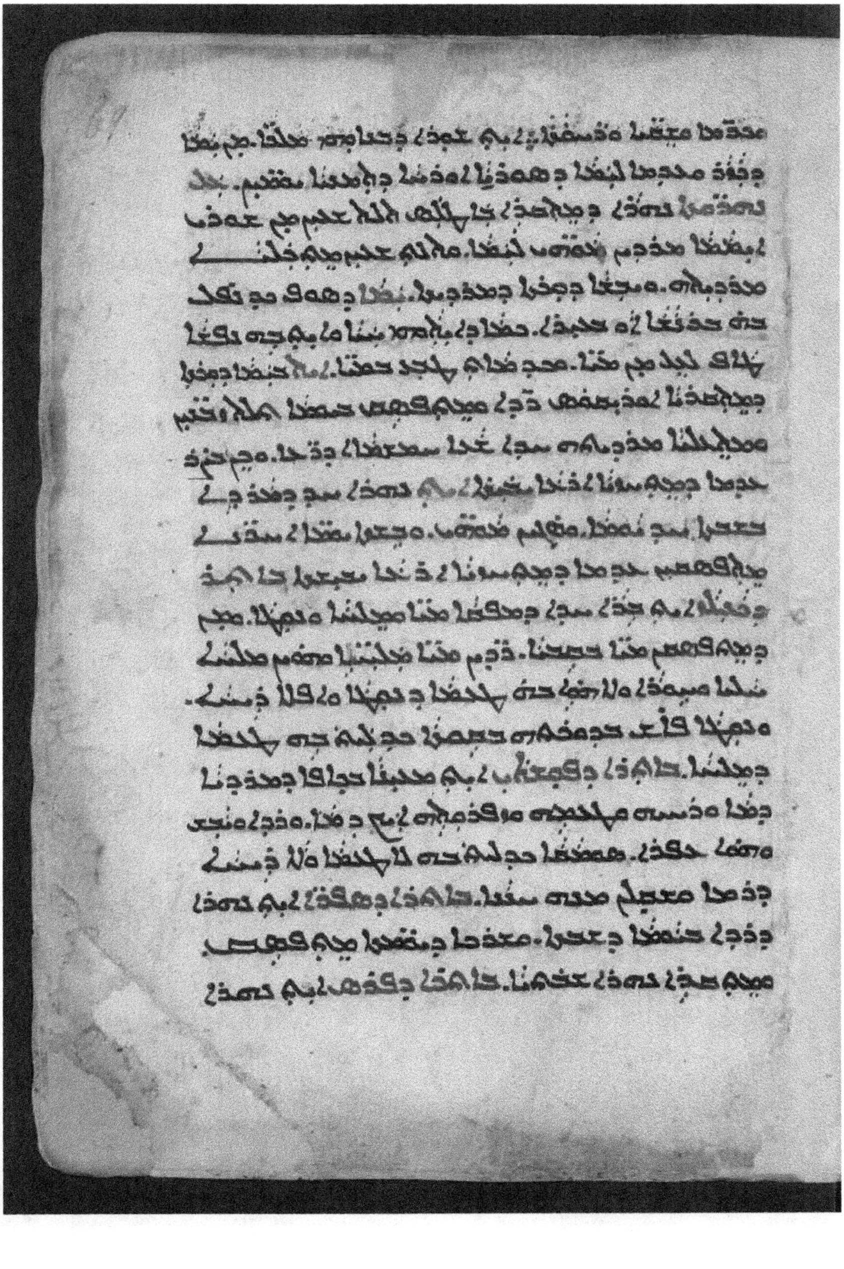

B1 fol. 69v

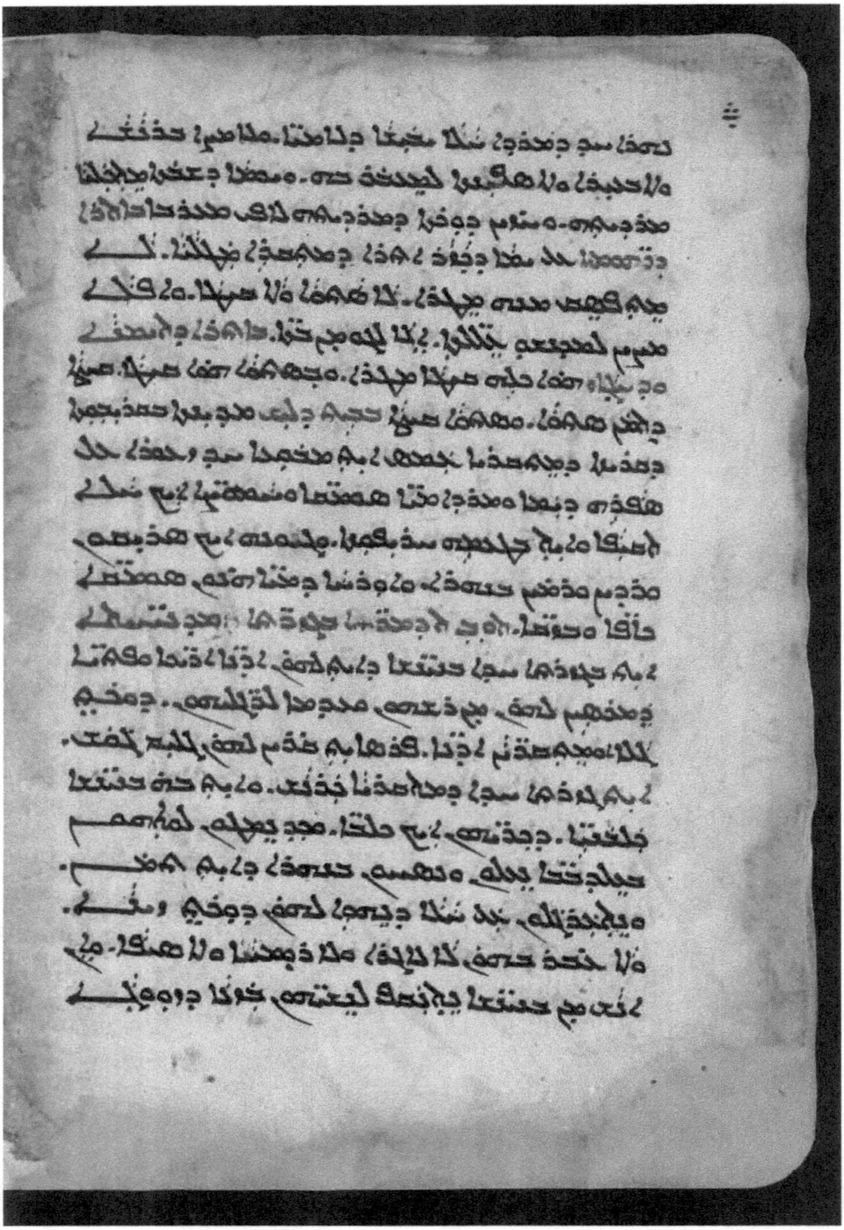

B1 fol. 70r

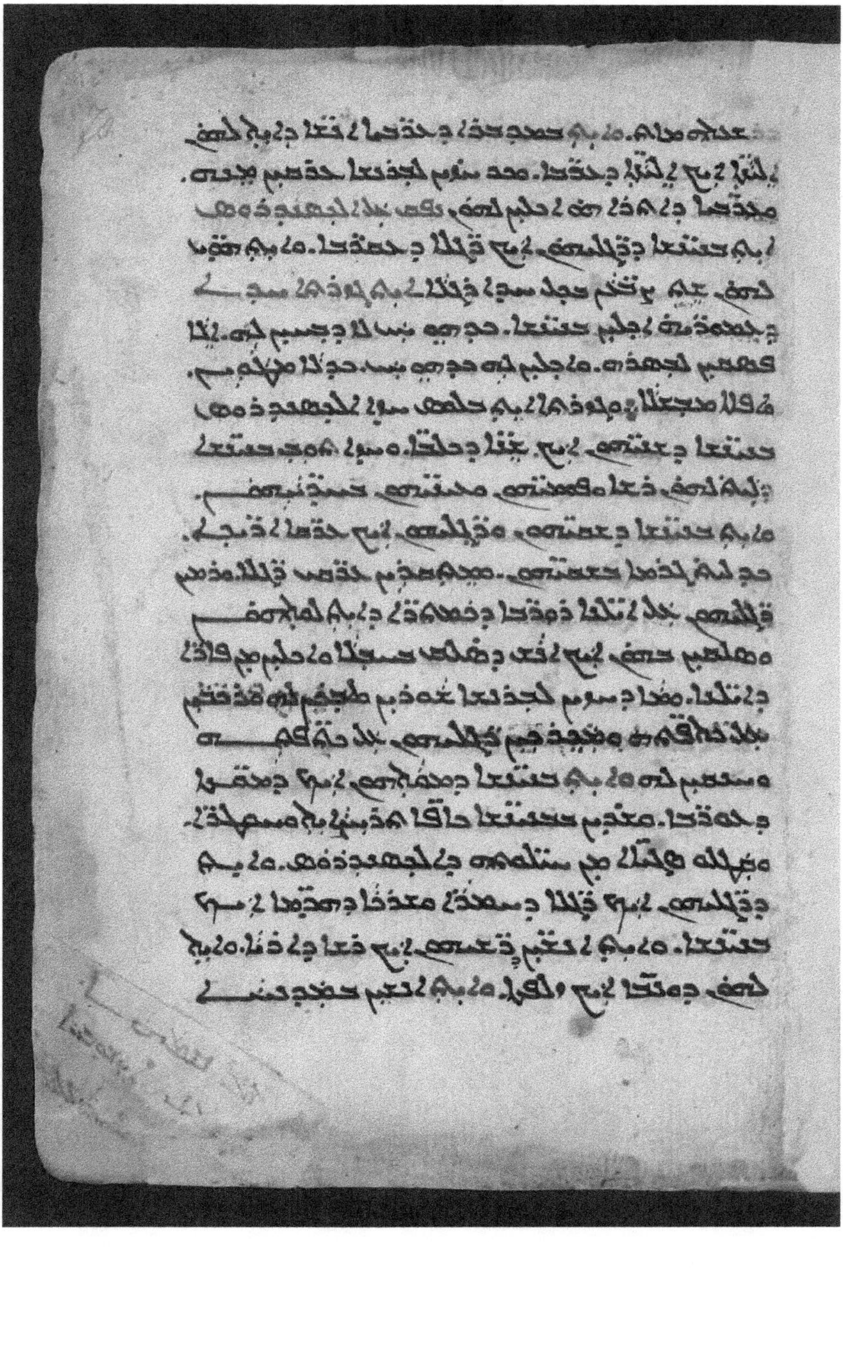

B1 fol. 70v

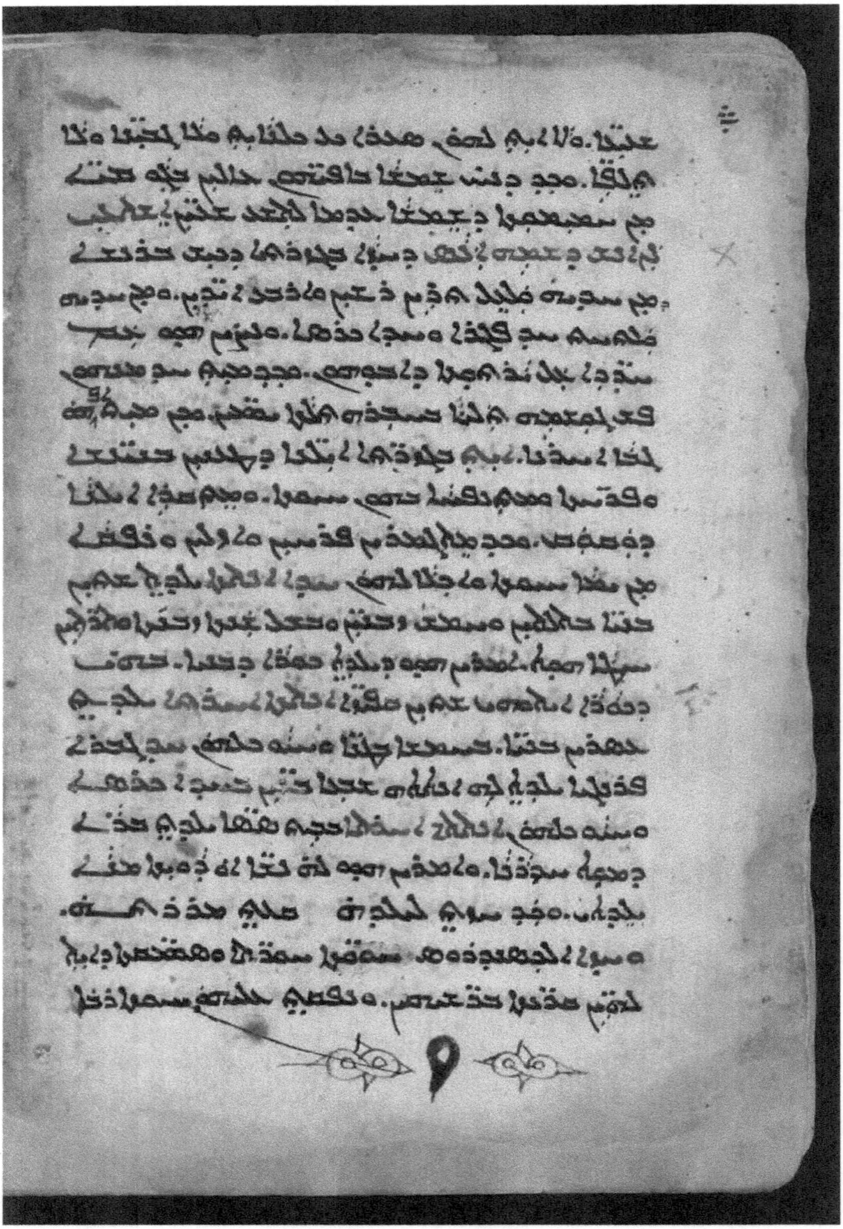

B1 fol. 71r

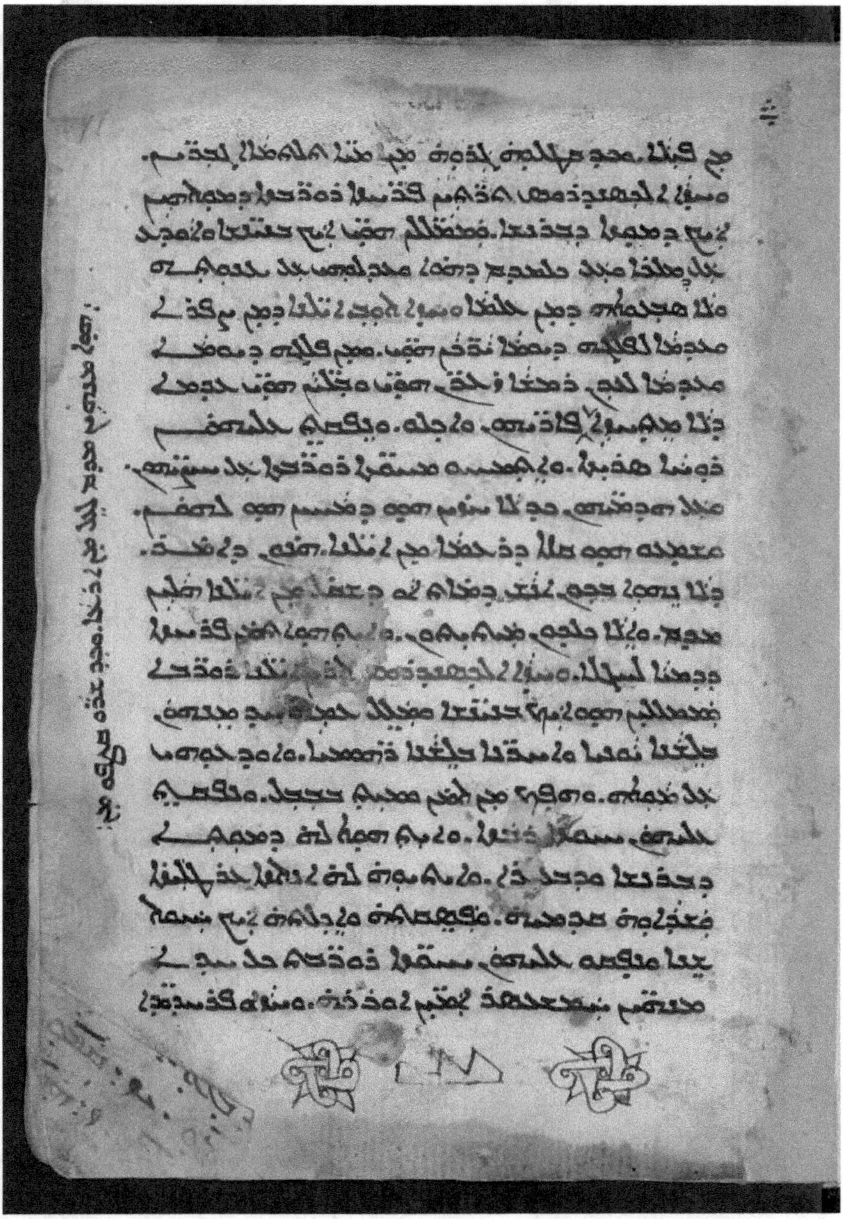

B1

fol. 71v

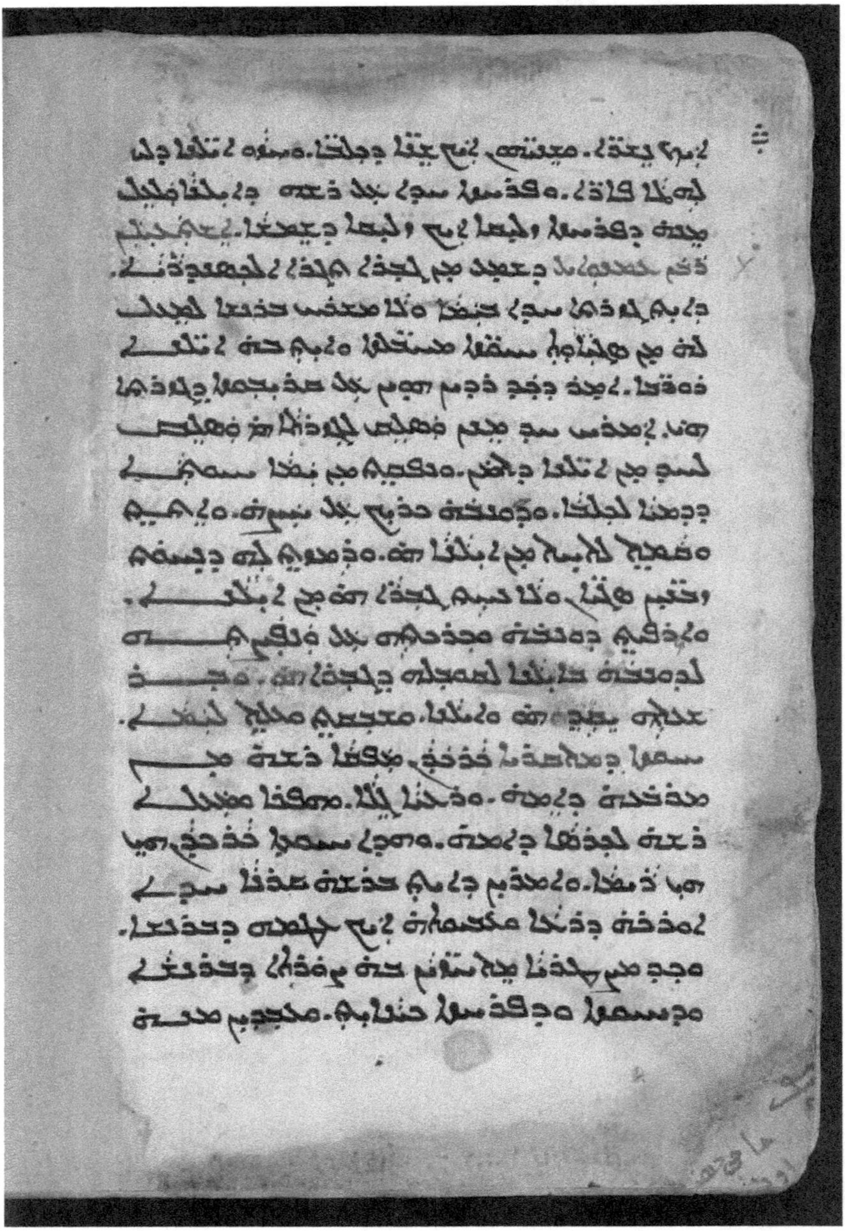

B1 fol. 72r

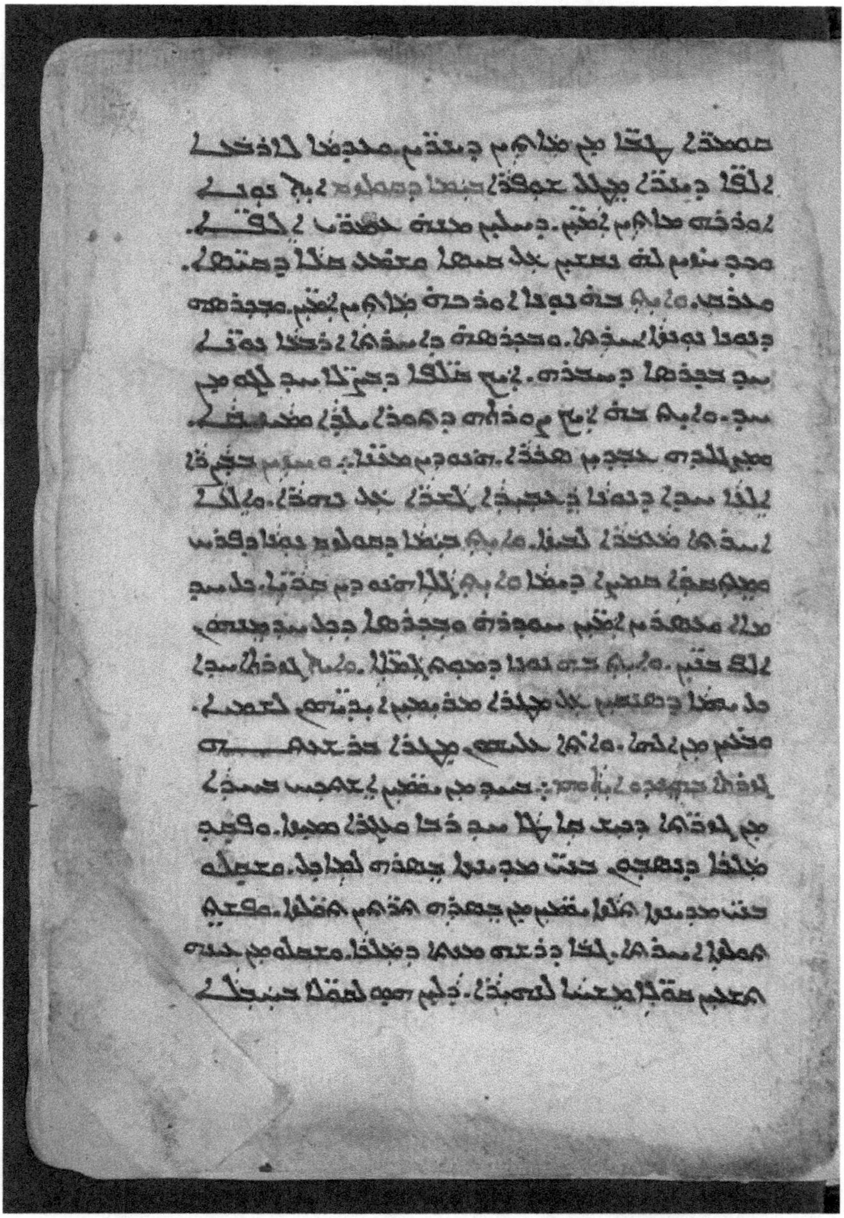

B1 fol. 72v

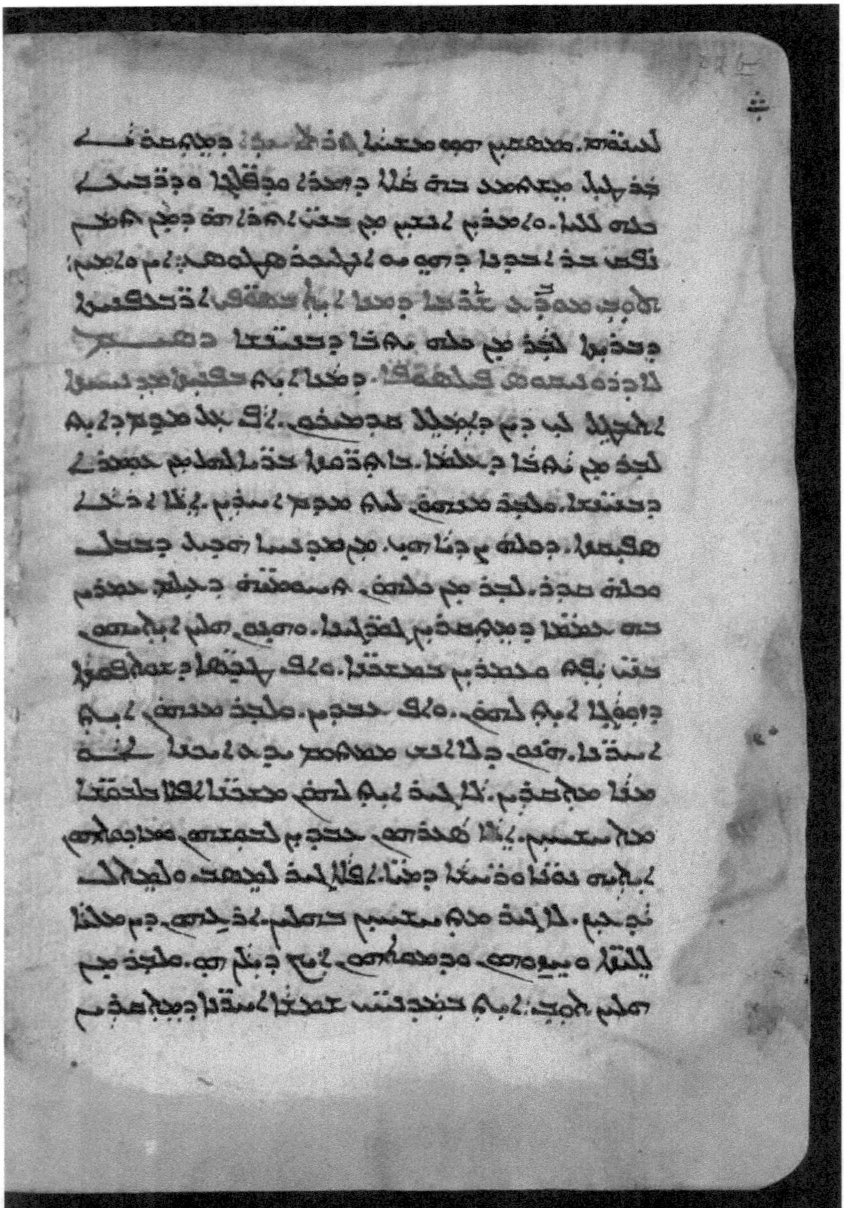

B2 fol. 7r

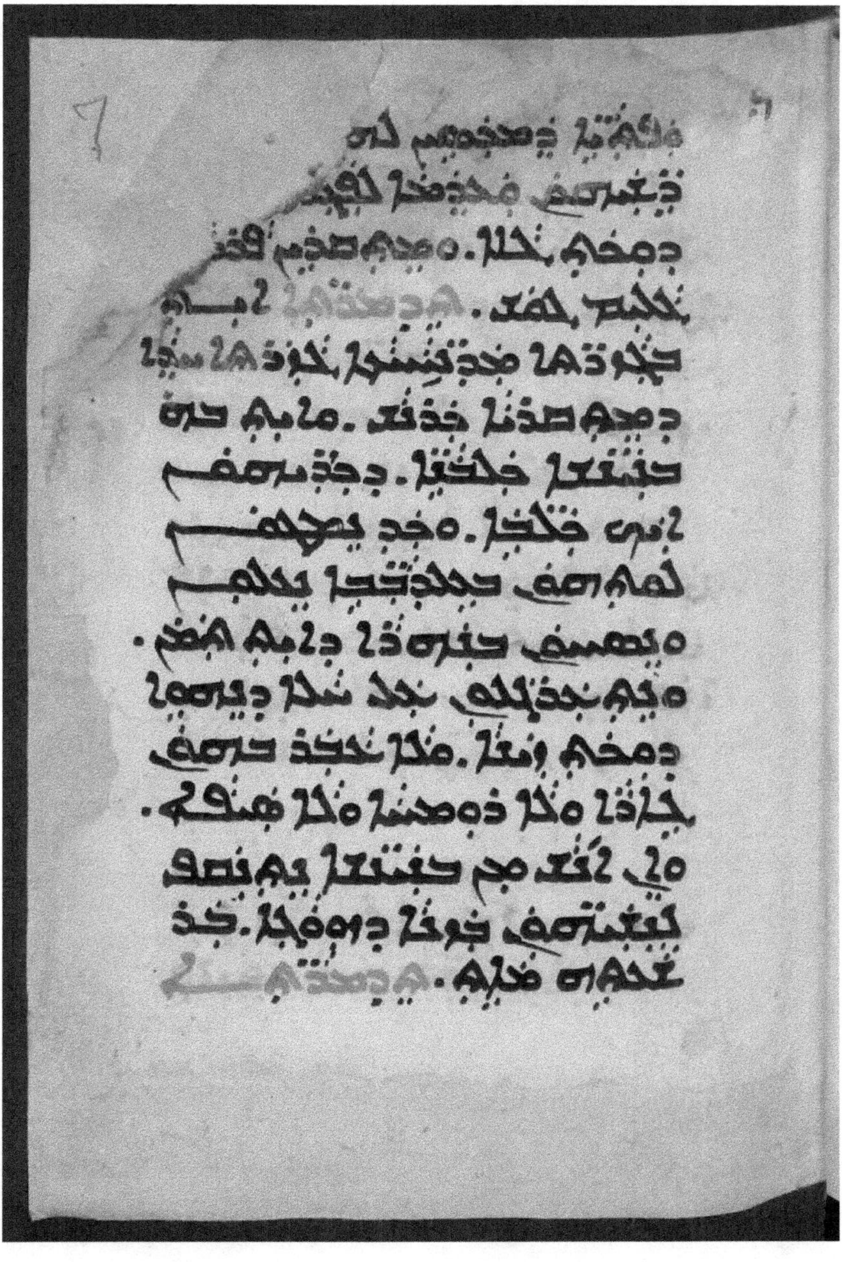

B2 fol. 7v

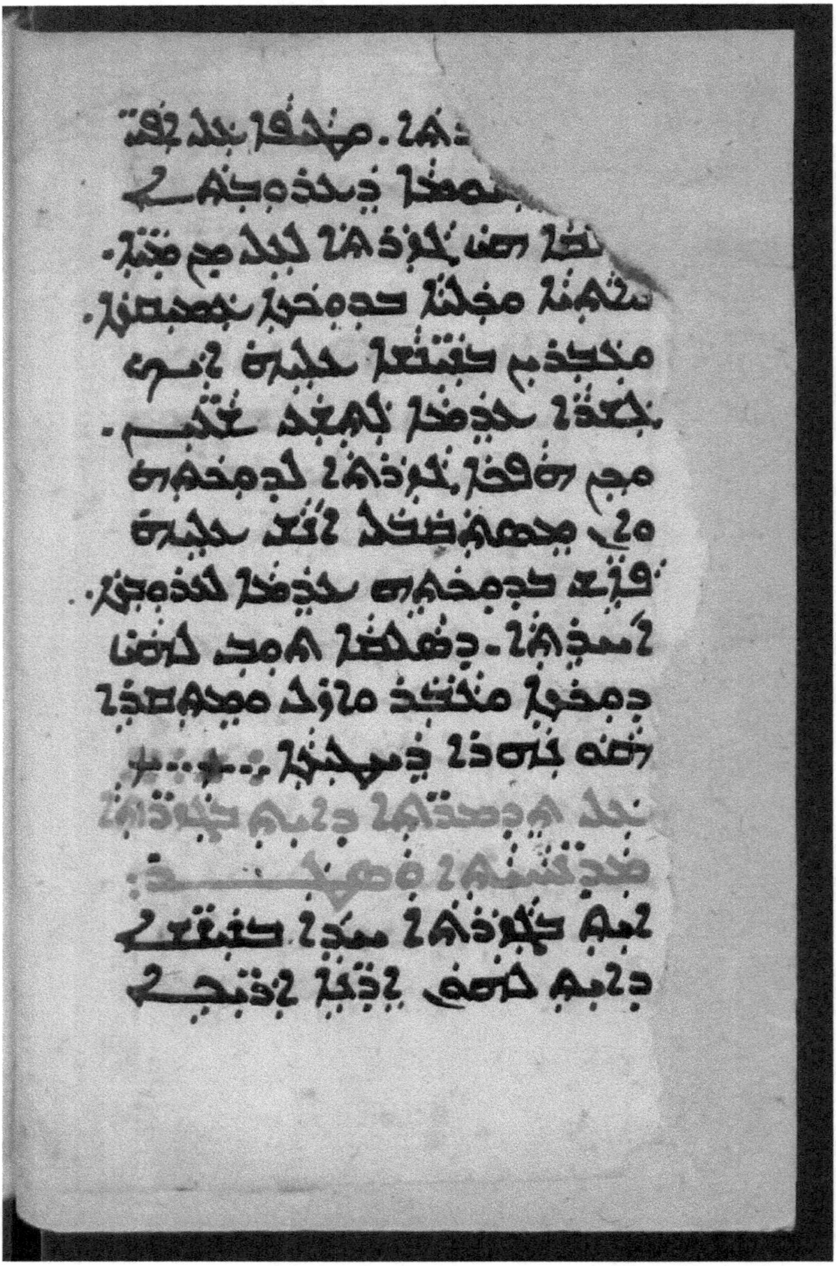

B2 fol. 8r

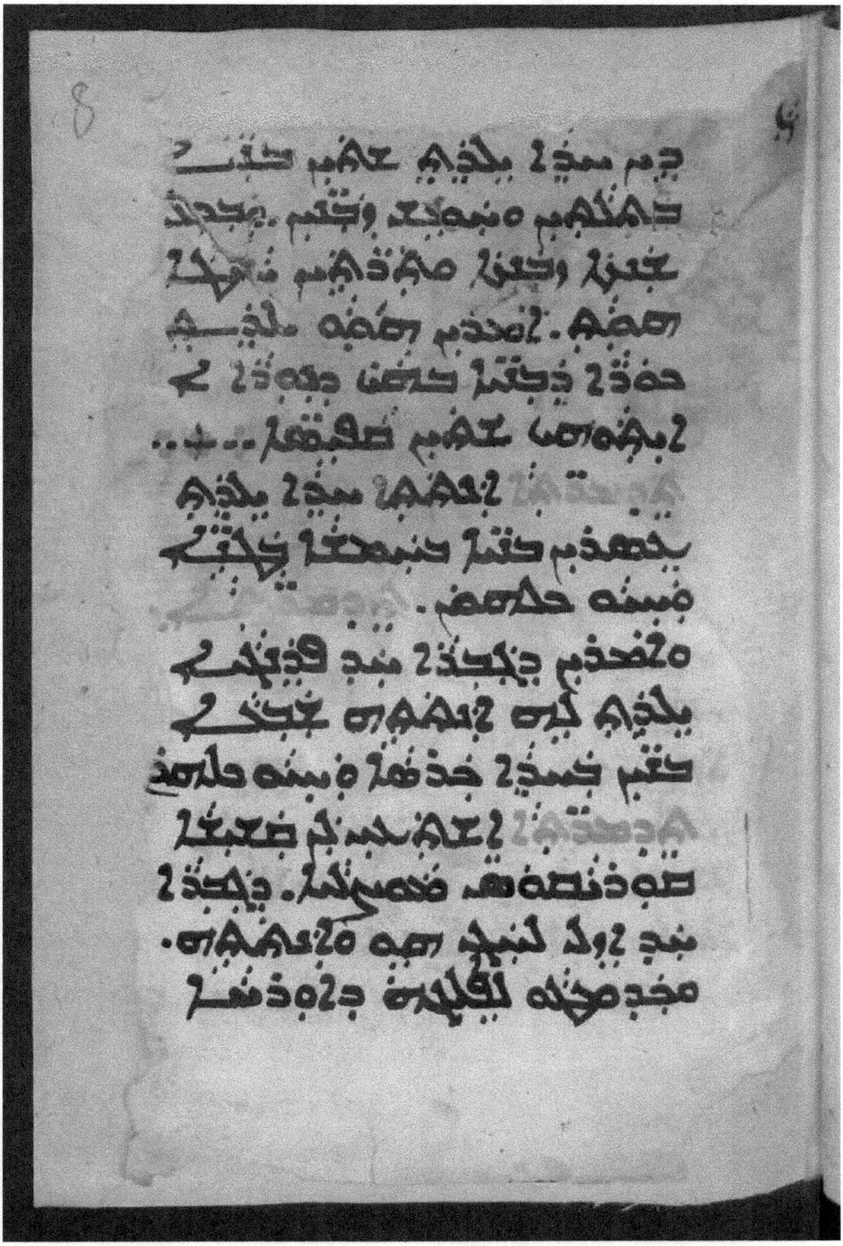

B2 fol. 8v

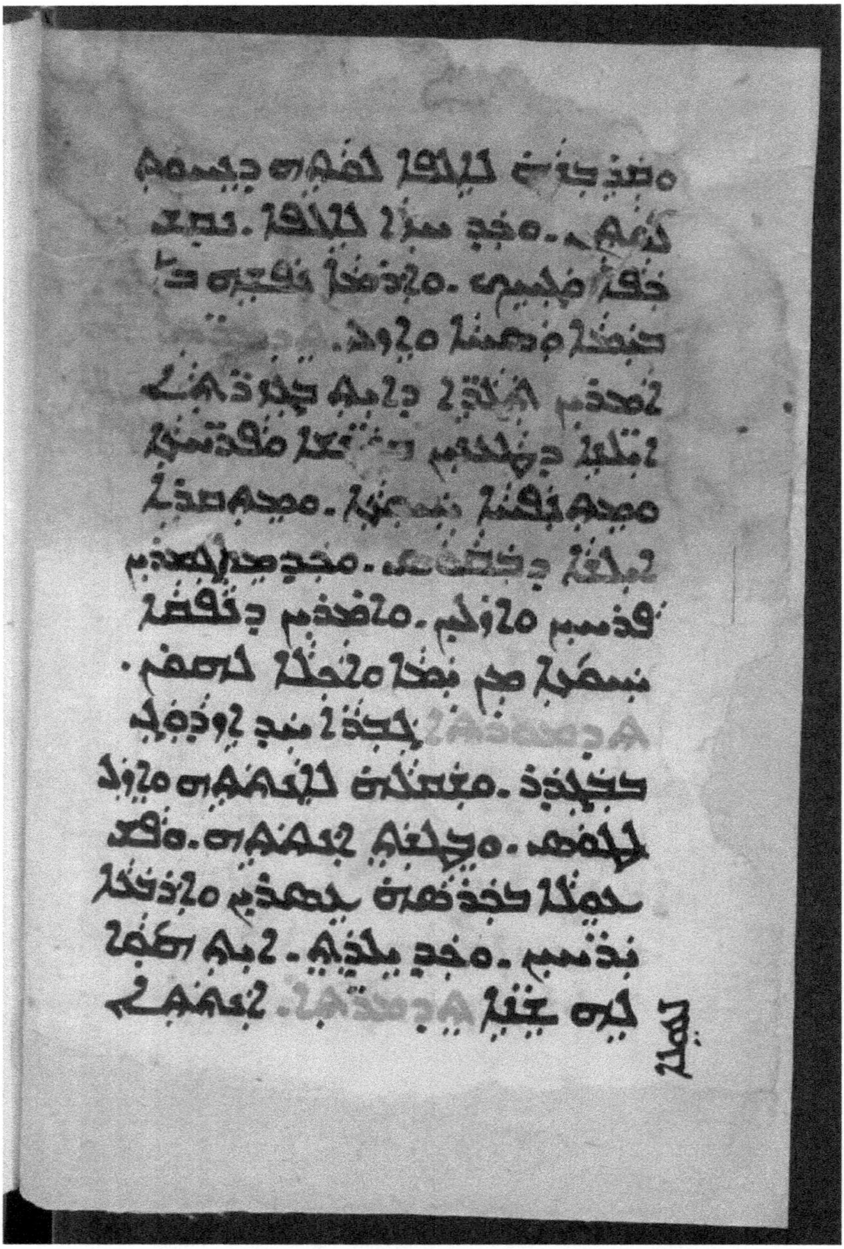

Cambridge Semitic Languages and Cultures

General Editor Geoffrey Khan

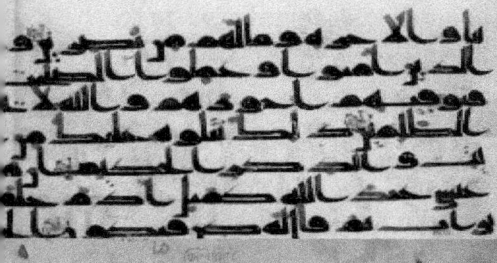

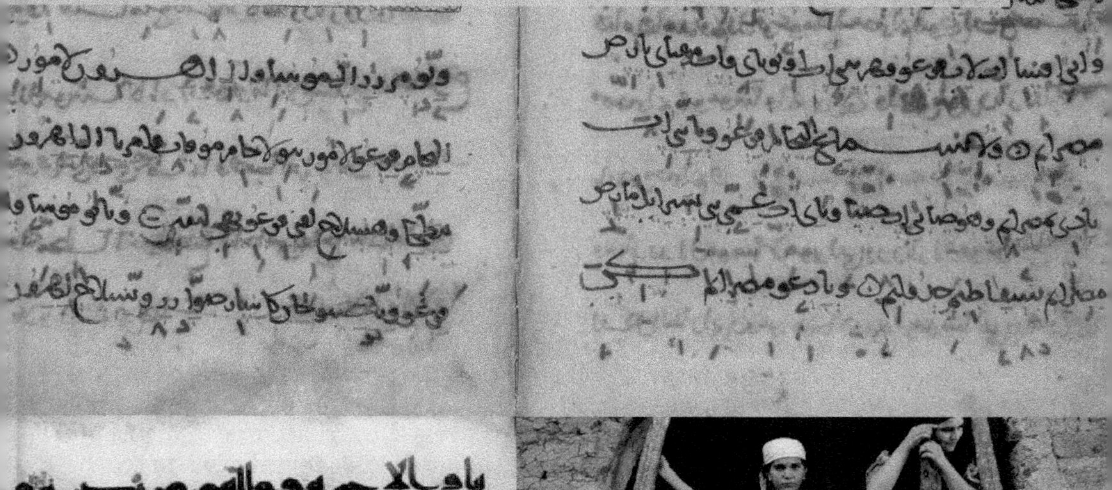

OPEN ACCESS

Cambridge Semitic Languages and Cultures

About the series

This series is published by Open Book Publishers in collaboration with the Faculty of Asian and Middle Eastern Studies of the University of Cambridge. The aim of the series is to publish in open-access form monographs in the field of Semitic languages and the cultures associated with speakers of Semitic languages. It is hoped that this will help disseminate research in this field to academic researchers around the world and also open up this research to the communities whose languages and cultures the volumes concern. This series includes philological and linguistic studies of Semitic languages and editions of Semitic texts. Titles in the series will cover all periods, traditions and methodological approaches to the field. The editorial board comprises Geoffrey Khan, Aaron Hornkohl, and Esther-Miriam Wagner.

This is the first Open Access book series in the field; it combines the high peer-review and editorial standards with the fair Open Access model offered by OBP. Open Access (that is, making texts free to read and reuse) helps spread research results and other educational materials to everyone everywhere, not just to those who can afford it or have access to well-endowed university libraries.

Copyrights stay where they belong, with the authors. Authors are encouraged to secure funding to offset the publication costs and thereby sustain the publishing model, but if no institutional funding is available, authors are not charged for publication. Any grant secured covers the actual costs of publishing and is not taken as profit. In short: we support publishing that respects the authors and serves the public interest.

Other titles in the series

Studies in the Grammar and Lexicon of Neo-Aramaic

Geoffrey Khan and Paul M. Noorlander (eds)

doi.org/10.11647/OBP.0209

Jewish-Muslim Intellectual History Entangled

Camilla Adang, Bruno Chiesa, Omar Hamdan, Wilferd Madelung, Sabine Schmidtke and Jan Thiele (eds)

doi.org/10.11647/OBP.0214

UNIVERSITY OF CAMBRIDGE
Faculty of Asian and Middle Eastern Studies

You can find more information about this serie at:
http://www.openbookpublishers.com/section/107/1

www.ingramcontent.com/pod-product-compliance
Lightning Source LLC
Chambersburg PA
CBHW050525170426
43201CB00013B/2092
9781800640320